D1603484

Praise for *Micro-Meltdown*

"Vikram Akula's first book, *A Fistful of Rice*, told the story of how he turned an idealistic vision into a thriving business that helped provide micro-loans to millions of poor women in India. What he couldn't know at the time was that there was a nightmare waiting on the horizon. He's now seen his dreams come crashing down before his eyes, and he's returned with grace and hard-earned wisdom. The lessons he has to offer are valuable to individuals in all walks of life. This is essential reading for every entrepreneur who wants to change the world for the better."

—Vinod Khosla, cofounder of Sun Microsystems and principal at Khosla Ventures

"If you're setting out to change the world, you need to be prepared for anything. That includes those disaster scenarios none of us want to imagine. Vikram Akula's eye-opening book provides absolutely necessary insights into what it's like to see your dreams come crashing down—and how to rebuild afterward."

—Van Jones, CNN commentator and founder of Dream Corps

"When Vikram Akula started his microfinance company, he had an admirable mission of tackling one of the world's most pressing problems: poverty. Initially, he had enormous success in blending the best of capitalism and philanthropy, but he also faced a fierce political backlash. Now, returning with an engrossing new memoir after surviving a genuine 'worst case scenario' disaster, he presents a vitally important cautionary tale."

—Klaus Schwab, executive chairman of World Economic Forum and founder of Schwab Foundation for Social Entrepreneurship and the Forum of Young Global Leaders

"Here's a book that no would-be entrepreneur can afford to skip. Reading *Micro-Meltdown* will stun you and teach you invaluable lessons about the storms one must weather in innovative business enterprises. An unforgettable true story told by a remarkable visionary, this is essential reading for entrepreneurs, especially for social entrepreneurs."

—Cheryl Dorsey, president of Echoing Green

"This absorbing book tells the story of how Vikram Akula turned an idealistic vision into a thriving business that today serves millions of poor women in India. Vikram also narrates the dramatic odyssey that his company took to get where it is today."

—Farzana Haque, global head for strategic group accounts at Tata Consultancy Services

MICRO-
MELTDOWN

MICRO-MELTDOWN

The Inside Story of the Rise, Fall, and Resurgence
of the World's Most Valuable Microlender

VIKRAM AKULA

BenBella Books, Inc.
Dallas, TX

BenBella Books, Inc.
10440 N. Central Expressway, Suite 800
Dallas, TX 75231
www.benbellabooks.com
Send feedback to feedback@benbellabooks.com

Printed in the United States of America
10 9 8 7 6 5 4 3 2 1

Library of Congress Cataloging-in-Publication Control Number: 2018003821

ISBN 9781946885104
eISBN 9781946885319

Editing by Glenn Yeffeth and Laurel Leigh
Copyediting by Elizabeth Degenhard
Proofreading by James Fraleigh and Cape Cod Compositors, Inc.
Indexing by WordCo Indexing Services, Inc.
Text design by Silver Feather Design
Text composition by PerfecType, Nashville, TN
Cover photo by Omar Adam Khan
Author photo by Ben Bloodwell
Cover design by Faceout Studio, Jeff Miller
Jacket design by Sarah Avinger
Printed by Lake Book Manufacturing

Distributed to the trade by Two Rivers Distribution, an Ingram brand
www.tworiversdistribution.com

Special discounts for bulk sales (minimum of 25 copies) are available. Please contact Aida Herrera at aida@benbellabooks.com.

This book is dedicated to the memory of Sitaram Rao, who brightened the world with his smile and compassion. He will always be remembered for his selfless devotion to helping marginalized communities and for how he gently guided so many of us in the development sector.

Sitaram, we love you and miss you.

CONTENTS

PART I: THE RISE

PART II: THE FALL

PART III: THE RESURGENCE

PART I
THE RISE

CHAPTER 1

AM I NOT POOR, TOO?

A couple years ago, I attended a Wall Street conference in Manhattan. The event was hosted by Credit Suisse, and the topic was microfinance—the practice of lending very small amounts of money to very poor people so that they can engage in income-generating enterprises. There were about fifty business-people in attendance, a few whom I recognized. I picked up my registration badge and found a seat in the back row. I wanted to blend in—anonymously—while I listened to the presenters and got a feel for current trends in the industry.

During the break, there was a scurry to the coffee table. I got in line as well. After the line of people filled their coffee cups, the participants stood chatting. I found myself talking with a twenty-something Credit Suisse investment banker who happened to be from India. He spoke with that precise British-Indian accent that is neither British nor Indian. His charcoal pin-striped suit had an elegantly folded white pocket square. His crisp white shirt and patterned blue tie somewhat mirrored my own attire, although I feel more at ease in a traditional *kurta*.

He said he had just joined Credit Suisse's microfinance group, having spent a couple years in the investment banking group.

I wondered if he would like the change—and the unique challenge.

"What do you do?" he asked me.

"I work in microfinance, too," I said. "I just launched a start-up called Vaya."

I explained that I split my time between the United States and India. Vaya is headquartered in Hyderabad.

He asked about the operational model I was using. I described the peer-group lending that Vaya uses and the focus on income-generating loans.

"That sounds like the SKS model," he said.

"Yeah, that's right," I replied, smiling. "It's like SKS."

SKS Microfinance is one of the world's largest microfinance companies. It serves close to seven million members in India and has disbursed more than $12 billion in microloans. It was one of the first microfinance companies in the world to do an IPO. In fact, Credit Suisse was one of the investment banks that helped take SKS public. Today, hundreds of microfinance institutions around the world emulate SKS.

I knew the company well. After all, I founded it.

The Credit Suisse banker did not know that. I didn't tell him. He wished me all the best and headed back for a second cup of coffee.

I was pleased in a way. The institution I had created—and to which I had devoted a good portion of my life—had transcended me.

As the banker walked away, my thoughts went back to one of the women who had been an early member of SKS. I met her twenty years ago, in 1998, soon after I founded SKS. Her name was Saailibai, and her world was very different from the mid-town Manhattan conference hall of Credit Suisse. Saailibai was a Banjara tribal woman in her early twenties who lived in a remote village called Kondapur in Telangana, the drought-prone region of southern India where my family is from and where I first started working in microfinance. The Banjaras are a tribal community and are among the poorest people in the country. Tribal people were historically marginalized and faced severe discrimination.

Saailibai's life was particularly difficult. She had been born into a very poor family and was the younger of two sisters. Her parents had been landless laborers, working on the farms of others. Her family was so impoverished that Saailibai and her sister did not go to school; instead, as each of them had reached the tender age of eight, they'd started working in the fields alongside their parents. Saailibai was married by the age of twelve. She had one son, Prahalad, but her husband died of tuberculosis soon after the child was born, leaving a teenaged Saailibai to raise the boy on her own.

I met Saailibai when we started a lending group in her village. In the initial years of SKS, I was fully involved in grassroots field work, and I had provided a group of five women that included Saailibai with our standardized training about our lending methods. The training involved using highly visual and tactile tools to explain the concepts of credit, principal, and interest in a manner that poor, semiliterate women could understand and remember. Saailibai and her fellow group members were intelligent, but the traditional culture in which these women existed denied them formal education and kept them sheltered from discussions of money.

Sitting on a patch of dirt in front of Saailibai's small, thatched mud hut, I used coins, seeds, and cardboard cutouts during the hourlong sessions that extended for a week, during the twilight of each evening. In the training meetings we spoke the local Telugu language.

At the end of the week, Saailibai and her group merged with other groups to form a village lending center of forty women. Saailibai took a loan for ₹4,000 (about $100) to buy a buffalo. Each day, Saailibai would milk the buffalo and sell the milk to a milk collector who would come by in the morning with two large tin milk containers draped on the sides of his bicycle. With the money earned from selling buffalo milk, Saailibai made her loan repayments at the weekly lending center meeting and paid off her loan in a year. She was left with the buffalo, a calf, and no debt. With her next loan, she bought farmyard manure and grew rice on a small plot of land that had sat neglected ever since her husband's death. She paid off that loan in a year. Then she took another, larger loan, for a second buffalo, which provided even more milk. With the profits from those early loans, she saved enough to build a home with stone walls and a corrugated tin roof to replace her thatched mud hut. Over the next seven years, Saailibai took larger loans to continue to farm her land and to purchase more buffaloes. With the profits, she was able to send her son to a private high school. He now has a job with the Indian government.

Since the lending center meetings took place in front of her house, I had developed an easy familiarity with Saailibai. She had a resplendent, wide smile. As part of our loan utilization visit I would go with her to her small farm plot in the fields surrounding the village. I remember how she stood proudly in front of her farm, scythe in hand, her bright orange *sari* in brilliant contrast to the rich green of the rice field. She, of course, had every reason to be proud. She was a single mother who was overcoming class, gender, and ethnicity barriers to stand on her own.

In those early days, when I came for the weekly lending center meetings, I would see her young son playing in front of the house while she was cooking or sweeping or engaged in some other chore. "How is school going?" I would ask him. "What did you learn this week?" In the midst of this banter, as other women strolled in with their passbooks for the meeting, Saailibai and I would catch up as well. Without pausing what she was doing—sweeping or cooking— she would look up and matter-of-factly ask me how I was. There was no stopping and standing at attention, as our relationship made her comfortable enough to shed the false deference that the poor often exhibit in front of people who are deemed "important." Instead, there were small gestures of concern that communicated her feelings. She would hand me a glass of cool water from the large clay pot, just inside her door. "Would you like some tea? Have you eaten?" We had an easy familiarity, as if I were a cousin from a nearby village who was passing through.

The start of my journey in microfinance began about eight years prior to meeting Saailibai. Though I was born in India, my parents immigrated to upstate New York when I was two years old. So, I grew up there. In 1990, after graduating from Tufts University in Massachusetts, I went back to India. I was full of idealism and determined to make a difference in the world. Taking very few possessions, I moved to rural Telangana to work with a small, grassroots nonprofit, the Deccan Development Society (DDS). After a year and a half as a field-worker with DDS, I returned to the United States to get a master's degree at Yale University, and then went back to DDS in 1994, working again in Telangana, this time on a Fulbright scholarship on an action-research project.

As head of a lending program serving thirty villages, I'd putter down dirt roads on an Indian-made Hero Honda motorbike, meeting with borrowers, disbursing loans, and collecting repayments. Each week, I talked with rural Indians who were pulling themselves out of poverty and despair—landless laborers who had started with nothing but were now launching their own small businesses, earning not only money but greater self-respect as well.

The degree of poverty in these remote Indian villages was unlike anything I'd ever seen growing up in the United States. Children with spindly legs and hungry eyes played in the mud alongside mangy stray dogs and farm animals. Piles of garbage dotted village roadsides, and sewage ran in trenches alongside homes. People lived in one-room mud huts, sweltering in the Indian sun. There was a smell of desperation in the air, a palpable sense of resignation that went back centuries. The poor had always been poor, and here in the Indian hinterlands, it felt like they always would be.

Working to help these villagers was incredibly gratifying, though there were definitely hardships to living in remote villages: sleeping on a straw mat on the floor in a small room, fetching drinking water from a distant well, and seeing the effects of poor nutrition and unhygienic conditions all around me was certainly a far cry from the middle-class comfort of Schenectady, New York, where I was raised. But I felt like I was really making a difference, really helping to end poverty in India.

Then, one day, a woman walked into our regional office. Barefoot, emaciated, and wearing a faded purple sari, she was obviously poor and from a lower caste. But she'd found her way to our office because she'd heard about our program and wanted to learn more. This was no small achievement, as she'd either paid to take a bus or had walked quite a distance to find us.

She asked some questions about our lending endeavor and then got quickly to her point. "Can you start this program in my village?" she asked.

I looked closely at her. She was probably in her mid-thirties, but like many poor Indians, she looked older than her years. Her face was worn and her skin weathered, but her eyes were alight with purpose. Life had beaten her down, but it hadn't beaten the hope out of her. This, I thought, was exactly the kind of person to whom we should be lending. So I promised to ask DDS's director later that day.

I got a disappointing answer. "Our grant cycle is coming to an end, Vikram," the director told me. "We don't have the funds to expand right now beyond the villages we're already in. There's nothing we can do."

The next day, I rode my motorbike to the woman's village to break the news to her. The sudden appearance of an Indian man speaking Telugu, the local language, with an American accent always caused a stir in remote villages, and it didn't take long for word to spread. The woman soon came outside to meet me.

"Here's the situation," I told her. "We don't have the resources right now to expand to new villages. We've got a set amount of money, and we've already committed it elsewhere." Even as the words came out of my mouth, I wished I could take them back. But all I could say was, "I'm very sorry."

The woman looked me in the eye, and with great dignity, she spoke the words that would change my life. "Am I not poor, too?" she asked me. I stared at her, jarred by the question, and she went on, "Do I not deserve a chance to get my family out of poverty?"

Am I not poor, too?

With these words, this driven, determined woman suddenly made me see how unfair—unjust, really—our microfinance program was. Yes, we were helping hundreds of poor Indians take the first steps to pull themselves out of poverty. But my program had just $250,000 to spend in thirty villages—that was all DDS had been given for the project. And once that money was disbursed, there would be no money left for other poor Indians who desperately wanted a chance, too.

This woman wasn't asking for a dole. She wasn't asking for a handout. She was simply asking for an opportunity. But we couldn't give it to her. I rode my motorbike home over those same dirt roads, but everything had changed. I had a new mission: to solve the problem of how to make microloans available on a mass scale, far larger than the few million people worldwide who were then being served. Microfinance as we were using it was a fantastic tool, but a deeply flawed one. There simply had to be a way to scale it beyond the constraints of how it was currently being practiced—to make it available to any Indian, or any poor person anywhere in the world for that matter, who wanted to escape poverty.

We had to find a way to change microfinance.

CHAPTER 2

MY UNEXPECTED QUEST TO END POVERTY THROUGH PROFITABILITY

Like many people, I believe microfinance is a core way of helping to address the global poverty problem. It provides poor people with the tools to find their own way out of poverty. It puts power squarely in their hands, giving them a larger stake in their own success than simple one-time donations of food, goods, or cash. And it offers innumerable side benefits—not only to the poor themselves, but to economies, banking systems, and political systems where microfinance is practiced. It is an incredibly powerful, versatile tool.

But unlike some, I believe that microfinance institutions, or MFIs, must be set up as commercial, well-managed for-profit entities if we have any hope of making a dent in poverty. This point of view puts me at odds with many of my colleagues—colleagues for whom I have great respect—but it's one I feel very strongly about. So strongly, in fact, that in late 1997 I started my own company, SKS Microfinance, to do just that. I launched SKS as a nonprofit out of necessity, but the goal was always to turn it into a for-profit company, which I did in 2005.

Many of the people I've worked with over the years—people whose opinions I respect, and whose love for India and desire to help the poor are deeply felt—have expressed keen disappointment in my choice. They say it's unacceptable, even unethical, to make money from charging interest on loans to the poor. But I believe the opposite: that doing well by doing good is not only acceptable, it's a way to make microfinance sustainable and therefore widely available.

I didn't come to these beliefs overnight. They're the culmination of a journey, one that took me through the worlds of academia, philosophy, nonprofits, and business. The very first step of that journey was discovering what poverty really was, as a young boy visiting India.

Though I was born in the south Indian city of Hyderabad, my family immigrated to the United States in 1970, as part of the "brain drain" that led so many educated Indians to seek their fortunes abroad. My father, Akula Krishna, a surgeon, brought us to upstate New York when I was two years old to start our new lives. Years later, when I went back as an adult to live in poverty-stricken rural India, my parents were baffled: Why would I return to such a place, after they'd taken great pains to create a better, more comfortable life for us in America?

The answer lay in a few grains of rice. When I was about seven, my parents took me back to India for the first time to visit with family. I had no memory of my first two years there and thought of myself as fully American. But during that trip, India made an impression on me that I would never forget.

I was at my aunt's house, a comfortable home in a middle-class Hyderabad neighborhood, when someone knocked at her door. The visitor was a woman with a half-dozen steel pots and a young boy in tow. She was selling the pots door to door. And by the look of her sari and her drawn, sallow face, she desperately needed whatever she could get in barter for them.

My aunt invited the woman in and began looking over her wares, while her son hovered near the doorway, unsure whether he was allowed to come in. As children do, he and I shyly sized each other up. It was clear from his dirty clothes and gaunt frame that he and I lived in completely different worlds, but he was about my age, so I felt a kind of connection with him right away. We didn't speak, but we continued to eye each other as my aunt and his mother bartered over what she would receive in exchange for the pots.

A price was agreed upon, and my aunt went into the kitchen to bring out rice for payment. I watched as the woman squatted down and held out her *pallu*, the folds of her sari. My aunt poured the rice grains into the outstretched garment, and a few grains— maybe fifteen in all—fell to the floor. The floor was made of dark, shiny *shabbad* stones, so the smattering of white grains stood out. I figured my aunt would just sweep them away when the woman and her son left.

To my astonishment, the woman reached down and pressed her finger against each grain to pick it up. My aunt was already heading back to the kitchen with her rice container, but this woman was carefully scouring the floor, making sure she hadn't missed a single grain. This, I suddenly realized, was what it meant to be truly hungry.

Like most middle-class American kids, I'd heard the refrain, "Don't waste your food! There are children starving in India." I was a conscientious child, so I always did try to eat everything I was served. But watching this boy and his mother, I understood for the first time that hunger was not an abstraction. These were real people—people not so different from myself—and fifteen grains of rice really mattered for them.

If I had grown up in India, I doubt I'd have been struck at all by the scene that unfolded in my aunt's house that day. But I was an Indian boy, growing up American in Schenectady, New York. I went to Cub Scouts, to birthday parties, to restaurants with my family. We lacked nothing, and we also weren't confronted with the daily reality of others' poverty: I was growing up in a happy, insulated bubble. But in India, poverty and hunger were right there for all to see—even right in my aunt's house. The contrast was stark and unforgettable.

We continued to go to Hyderabad over the summers, when I was out of school. I practiced my rudimentary Telugu and kept learning more about India each time we visited. But I still considered myself 100 percent American and even had asked my friends to call me Vic, rather than Vikram, so I could fit in better as I moved up through junior high school. Then, the summer I was twelve, I witnessed another incident in India that struck me as powerfully as had the rice grains incident five years earlier.

We had gone back for a family wedding, which in India, as in many parts of the developing world, is quite a lavish affair even if you're solidly middle class. Families will save money for years to put on the most extravagant celebration possible, with multiple courses served at the meal, fancy decorations, expensive gifts, and even rented horses or elephants for the groom to ride in on.

Everyone was dressed in beautiful silk saris and ornate kurtas, with the women's gold jewelry glinting in the evening light. When we sat down for dinner, waiters brought out the food on traditional leaf plates. Course after course was served—piping-hot chicken biryani, glistening ghee-laden curries, sweet meat, dal, paneer, and sugary jalebi—with the waiters swiftly refilling each half-empty plate, as everyone ate and drank and the volume of the party increased.

Finally, the last course was finished. The happy, sated guests rose to begin migrating from the dining tent to another tent for the continued celebration. As I walked away from my table, I happened to glance back as the last leaf plates were being cleared.

Two boys about my age, in threadbare clothes and with lean, hungry faces, had made their way into the open-air dining tent. I watched as they took as many leaf plates as they could and carried them a short distance away, to the top of a hillock. They sat beneath a tree there, and then quickly got to work: One boy scraped the leftover food off plates while the second, older boy held another plate to collect it all. Then the two boys, clearly ravenous, began scooping the leftovers into their mouths.

I stood and stared. I couldn't believe their desperation, literally eating our castoffs, our waste. In Schenectady, I thought, these boys might be my friends, or on my soccer team. Here, they were scavengers, too hungry to care who might see them filching the scraps of food we didn't want. It felt so unreal to me—and yet I was standing here, watching it happen. I almost couldn't stand that such desperation existed, and that it was on view, right there in front of me.

That was the moment I knew, beyond doubt, what I would do when I got older: I would come back to India and help people like those boys get out of poverty. Why should I have an easy, comfortable life while others, by luck of the draw, had to struggle so hard to survive? It's probably too clear-cut, or too romanticized, to say I made a vow right then to try to eliminate poverty in India. But that was the moment when what I'd seen lodged so firmly in my consciousness that I couldn't imagine doing anything else.

India is a land of breathtaking beauty, deep history, and astonishing diversity. It's a land with so many languages and dialects that fewer than half its people claim the national language, Hindi, as their native tongue. Depending on which city or village you go to, you're as likely to hear Bengali, Telugu, Tamil, Urdu, Punjabi—or English—as you are Hindi. All told, the country has twenty-three official languages and hundreds of distinct dialects.[1]

It is also a land of amazing religious and ethnic diversity. Though more than 80 percent of Indians identify as Hindu, a walk down any street in any city will take you past Muslim mosques, Sikh temples, Zoroastrian shrines, and Christian churches. And even within the Hindu religion, a plethora of gods vie for attention: Shiva, Ganesh, Krishna, Rama, and literally hundreds of others. Hindu temples, from sprawling complexes to tiny roadside shrines, pay homage to a vast and vibrant religious culture.

To be Indian is to share in a heritage that is at once common to more than 1.3 billion others and unique to each family, region, or faith. India is impossible to characterize in a few words; it is as colorful and chaotic as the wild, lurching traffic that flows through its streets. It is full of the hope and potential of an emerging economic power and the excitement of becoming a potent new force in the world. And with its call centers, software developers, and eager embrace of the technology age, it is leading the world into a new era.

When I went to India in the 1990s, it was a land of extreme poverty. In 1993, 433 million people or 46 percent of the population lived in extreme poverty, defined by the World Bank as the purchasing-power equivalent of less than $1.90 per day. If that's not bad enough, the numbers spiked even more when you consider how many Indians lived below the next level of poverty, the purchasing-power equivalent of less than $3.20 per day: 764 million people or 81 percent of the population lived on less than that. Things have improved since then, but tremendous poverty remains. The most recent figures at the time of this writing, released by the World Bank in May 2014 and based on the results of the 2011 International Comparison Program, indicated that 268 million or 21 percent of the population lived on less than $1.90 per day. So, India has 27 percent of the world's poorest people; that group is part of the 763 million people, or 60 percent of the country's population, who survive at the next level of poverty, which is less than $3.20 per day.[2] In sum, India has more poor people at the level of $3.20 per day than the combined populations of the United States, Russia, France, the United Kingdom, Italy, Spain, and Canada—roughly 11 percent of the Earth's population.

It's not simply that you notice the poverty when you visit India. It is all around you, so prevalent and insistent that you can see it, smell it, feel it. From the dusty villages scattered over bone-dry plains to the crumbling slums of the cities, the culture of poverty is embedded in the land. Anyone who's spent time in India returns home with stories of beggars lining the streets and mothers with hungry children in their laps, hands held out for a coin or two. In India, tragically, poverty continues to be a part of the landscape, as natural and unchanging as the vast Deccan plains and the flow of the Ganges River.

When I enrolled at Tufts University in Massachusetts, at age seventeen, I began thinking in earnest about how to help India's poor. I devoured the works of the great philosophers, searching for clues on how to live my life and make a difference in the lives of others. Like many college students at the time, I was drawn to leftist ideals, but I also craved the order and drive associated with the right. During my freshman year, in a moment of teenage zeal, I wrote in my journal that I wanted to "eradicate poverty with the discipline of a Marine." It was a strange, and rather corny, thing to write. But I was anxious not simply to *do* something but to do it well and efficiently.

I became the do-gooder to end all do-gooders, spending my time studying, playing for the college tennis team, and working with the campus community service organization. While my classmates went out on Friday nights, I volunteered at a local homeless shelter, as if trying to make up for the fact that I had so much while others had so little. I was driven by guilt, buried under the weight of my good fortune and the memory of the poverty I'd seen. And my overheated conscience was further pricked by reading the philosophical writings of Friedrich Nietzsche my freshman year. Suddenly, here was this new notion that morality was constructed; there was no absolute moral truth. I did not need to feel guilty or worry too much about others. For an idealistic teenager, reading Nietzsche felt a bit like getting kicked in the head.

The summer after my freshman year, I decided I'd personally prove Nietzsche wrong. Of course there was universal truth in morality and in moral feelings like kindness and sympathy! If you showed people unconditional love, I believed, they would reciprocate. Convinced my theory was true, I devised a way to test it: I walked out of my parents' house in Schenectady one June morning with just $20 in my pocket and set out to hitchhike around the country. Hitchhiking, I thought, was the ultimate expression of trust. I would be putting myself at the mercy of total strangers, and I was excited at the prospect.

I hitchhiked my way to New York City, walked through Harlem, slept in Central Park, and joined a peace march down to Washington, D.C. I sold turkey legs at a carnival booth in Norfolk, Virginia, went hiking in eastern North Carolina, caught rides with everyone from an older woman in a sporty red Karmann Ghia to rednecks in pickup trucks. Even as a dark-skinned, long-haired stranger in the rural South, I was almost always treated with respect and trust. I slept undisturbed under the stars. An optometrist I met at a diner in a town called Blowing Rock gave me the keys to his house, to stay there while he was away. And a student at the nearby Appalachian State University took me mountain climbing, which led to the most memorable experience of the trip—the experience that encapsulated exactly what I had set out to prove.

While we were mountain climbing, a spider bit me on my upper thigh. Over the next couple of days, the spot became swollen and tender, an angry red lump. It got so bad I feared I'd have to go to the emergency room—not an attractive option for a broke student with no health insurance card on him. I was calling my parents every week or so from pay phones, but they were worried enough as it was; I couldn't stand the thought of telling them I was suffering from an infected spider bite, too.

So I pressed on, catching a ride with a heavyset, dark-haired guy outside Asheville, North Carolina. I slung my backpack into the backseat of his dark green Buick and started making small talk as we sped down the highway. After a while, I mentioned the mountain climbing—and the bite on my thigh.

To my surprise, he immediately pulled the Buick over to the side of the highway. "See those leaves over there?" he asked, pointing a burly finger. "Go grab a handful."

What should I do? If I got out, this stranger could just drive off with my backpack, leaving me helpless by the side of the road. But if I grabbed my backpack before getting out, he would know I didn't trust him, and the fragile bond we'd begun to establish would be broken. This was exactly the kind of moment that I'd come on the trip to experience—the kind of moment that could prove or disprove my theory. After a brief hesitation, I opened the door and got out.

As I'd hoped, and even dared believe, the man stayed put. I grabbed a handful of the leaves, got back in the Buick, and we continued down the road. Soon we exited the highway, drove past a small town, and ended up in an even more remote area. He turned down a dirt road and took me deeper into the woods, finally stopping in front of a modest one-story house with a couple of battered vehicles parked in front. The house was rundown, even foreboding. *Oh, boy*, I thought, *here we go*. Nobody had any idea where I was; I was completely at the mercy of this man. Now I felt the stirrings of real fear.

We walked into the house, and the man went straight to the kitchen. A few minutes later, he came out and said to me, "Okay, drop your pants."

Every corpuscle in my body told me to run. But this was it: the ultimate test. Would my trust be repaid with trust? I dropped my pants. And this big, burly, backwoods man took a few steaming leaves from a boiling pot and pressed them to the swollen lump on my thigh. A chemical property in the heated leaves "sucked" out the eggs the spider had laid there after its bite. Within a day, the sore had healed. Strange as it may sound, this encounter was the epitome of so many instances where trust was freely exchanged during my travels.

Those experiences colored my worldview forever. They solidified my belief that putting out love and trust into the world is ultimately repaid in kind. That belief became a cornerstone of what I've tried to do in India. While it's true that my good fortune on the road was partly the luck of the draw, I still believe there's a fundamental level at which trust is repaid with trust—and anyone who's ever experienced the kindness of a stranger knows exactly what I mean. At every level, the work SKS did in India required trust: We had to trust our borrowers to repay unsecured loans. The borrowers had to trust others in their group to make payments, as no one received a new loan unless everyone made their payments. Our lenders had to trust that we would protect their funds. And our investors had to trust that we would steward their money in a way that would bring returns. Trust was the essential element of everything we did, and I had learned it that summer while hitchhiking.

Back at Tufts, I continued studying philosophy and pondering how to get back to India after graduation. I spent my summers seeking out new experiences—working as a carny in Canada, selling soda at Albany Yankees games, volunteering with Meals on Wheels. And I continued to explore the question of morality in my senior thesis, "Why Be Moral?"

Ultimately, it was the seventeenth-century English philosopher Thomas Hobbes who helped me reconcile the idealistic notion of being moral with the hardcore realities of everyday life. Hobbes, who famously wrote that life in the state of nature is "solitary, poor, nasty, brutish, and short," believed that human beings are, at their core, selfish. But, he argued, it was rational for humans to accede to a social contract, or follow a moral code, because doing so helped bring about a stable, functioning society. Moral guilt was useful, as it created a sense of responsibility toward others.

Though Hobbes's conclusion was, at the time, a justification for surrendering rights to the authority of a political ruler, for me what was striking was that this wasn't some mushy philosophical theory rooted in abstract universal truths. Following moral rules had a more prosaic, logical purpose: enabling society to function.

This was the perfect intersection of idealism and realism. The fact that these two notions could coexist side by side made a lasting impression on me. It was the root of my realization that ethics didn't have to trump everyday living but rather could complement and enhance it. This led me to my own philosophical view that doing good and doing well could, and in fact should, coexist. This idea would later form the root of SKS.

As I finished my studies at Tufts, I was excited to get out into the world and test my theories. At long last, it was time to go to India and start working with the poor! The only problem was, I had no idea what I might do there, or who would hire a fresh-faced college graduate like me. Back in those pre-internet days, these questions were far more difficult to answer.

I went to the women's center on campus, knowing that groups working specifically with women were more progressive. I began flipping through magazines in hopes of finding a nonprofit located in drought-prone Telangana, which was then part of the state of Andhra Pradesh. Because I spoke rudimentary Telugu and had family there, I figured that would be the best place to start. There weren't as many options there as in cities like Delhi, Mumbai, or Kolkata, but eventually I tracked down the contact information for a few nonprofits. I sent off a raft of letters and waited.

Only one organization, the Deccan Development Society, responded. And even their letter was decidedly lukewarm. The director, a man named Biksham Gujja, basically said, "Okay, if you come here we'll meet with you, but we're not promising anything."

Relieved to have gotten a reply, and determined to convince Biksham to hire me, I bought a one-way plane ticket to Hyderabad and packed a single gym bag with clothes. I wanted to travel like Mahātmā Gandhi—no unnecessary attachments, no excess of material goods. I had read about Gandhi's experiences in South Africa as a young man, when he was first developing his ideas, and I wanted to experience that same kind of awakening. I knew I couldn't do it sitting in an academic environment in America.

So, this was it—I was finally going to India to help the poor! I was excited and a little nervous. I would have been more so if I'd known what a rude awakening awaited me on the other end.

CHAPTER 3

PUTTING THE LAST FIRST

V ikram," said the man sitting across the table from me. "You cannot help the poor. So don't even try to approach it that way."

After four flights and twenty-four hours in transit from
Schenectady to Hyderabad, one day to get used to the time change,
and a nervous Monday morning auto-rickshaw trip across town, I'd
finally made it to the offices of the Deccan Development Society—
where I met Biksham, a calm, laconic man with a thick mustache and
a head of thinning hair. I had come on a mission, but here in my very
first meeting, Biksham was shooting it down.

He'd seen my type before: eager young American, coming to India
expecting to change the world. In his experience, most young people,
no matter how dedicated they believed themselves to be, ended up
moving on to other things when faced with the reality of working in
India's poorest rural areas.

"The poor know a lot more than we do about how to help themselves," Biksham went on. "We're not all that much use to them, in
that sense."

I heard his words, but I didn't believe what he was saying. Of
course we could help the poor! We could teach them how to improve

their lives. I could get access to information on new, more modern agricultural techniques, or study scientific dairying procedures, and go out into the villages and teach people what I'd learned. The poor obviously needed us! They were uneducated, and we were in a position to bring them knowledge.

I decided Biksham was just being modest, as DDS had been working with India's poor for about seven years by then. Their work included agricultural programs, immunization drives, and other social projects, and they had established a thriving set of women's groups that met regularly in the region where DDS worked, a few hours' drive outside Hyderabad. So I just brushed aside his comment and asked again whether I could volunteer with DDS.

"Sure," he said, a half-smile on his face. "Be ready at six-thirty tomorrow morning. We'll go out into the field, and I'll show you what we do."

The next morning I was up and ready to go, excited at the prospect of traveling to remote villages and meeting the people I hoped to serve. Biksham picked me up in a jeep, and we made our way through the streets of Hyderabad just as the sun peeked over the rooftops and the traffic started flowing. We drove to the city's outskirts, then continued on a long, straight highway out of town.

There's a stark beauty to the Telangana countryside. It's extremely dry, so there are long stretches of dusty roads, yellowed brush, and withered, knotty trees. The earth in some areas is a deep red color, rich in iron. Tiny villages dot the landscape, and rutted dirt roads snake off into the odd copse of trees. The occasional roadside stand offers fresh fruits or cold drinks. And as you get farther and farther from the city, the air gets clearer and the sky bluer.

The roads in rural India are much rougher than those I was used to in the West, with potholes, accidents, and the occasional intrusion of farm animals slowing traffic. It took us about three hours to cover the ninety miles, but we finally pulled up to a collection of warm red mud-brick buildings in the center of a small village. "This is DDS headquarters," Biksham said. We got out of the jeep, and I took a look around.

The DDS buildings were impressive, stately almost, amid the modest dun-colored village huts with thatched roofs. A tamarind tree stood sentry, giving shade, and a large well had been dug for fresh water. The main buildings were a couple of stories tall, with ornate mud-brick carvings and balconies overlooking the courtyards, and they were well kept and inviting. We walked into one, and Biksham began showing me around.

A large hand-painted map hung in the front hallway, dividing nearby villages into clusters. A small office off to one side was crammed to the ceiling with dusty ledgers and stacks of paper and folders—a forest's worth of paperwork. Straight ahead was a cavernous meeting room, its white-washed walls and open windows giving it a bright, open air. And seated on the floor in the room was a group of about forty women, all of whom began nodding and greeting Biksham as soon as we walked in.

"This is our village leaders group," Biksham told me, then gestured for me to sit down with them. "Have a seat. Observe."

I sat among the women, and they started their meeting; they obviously had been waiting for us to arrive. The first thing they did was sing a song—a simple tune, in unison, that opened each meeting. Though my Telugu was rusty, I could make out the theme of the song: unity, the poor banding together to help each other.

Looking around the room at these women in their bright saris, their voices reverberating off the bare walls in the morning sun, I felt almost overwhelmed. This, I thought, is exactly where I want to be. I must have had a goofy, dreamy grin on my face when the song ended and Biksham spoke up. "This is Vikram," he said, gesturing to me. "He's going to spend some time with us. You all need to teach him Telugu."

The women laughed, and I looked around sheepishly. The challenge had been laid. Would I be disciplined enough to really learn Telugu? Could I take living in a remote village—away from television, telephones, newspapers, English-speaking friends, restaurants, and all the other comforts of home? Biksham clearly didn't think so, but later that day he showed me to a spartan dormitory-style room in the compound, and invited me to spend the night—and as many nights as I liked.

That whole first week, I watched and learned. I wanted to have a specific job to do, but that wasn't how Biksham operated. He wanted to see how I would comport myself with everyone, what I'd be drawn to, how I would spend my time. So, I just tagged along with others wherever I could. I hitched a ride with one DDS worker, Raghu, as he rode his motorbike out to check on an organic agricultural project, and we got drenched in a sudden downpour on the way back. I spent time at the DDS children's center, practicing my Telugu with the kids who'd drop by after school. And I went to a night meeting in one village with another DDS employee named Ranga, which gave me my first taste of what to expect while working with villagers.

I suppose I'd expected poor village women to be docile and easily led. I had an image of women nodding deferentially, looking to us for help, gratefully accepting whatever wisdom we could impart. This was ridiculously, completely, embarrassingly wrong. When I went with Ranga to the village meeting, I saw just how ambitious and aggressively outspoken the women really were. If they didn't like something, they let you know right away. And they would not countenance being talked down to. It was fascinating to watch Ranga interact with the women. Very quickly, my stereotypic notions were being stripped away.

At the end of that first week, I heard DDS was starting a new immunization program. This entailed sending volunteers and workers out to villages, where they'd knock on doors and ask whether the children of the house had been immunized. It was a straightforward task, with a simple set of standard questions—the perfect opportunity for me to get involved. I asked Biksham if I could work on the immunization project, and, to my relief, he said yes.

For the next month, I rode around to the surrounding villages in a jeep, working on both the immunization project and a DDS organic agriculture project. I spent time with community organizers, seeing how they worked, and got to know the rhythm of rural life. On occasion, if I was out late at night, I would stay over in the hut of a village family. I drank chai in village stalls, ate in small roadside *dhabas*, and talked and listened as much as I could. I slept in my small bedroom at DDS and ate the community meals at the compound. The more I did, the more I wanted to do—there weren't enough hours in the day to have all the conversations and see all the sights I was drawn to.

At the end of that first month, Biksham decided I was doing enough to warrant a salary. I hadn't asked for one, and I knew DDS didn't have any extra funds floating around, but Biksham came up to me one afternoon and said, "We're going to pay you a thousand rupees a month for your work." I was thrilled at his vote of confidence, but when I told my grandmother in Hyderabad about it, she punctured my bubble quickly.

"I pay my watchman more than that," she said and shook her head.

I wasn't surprised by her lack of enthusiasm—1,000 rupees was the equivalent of about $55 in 1990. But quite by accident, I soon discovered another reason why she, and my mother, were so dismayed by my new choice of profession.

After I started living at the DDS compound, I'd occasionally travel back to Hyderabad to visit with my grandparents, aunts, and uncles. In fact, whenever I was there, I stayed at the same aunt's house where I'd seen the woman pick up those grains of rice all those years ago.

On one visit, I happened to read a newspaper article about one of my uncles, V. Hanumantha Rao, who was then in the running for chief minister of the state of Andhra Pradesh. A chief minister in India is the equivalent of a U.S. state governor. A charismatic grassroots politician with a deep, commanding voice, this uncle was close to former prime minister Rajiv Gandhi, son of the slain prime minister Indira Gandhi, and was considered an up-and-coming young Turk in Indian politics.

But what caught my eye was a piece of information I'd never heard before: My uncle—my whole family, in fact—came from a "backward" caste. This was a significant detail in the story, as historically, members of backward castes had only been allowed to undertake manual labor or serve as craftspeople. Those strict prohibitions had begun breaking down, but even my uncle and father's generation had had limited educational and career opportunities—and those were the result of affirmative action–style programs. Backward caste members were not historically politicians—or surgeons or philosophers. In fact, they were the lowest in the four-tier Indian system, higher only than the Dalits, or untouchables.

The caste system is an ancient and enduring part of Indian society, set forth in sacred Hindu texts and long enshrined in the culture. There are four castes: the Brahmins, who are priests and scholars; the Kshatriyas, who are warriors and nobility; the Vaishyas, who are the merchant class; and the Shudras—the so-called backward caste—who are the laborers and tradespeople. Below all these are the "scheduled" caste, the untouchables, so named because the British government "scheduled" them for equal opportunity programs as the era of British rule came to an end. Yet even today, members of the scheduled caste suffer horrific discrimination, including physical and psychological abuse, for their social position. Untouchables are still considered by some Indians to be subhuman, and are at times treated as such, being threatened, beaten, forced to humiliate themselves publicly, and sometimes even murdered simply for their status.

The system is deeply rooted in Indian consciousness, and although India's constitution makes it illegal to discriminate according to caste, the reality is that it happens all the time. It is a shamefully prejudicial way of dividing people, and over the years the Indian government has enacted various affirmative action programs intended to mitigate the effects of centuries of discrimination against members of backward and scheduled castes.

I had always believed we were Vaishyas, or the merchant caste, as I knew my grandfather had run his own sari shop. Stunned by the revelation in the newspaper article, I asked him about it. And that was the first time I learned of my own family's struggle to overcome poverty.

As it turned out, my grandfather had indeed started out as a laborer. Born in 1916 in a village outside of Hyderabad, he was left fatherless at age three when his father died, leaving him and his mother in a precarious economic position. Not able to cope alone, they moved from their village to Hyderabad city to stay with relatives. And although my great-grandmother found work at a general store run by a family member, she earned just 4 rupees per month—about $6 in today's terms, barely enough for them to survive. My grandfather was forced to drop out of school in the fourth grade to work.

He started working as an errand boy in a cloth shop, earning a monthly salary of 50 *paisa*, roughly 75 cents. But my grandfather wasn't satisfied with the life that society, culture, and centuries of history had dictated for him. Ambition burned in him, and he began plotting his move out of poverty. He learned everything he could about textiles and the customers who came into the store, and eventually he worked his way up to salesman.

By the time he turned fifteen, he had developed a real knack for sales, helped along by his warm and affable nature. He managed to land a job at a different textile store at a higher salary, this time earning 3 rupees a month, about $4.50. Yet despite the raise, this was still not enough money to survive. So, he took an additional job, working part-time in the private army of the Nizam, the head of the traditional ruling dynasty of the Hyderabad region. He'd leave before dawn to go to the palace grounds, then get to the store by late morning and work into the night. The days were long and arduous; at age sixteen, my grandfather was working twelve to fourteen hours a day, six days a week.

Despite this rigorous pace, my grandfather kept trying to learn as much as possible about the textile business, even traveling with the shop manager to Mumbai to purchase saris. At the age of nineteen, he was ready to make his move: He asked the shop owner if he could start his own business. Not having any start-up capital, my grandfather proposed taking saris on credit, bicycling through neighborhoods, and selling them door to door. The owner agreed, and my grandfather quickly built up a loyal base of customers. Finally, in 1942, at age twenty-six, he was able to forge a partnership with a financier and start his own sari shop, Prabhat Cloth stores in Hyderabad's Sultan Bazaar. At the time, this was an amazing leap for a member of a backward caste.

My father grew up seeing the example of my grandfather's ambition. He, too, wanted to break the chains of our cultural heritage, and with the advent of affirmative action–style programs for lower castes in the 1950s and '60s, he was able to push ahead even further. After my father finished high school, he studied medicine—the first person in our family to reach such heights in education. And when he became a doctor, he took the first opportunity he could to move to the United States, where he and my mother could raise a family in a society that didn't care what caste we came from.

The leap my own family took, in just two generations, was astonishing. It was emblematic of the changes taking place in India during that time. It was also the reason my mother, Padma, in particular, was aghast at the career choice I was now making. She simply could not understand why, when she and my father had struggled so hard to create a better life for us in America, I would ever want to come back to live in a village and work with dirt-poor people in India. She was confused and disappointed, and she didn't hesitate to tell me so. In fact, the first time she and my father came to visit after I started working with DDS, she not only told me exactly how she felt about it, she showed me—in a most unexpected way.

My parents had flown into Hyderabad, and I was eager to take them out into the field and show them the work I was doing. I had been in India about two months then, and I was proud of my progress: My Telugu was improving, I was learning the rhythms of village life, and I had many friends, colleagues, and DDS members I wanted them to meet. We headed out to the villages, my mother reluctantly climbing into the jeep for the three-hour trip.

When we arrived at the DDS compound, I took my parents into the meeting hall, where several of the older women I'd become close to had gathered. This was a big moment for me—I was excited to introduce my mom to the women who were more or less my mother figures here in India. As a sign of respect, the women all sat on the floor and offered my mom the only chair in the room. This was a typical gesture, but my mother was mortified. It was obvious to everyone that she was fighting back tears. Why would her son choose this place, moving backward to poverty when there was so much promise elsewhere?

My mother tried to compose herself, and though I hoped they didn't pick up on the real source of her distress, the truth is that poor people know better than anyone when they're being judged. Yet the women were absolutely gracious, with one, Narsamma, offering a gentle running commentary to try to break the tension.

"What mother wouldn't be upset when her son goes far away?" she asked, smiling. "Of course, she misses Vikram. Of course, she wants him near her." The other women offered up similar banalities, until mercifully it was time to take my parents into the villages.

Unfortunately, out in the field things got worse rather than better. I walked my parents around a couple of villages, introducing them to people I'd been working with and proudly showing off my language skills. It was a brutally hot day, which I apparently hadn't taken into account, because all of a sudden my mother keeled over and dropped to the dirt with a thud.

My god! I thought. *What have I done to my mother!* I knelt beside her and put my hand on her face. "Mom!" I shouted. "Are you okay?" At which point my physician father piped up.

"Ah, she's just fainted," he said. "Give her some water. She'll be fine."

The combination of sun and emotion had gotten to my mother, but my father actually seemed to be enjoying the field visit. He didn't say it in so many words, but I think he was proud of me. Though he's a surgeon, he's not your typical wealthy doctor—in part because, before he retired, he always voluntarily treated indigent patients, never refusing to see people just because they couldn't pay. He also volunteered at a local community center, and he treated prisoners in his practice—I remember occasionally seeing big men in orange jumpsuits when I went to his office. My younger brother and I learned what it means to have a community ethic by watching my father at work. For my brother, that ethic translated into joining Teach For America and then leaving the United States to teach in war-torn Beirut, Lebanon; for me, it meant coming back to India.

We managed to revive my mother and soon got her and my father on the road back to Hyderabad. This was probably best, as very soon I would make a move into an even more remote part of India—a place where no one else in DDS would volunteer to go.

A couple of months into my stay at the DDS compound, Biksham told the employees that we'd gotten funding to expand into forty more villages. He wanted someone to head up this new program, but the person would have to move to a tiny speck of a village in an even more poverty-stricken area.

Though my mother had been unimpressed, the DDS compound actually had many comforts—a staff of women who cooked communal meals, a continuous schedule of meetings and activities, and the children's center, to name just a few. And although it was located in a small village, the compound wasn't far from a larger town, which had a couple of restaurants and even a movie theater. This new assignment, by contrast, would involve moving to an area that was not only miles away but lacked basic modern conveniences such as running water and electricity. And none of the DDS employees who were qualified to run the program had any desire to take it on.

To me, it sounded idyllic. "I'll do it," I told Biksham. "I'd like to run this project."

Biksham sized me up. Over the last couple of months, I had proven I was committed to working in rural India. I'd done everything he'd asked of me. And now I was asking for more. Besides—no one else would do it, so what choice did he have? "Okay, Vikram," he said. "Here's your opportunity."

I had arrived in India with only my gym bag of clothes, but the women at DDS weren't about to let me go off into the sticks without some essentials. They quickly rounded up pots and pans, a few dishes, some utensils and basic tools, and sheets and a pillow. A DDS driver and I loaded everything in the back of a jeep, and off we went.

Eventually, the driver rolled to a stop in front of a small, abandoned one-room building in the middle of a huge field. "Here we are!" he said. As I got out I saw where "here" was: essentially, the middle of nowhere. He helped me unload my things, and together we carried them into the small room that would serve as my new home.

The first thing I noticed was that there was no door, which meant no way to keep out mosquitoes and flies, wandering animals, or other intruders. The second thing was that this was the most austere room imaginable. There was nothing in it; the walls were utterly bare, without even any windows. Outside, parched fields stretched around me in every direction, and, in the distance, there was a rock quarry. There was no one around, though a small village was visible in the distance.

The driver walked me to the village and introduced me to a few locals. In any rural Indian village, word spreads quickly when something unusual happens—or, as in this case, when someone unusual shows up. Soon enough, a small group had gathered, asking what I was doing there. "I'm from the Deccan Development Society," I told them. "We're starting a new project in your area."

Most were simply curious, though one man seemed concerned for my safety. "I will stay here with you until you get a door," he said. I was grateful but also felt a little silly. Here I was trying to head up a big new project, and I was being looked after like a little boy. It was mildly embarrassing—but it was hardly the last time I'd end up feeling embarrassed in this village.

As I quickly learned, I pretty much didn't know how to do anything I needed to do. The man who'd volunteered to stay with me ended up helping me build a small fire, so I could at least boil some water and make some rice and dal for dinner. But where would I get water? There was obviously no running water in my little room, and I had no clue where the nearest well was. He walked me to the well and showed me how to draw water. When I asked about where to use the bathroom, he gestured to the vast field.

"There's a quarry down the way," he said. "Just go down there. Everyone does." As it turned out, the little building that would serve as my new home was originally part of a weigh station for trucks headed to and from the quarry. After excavation there had stopped, the weigh station was abandoned, and it had sat unused since that time. The first thing I needed to do was get some doors made—but how do you go about that in a village you've never been to, with no obvious way to find out? Fortunately, a DDS staff person lived in a village nearby, and Biksham told him to stop by to help me out. Within a week, he helped me get some doors made.

The other person who helped me out was the village "fixer"—a local resident who acts as a dealmaker and general conduit between those who need something and those who can provide it. The first thing the fixer did was find a woman to cook for me. I had never imagined I'd have my own cook, but the reality was that it was just too time-consuming to have to gather firewood, make a fire, haul water to boil, and prepare food every day. I had no refrigerator or icebox, so everything had to be made fresh. The simple process of existing consumed far more energy and time than I had ever imagined.

Anyone who thinks poor people are lazy should spend a week living as many of them do. With none of the conveniences the developed world takes for granted, every chore takes inordinate amounts of time and energy. From cooking to bathing to cleaning, nothing was easy. And I found that, embarrassingly, I had no clue how to do the simplest things. "No, no, no!" the local women yelled the first time they saw me trying to wash my clothes. They explained the process to me: First, soak your clothes with either soap powder or a hard soap cake. You do it by the well, so the water will run off in drainage. Then, you wring out the sudsy water and whack each item hard against the well stones, to get the dirt out. Finally, you rinse the clothes, tie them together, and hang them off a nearby tree. I didn't want to admit it, but the first few times I washed my clothes, I was sore the next day from the exertion.

Even more embarrassing was learning how to use the bathroom, village-style. As I'd been told, I would need to head down to the quarry and just find a place to go. But Indians, unlike Westerners, don't use toilet paper—they simply bring a small pot of water and use their left hand to clean up (hence the intense cultural taboo against ever eating with your left hand or offering it in a social setting). Until I got the hang of it, I needed to bring a good deal more water out to the quarry, which led to snickers from villagers whenever I passed by with my bucket of water.

I also set about trying to dig a well. We were hoping to turn the old weigh station into another DDS compound, with a plan to reforest the land surrounding it, so we'd need a closer source of water than the existing well. What did I know about digging a well? Nothing—that wasn't something they taught at Tufts. I decided to hire a local laborer to help me do it. I had someone in mind but had no idea what such a job should pay. And unfortunately, such a direct question will never result in a direct answer in an Indian village. "How much should I pay him?" I asked a few locals. "Well," they would reply, wobbling their heads in a common Indian gesture, "You know how much!" I didn't, but I decided to wing it. So, I hired several more laborers, both men and women, to get the project going. The men would use pickaxes and shovels, slowly descending into the deepening hole, and the women would haul the dirt away. They dug and scraped and sweated, toiling for hours in the hot sun until finally hitting bedrock, at which point I hired a couple of guys to come in with dynamite to finish the job. They blew the bedrock to smithereens, and the laborers descended even farther down to cart out the rubble. Soon, we had made a giant, gaping hole, deep enough to require carving a set of steps to get out. It was incredibly impressive. And dry as a bone.

I felt disappointed, even a little silly. But fortunately, Biksham had given me an extremely valuable piece of advice when he'd sent me off into the hinterlands.

"Don't worry about making a mistake," he'd told me. "It'll be okay. Just do what you think is best."

I really had no other choice, since there was no telephone in the village, and I had no way of checking in with Biksham to debate my decisions, large or small. Every other week or so, I'd ride my Hero Honda motorbike back to DDS headquarters to meet with Biksham and give him updates on the project, but other than that, I just had to make decisions based on my not-so-vast twenty-one years of life experience. It was extremely helpful to know I wouldn't be criticized in the inevitable event that something went wrong.

In the meantime, I was starting to understand what Biksham meant when he said, "You cannot help the poor." India was rife with well-intended but badly conceived projects that misguided elites had inflicted on the poor.

Bureaucrats gave subsidized loans so the poor could buy high-milk-yielding Jersey cows—but the exotic cows couldn't handle drought conditions and died. A project that introduced capital-intensive agriculture led to a drop in the water table, so although a handful of farmers benefited, everyone else in the community suffered. Educational programs for poor children failed to prepare them for the formal economy but succeeded in alienating them from their traditional economies, leaving them ill-equipped for either situation. In fact, it seemed that most efforts to "help" the poor ended up harming them in some way instead.

There was a strikingly wide gap between the conversations I had with educated Indians in Hyderabad and the Indians I knew in the villages. The longer I spent in the field, the clearer it became that the people who knew most about how to help the poor were the poor themselves. It made me wonder why those in a position to help always seemed to avoid asking those they wished to help what they truly needed.

Around this same time, I began reading a book called *Rural Development: Putting the Last First*, by Robert Chambers. Its central point was that the development community takes a top-down view of rural poverty, with executives and bureaucrats from nonprofits getting their information from either large-scale survey questionnaires or brief and hurried visits to villages located just outside of cities. Because they have limited direct engagement with poor people, they get incomplete information, so they end up designing inadequate, and sometimes downright harmful, programs. Poor people themselves are actually far more knowledgeable about their situations than outsiders, and they also have ideas about how to improve things.

As a liberal college student, I had bought into the notion that the poor aren't terribly knowledgeable and that they need education from outsiders. But from my experience of living in Indian villages, I quickly realized that they generally knew far more than I did. During my first few months in the village, I was the one always looking for help, support, and ideas from them, not the other way around.

Putting the Last First forever changed the way I approached the poor. It was the final piece of the puzzle; reading that book while simultaneously watching the poor in their own environment convinced me that Biksham was absolutely right. We couldn't help the poor—but what we could do, and had to do, was help the poor to help themselves. Every product, every system, every program that was designed to help the poor had to be designed by the poor themselves. This became my new goal.

I also came to one more equally important realization at this time. No matter what I was doing at DDS headquarters or in the villages—immunization, agricultural initiatives, health, education, whatever—the conversation always came back around to the same thing: money.

I began noticing that, whenever I'd go to a village to talk about launching a DDS initiative, there would be a brief flurry of conversation among the village leaders. As my language skills improved, I could glean what these conversations were about: People were discussing who I was and what I was in the village to do. Was I the guy who could give out microloans? No? Then who was?

Villagers cared about social projects such as educational and health initiatives, but only to a point. What they really wanted was loans for entrepreneurial activities. They wanted to be able to take care of themselves; everything else was secondary.

This realization was a huge revelation for me—the second one I'd had since coming to India. Now I knew these two things: First, that the poor must control their own ascent from poverty. And second, that money was the root of all self-empowerment solutions. Now the question became, how could I bring these two ideas together to help eliminate poverty?

I wanted to stay in India and keep searching for the answer, but after more than a year and a half in the field, Biksham gave me a piece of advice. "You should go back to America," he said. "You will burn out if you stay here. Go back and get a graduate degree."

He was right. Living in India was exhilarating but exhausting. With reluctance, I returned to the United States to continue my studies, counting the days until I could return to Telangana villages.

CHAPTER 4

THE STORY OF MY EXPERIMENTS WITH GRAMEEN

In the fall of 1974, when I was a boy happily playing soccer in Schenectady, a man named Muhammad Yunus was watching a catastrophe unfold in his native Bangladesh. Famine had struck the land, and hundreds of thousands of people were suffering, and dying, for lack of food. Professor Yunus, then a thirty-four-year-old economist, had gotten his PhD at Vanderbilt University in Nashville and had stayed active in Bangladeshi politics even while living in the United States. But in 1974, he returned to southeastern Bangladesh, where he joined the faculty of Chittagong University in Hathazari Upazila to teach economics. That fall, his fate—and the fate of millions of poor people—changed forever when Professor Yunus, moved by the plight of a group of starving families, gave a $27 loan to help them launch a small business. It was a minuscule amount by Western standards but a lifeline for his starving compatriots. And it sparked an idea.

Within two years, Professor Yunus launched an experiment: a project to determine the feasibility of offering very small loans to very poor people, to help them out of poverty. He started in a village called Jobra and quickly expanded to other nearby villages. What he found was that not only were poor Bangladeshis eager to start their own enterprises, they were surprisingly good at it, too. The project, called Grameen, from the Bengali word for "villages," continued to expand.

By 1983, the Grameen experiment was spreading like wildfire, with more and more Bangladeshis clamoring for loans. That year, the Bangladeshi government granted the Grameen project official bank status, and the newly incorporated Grameen Bank continued to expand. Over the next thirty-five years, Grameen would reach almost nine million borrowers.[1] Grameen Bank wasn't the first-ever microfinance institution, but it was certainly the most influential, as new MFIs that cropped up in the ensuing years often borrowed its innovative practices. For his vision and effort in spreading the practice of microfinance, Professor Yunus was awarded the Nobel Peace Prize in 2006.

Muhammad Yunus was already a legend when I began working in microfinance in the early 1990s. I had read all about him and thought what he was doing was incredibly visionary. After spending a year and a half in remotest India, seeing for myself how entrepreneurial and energetic the villagers really were, I realized that I wanted to do what Professor Yunus was doing. Microfinance gave poor people the power to help themselves, rather than bestowing misguided help on them from above. My next foray to India would be a perfect example of trying to correct such misguided aid.

I had returned to the United States at Biksham's urging to embark on graduate studies, but for the whole three years back in the States, I was plotting a return to India. My studies were a bit haphazard—I bounced from Harvard Divinity School to the Worldwatch Institute to a master's program at Yale University—but I was fortunate enough to win a Fulbright scholarship in 1994, enabling me to return to DDS and the villages. The new project I'd be working on demonstrated exactly how misguided programs designed to "help" the poor could be updated and improved.

In its year of independence in 1947, the Indian government had set up a food grain distribution program. Essentially, the state would buy grain and give it to people at a subsidized cost. It was a well-intentioned project, but not very practical in terms of sustainability, as the money flow was all one way, from the government to the people.

So DDS came up with an alternative. Instead of simply using the subsidy to give poor people grain, why not give them that same subsidy money as a no-interest loan? Then they could plant and grow their own grain, sell some of it and keep some for themselves, and repay the government its money. This would be far more sustainable than the existing program—and on top of it all, it would also create jobs for agricultural field-workers and regenerate lands left fallow for lack of capital.

The government agreed with DDS and funded the project to the tune of $250,000. And I was offered the chance to head it up. This would be my first time working on a project that was purely about microfinance, and I was excited. What I didn't anticipate was that the new program, well intentioned as it was, was a bit of a mess.

I recruited several loan officers to help me cover the thirty villages in our purview. Their task was theoretically simple: Set up meeting times in each village, then travel there at the appointed times to hand out loans, collect repayments, and discuss any problems with borrowers. In reality, it became a nightmare.

Some borrowers repaid their loans in grain, but for those who repaid in cash, several problems arose. For one thing, the various people who had received loans had different schedules for repaying. Some were supposed to make payments periodically throughout the growing season, while others made a lump-sum payment at the end of the season. And because these were zero-interest loans, provided with government subsidies, some borrowers didn't seem terribly concerned about repaying at all.

Meetings in villages were typically scheduled for evenings. A loan officer would ride his motorbike into a village, sometimes with a backpack full of cash—either from previous repayments or for new loans. It wasn't safe to be carrying that much cash at night, but there wasn't really an alternative, as the agricultural work the loans were paying for had to take place in daylight hours.

Because the loan repayments were all in differing amounts, each loan officer had to keep careful track of who paid how much, counting out crumpled bills and sorting through handfuls of coins, then writing the varying numbers down in a ledger. He'd then record the amounts on a receipt for each borrower, again writing everything by hand, on the spot, as there weren't standard preset amounts. The process wasn't automated at all—not in the field, and not back at DDS headquarters, where information from the ledgers was painstakingly hand-copied into other ledgers and stored in giant stacks of books.

With thirty villages in our program, we were manually tracking thousands of transactions. And with differing amounts and differing dates of repayment for everyone, the process was far more complicated than it needed to be. But for the whole year and a half I headed the project, that was how we did it, even though one thought kept creeping into my head: There has to be a better way to do this. At the time, however, this was how everyone in microfinance kept track—by hand, in ledgers, with all the mistakes and inefficiencies that entailed.

And this still wasn't the biggest problem with microfinance. The biggest problem was revealed that summer, when I had to tell that determined, hopeful woman in the faded purple sari that we had no money to expand to her village. Her response—"Am I not poor, too?"—pushed me to the next level: I realized then that I didn't simply want to practice microfinance; I wanted to improve it. I wanted to make it possible for *everyone* who desired a loan to get one.

But how would that be possible? When I returned to my studies in the United States after eighteen months of running the DDS microfinance project, I resolved to answer that question once and for all.

On returning to the States in 1996, I enrolled in a PhD program at the University of Chicago. In reality, I didn't much care about getting a doctorate; I just wanted to have time to plot my move into full-time microfinance. Chicago was very strong in South Asian studies, and it had an excellent political science department, so that's where I headed. Studying political science gave me the greatest latitude in finding a dissertation topic, but there was another reason why I chose it.

Although microfinance is, on the surface, about loans and business and interest rates, my time in India had convinced me that, at its core, it's really about power. Success in microfinance wasn't measured only in numbers. It was measured in the changing power dynamics. It was about changing historical and cultural norms, shifting centuries-old power structures in a way that would help the traditionally downtrodden. While perhaps not the most obvious choice, a political science doctorate seemed a natural fit for what I was trying to accomplish.

The more I thought about the problem of how to scale microfinance, the more I realized there were three essential problems with the way it was practiced. First, there was never enough money to go around—the problem I'd faced with the woman in the purple sari. Second, the haphazard way it was practiced, with differing loan amounts and dates of repayments, for example, made the process highly inefficient. And third, the cost of doing business was too high—with so many tiny loans, and so much time and energy required to collect on them, the transaction costs were too high and the margins too low to be sustainable.

I began to think of these problems as the "three Cs": capital, capacity, and costs. I didn't know yet how to solve them, but I believed that if I could, microfinance could expand to serve tens of millions—even hundreds of millions—more people than it was then serving. Yes, existing MFIs were doing a lot of good, but with more than 750 million poor people in India alone, "good" was never going to be good enough.

In the midst of all this pondering and planning and studying, I hit on a simple but powerful idea: Why not make the practice of microfinance operate more like a business? After all, I'd seen firsthand how borrowers were able to generate significant profits that they could not have created without access to finance. They would have been happy to give a portion of that profit in the form of interest if it meant they could have continued access to larger pools of finance. Meanwhile, with the interest earnings, an MFI could sustain itself and even earn a profit. It was a win-win. In this way, I thought, microfinance could potentially become a highly profitable business, which would generate income and even make enough money to attract commercial capital. That way, the pot of money could continue to grow, even as more and more loans were given out.

Some other emerging microfinance leaders had similar ideas, but my notion of highly commercial microfinance was pretty radical for the time. There seemed to be an unspoken law that microfinance providers had to function as nonprofits—they could offer loans to the poor and charge interest, but only as much as they needed to cover the bare-bones minimum cost of supporting the work. Money for microcredit typically came from government grants, foundations, or donors, and when it was lent out, it was gone. Sure, it eventually came back in the form of repayments, but there was no way to grow the programs beyond the number of people those finite donations could serve at any given time.

Turning microfinance into a commercial venture seemed to be the perfect solution. If a microfinance institution could be run as a profitable enterprise, it could attract investment from private investors—those who expected a return. Since private investors are a virtually unlimited pool—after all, everybody wants a return on their investments—there would be no limit on the amount of funding available. And inviting private investors would have another benefit: Once we had the equity provided by their investments, commercial banks would be willing to lend us even more money, giving us a vastly bigger pool of capital. The only catch was that interest rates would have to be fair for borrowers but high enough to not only cover costs but provide investors a healthy return.

This seemed an acceptable trade-off to me. Why did "doing good" necessarily have to be a nonprofit activity? Why did the money flow have to be in only one direction, from donors to the poor? Why not bring things full circle, making it possible for donors—or investors, as the case would be—to make money from supporting microfinance? There was an artificial wall between nonprofit and for-profit ventures, but there didn't have to be.

I was excited about this idea and started writing a business plan. The notion of starting a company was too daunting—especially since I'd seen the level of bureaucracy and corruption I'd have to navigate in India—so initially, I just wanted to start an experimental for-profit branch of an existing MFI. I started putting together funding proposals while still doing my PhD coursework, setting a crazy pace that, unbeknownst to me then, wouldn't slow down for more than fifteen years.

The idea of raising equity for microfinance was unheard of at that time, so initially I looked for donations. For me, raising donations did not contradict my commercial philosophy because my intention was to convert those donations into equity (not in the name of the donor but in the name of the foundation to which they donated), after the for-profit venture became profitable. So, I started to raise funds.

I didn't know anything about raising money, but my efforts got a jump start when the Chicago-based India Development Service, a volunteer group formed to support Indian nonprofits, made me an offer. I had asked them for $10,000—more than their typical grants of $5,000 or so—and they said they'd give it to me, on one condition. I had to raise $10,000 from other sources to match it.

This instantly put me into high gear. With $20,000, my crazy idea just might become a reality. I picked up the phone and started dialing people—colleagues of my father, friends of my mother, parents of my Indian friends, anyone who I thought might be willing to give a few dollars.

It was tough going at first. I had no idea what I was doing and felt slightly cowed about asking people for money. I'd spend a half hour on the phone with a wealthy Indian-American doctor, listening to him pontificate about "what India needs," and then at the end he'd offer me $50. I went to an event my late uncle, Chandrashekhar Thunga, put together at his house in Chicago, and when I felt too timid to ask for money outright, he pulled me aside and said, "Vikram, your idea is good. But you have no idea how to raise money from Indians. You have to say, 'Give me a check for one thousand dollars now!'" This wasn't the first time, nor would it be the last, that someone told me I needed to be more direct with Indians.

My parents stepped up, too, holding samosa-and-tea parties for friends so I could come and do my song and dance, complete with a slide presentation. Having seen my mother's reaction to my work in India, and knowing how much she wished I would pursue a different career, I was really touched by her show of support. With their help, the money continued to trickle in on my visits home to New York. People would hand me $51 or $101 at the end of a samosa evening (superstitious Indians never give an amount ending in zero, as it means the funding will end there). My parents also gave money, as did my uncle in Chicago, who pitched in $5,001 himself.

I also filled out applications for start-up funding from foundations, which was another thing I'd never done before. So I sought some outside help. One afternoon in the spring of 1997, I made my way to the basement office of the university's associate dean of student services, seeking guidance for writing these proposals. I walked into a modest room ringed with piles of paperwork—a typical no-frills student services office—and greeted the woman seated behind the desk. Her name was Michelle Obama.

At the time, Barack Obama was running for the Illinois State Senate, and Michelle had recently left her position with the non-profit organization Public Allies. She was developing the university's Community Service Center, and she was the most accessible and knowledgeable adviser I could think of to ask for help.

Over the course of several meetings, she advised me on a proposal I was writing to the Echoing Green foundation, giving me valuable feedback on drafts. She suggested that I offer more concrete details in my proposal, as I had a habit of telling the stories of the poor women I'd met but sometimes fell short on enumerating what exactly I needed. "You need to be more specific," she told me. "How much money are you looking for in the first and second years? You need to work out your budget." With her help, I realized I needed to show the foundation that I knew what I was doing operationally, not just philosophically.

With all the fundraising parties, grant applications, and course-work, the academic year passed by in a blur. I hit up everyone I knew, and donations trickled in from more than 300 people, some of whom gave as little as $11. But by the end of the year, I had managed to raise about $52,000, including the $10,000 matching grant—far more than I had dreamed possible.

The next step was finding an existing microfinance institution that would let me open a for-profit branch as an experiment. This shouldn't be too hard, I thought, since I was bringing donor money to fund the project. But as I soon found out, money alone wasn't enough to break down the entrenched thinking among existing MFIs.

In early February 1997, the first-ever Microcredit Summit was held at the Sheraton in Washington, D.C. Three thousand people came from all over the world, and First Lady Hillary Rodham Clinton gave the keynote address. I knew Professor Yunus was going to be there, as well as the leaders of MFIs operating in India, so I packed up my only suit and tie and headed for the capital.

Despite having raised $52,000 for my project, I had no money myself, so I got into the summit by volunteering to be an official timekeeper for the sessions. As soon as the volunteer schedule came out, I jockeyed with the other timekeepers to get into the sessions I wanted. While the perfect way to attend the conference for free, being a timekeeper made it difficult to approach the panelists as a colleague when they saw me as merely a student volunteer. However, this was my big chance, so I took every opportunity to tell others about my project.

I approached David Gibbons, who was launching a microfinance initiative called Cashpor in the Indian state of Uttar Pradesh. I talked to Udaia Kumar of Share Microfin, which had been operating in India since 1989. I met Ela Bhatt of the Self-Employed Women's Association, or SEWA. I approached Alex Counts of the Grameen Foundation USA, as I couldn't even get close to Muhammad Yunus, who even then had a kind of rock star status. I hustled and talked and introduced myself to anyone who I thought might be interested in my for-profit experiment.

Everyone said no. No one wanted to take a chance on an untested theory cooked up by an eager graduate student. I was told I was "too young," "not experienced enough," and, in two cases, "too American" to make the project work. No matter how persuasively I argued, no matter how much I tried to charm my listeners, nothing worked. I left the summit disappointed and embarrassed that no one seemed to take me seriously. But I also felt the stirrings of something else: a determination to prove them all wrong.

If no one wanted to take a chance on me, then fine. I would do it myself! I hadn't planned to start my own organization, and I didn't relish the idea of all the paperwork and bureaucratic hassle it would entail, but I believed so strongly in my idea that there was no other choice. I decided to call it SKS, for *Swayam Krishi Sangam*, a

Sanskrit phrase meaning "self-cultivation society," or, more loosely, "self-help society."

I returned to Chicago, feeling exhilarated and daunted. Raising money was one thing, but launching an independent organization—in India, no less—was quite another. I spent the rest of the spring and summer doing research and asking as many people as possible for advice. Given its status as a pioneer in the field, I knew I wanted to follow the example of Grameen Bank. So, in November 1997, I traveled to Bangladesh for a two-week training session with Grameen.

The Grameen Dialogue program was designed for people who wanted to learn the Grameen system for distributing loans and collecting payments. Over the nearly two decades Grameen had been in business, its management had plenty of time to try out different methods and see what worked best. From what I saw in the field, the basics of their system were elegant and efficient, so I resolved to borrow their ideas for SKS.

Grameen lent almost exclusively to women, as men had proven more likely to spend cash in hand on personal items rather than on their businesses or households. Also, women had shown themselves to be excellent entrepreneurs, despite cultural biases to the contrary. Putting women in charge of a household's loan was a way of empowering them, too, though that was a welcome by-product of the system rather than a goal of it.

The Grameen system was based on an ingenious combination of trust and peer pressure. Borrowers were divided into subgroups of five, and within a given village there might be as many as eight of these subgroups, making a total of forty borrowers. Each woman in the group was responsible for her own loan repayments, but if any one woman missed a payment, no one else in the group could receive a loan until it was paid.

In this way, all the women looked out for each other and likewise kept each other in line. They shared a community bond—a bond the weekly meetings were designed to strengthen. The women would gather each week at the appointed time, opening their meeting by reciting, in unison, a series of pledges—to follow the rules of the lending program, to look out for their fellow borrowers, to send their children to school, and so forth. And the Grameen loan officers would collect payments, approve new loans, and address any questions the borrowers had.

Sitting in on a borrowers' meeting is a powerful experience. Taking my place in the group, looking around at these entrepreneurial poor women in their colorful saris and bangles, I remembered the feeling I had on my first visit to DDS, seeing the village leaders sing. These meetings are the most basic building blocks for ending poverty: They represent poor people taking control of their own destinies, pulling themselves up and creating not only economic betterment, but hope for themselves. Seeing this in action is nothing short of inspiring.

It's easy, and common, to assume that poor people are not very smart. Why else would they still be mired in poverty, after all? But the truth is that huge numbers of poor people are both very smart and very entrepreneurial, as we've seen time and again in the microfinance world. The expression "a fistful of rice" (a phrase I chose as the title of my 2010 memoir) comes from an entrepreneurial practice of the poor: A woman cooking a pot of rice will typically take one handful of grains and put it away in a separate place. This "fistful of rice" is an investment, a hedge against possible shortages later.

The beauty of microfinance is that it provides tools for the poor that they've never had access to before. That lack of access has been devastating: It's like trying to play tennis without a racquet, or becoming a great musician without an instrument. No matter what innate talent you may have, it's useless without the simple tools needed to express or develop it. Over the years, Grameen's borrowers had launched all kinds of successful enterprises: small home-front stores, tailoring, potato farming, selling goat milk. People could choose to invest in something they were already good at, rather than something that was dictated to them.

I took in everything I could during that two-week program, scribbling notes and asking numerous questions. The Grameen model would serve as a perfect basis for SKS, but I already saw a few things that needed changing. One particularly jarring example came when I asked a Grameen loan officer for a loan history of one of his members.

"Give me a day," the loan officer said.

I assumed he asked for some time because he was busy, but to my astonishment, he needed the time to pull down dusty ledgers from previous years, so he could look up and then scribble down by hand each loan and repayment this member had made. We had similar manual accounting at DDS, but I assumed that Grameen Bank was more advanced. Imagine walking into any Western bank—even back in the '90s—and asking for records pertaining to a client's loans or deposits. No modern bank would have to page through handwritten ledgers to produce those figures. It was utterly primitive, shockingly so. I knew we would have to find a way to automate our recordkeeping, even if it meant developing a new software program to do it.

At the end of the two-week session, I finally got to meet the man I thought of as a personal hero: Muhammad Yunus. He was the closing speaker for a small group of us, and afterward we all got a chance to spend a few minutes talking with him. I was excited at having the chance to meet him—and cocky enough to tell him I planned to improve upon his methods.

"You know how Gandhi called his autobiography *The Story of My Experiments with Truth*?" I asked him. "Well, one day I'm going to write my autobiography and call it *The Story of My Experiments with Grameen*." Professor Yunus just smiled, no doubt amused at the hubris of this twenty-something upstart who had yet to distribute a single loan from his own organization.

Despite my seeming arrogance, I was starstruck enough that I bought three traditional handwoven Bangladeshi shirts from Grameen's borrower-run textile company, so I could dress like him. I still have one of them—the other two wore out from overuse. I also still have the small, intricately decorated hand fan he gave to each of us, handmade by one of Grameen's borrowers. Meeting Professor Yunus was a thrill, and I made no secret of wanting to emulate him. But I wanted to outperform him, too.

In December 1997, shortly after finishing the Grameen program, I made my way from Bangladesh to Hyderabad. This was it—time to start SKS and get the ball rolling on what I was convinced would be a better, stronger, more efficient microfinance system. However, the process of getting permission to bring my $52,000 into India would prove slower, less efficient, and more frustrating than I ever imagined.

I enlisted DDS cofounder Vithal Rajan as chairperson and went to register SKS as soon as I arrived in India. I ran into the first snag when a government official asked me for a bribe to complete the paperwork. This wasn't terribly surprising, as Indians have for centuries followed a tradition of handing out *baksheesh*, or small bribes, to get things done. Even though it's absolutely ingrained in the culture, and taken for granted by many Indians, I was determined not to grease anyone's palms for any reason. Whatever money I had was earmarked for the poor, and I resented the notion of paying extra for ordinary services. Besides, though the culture of petty bribery was accepted among Indians, I knew that it was the poor who were the ones least able to afford such bribes and thus are hurt most by a culture of bribery. How could I participate in bribe-giving when it would disadvantage precisely those people I wanted to help? The end could not begin to justify the means; in this case, the means would in fact subvert the end.

So, instead of paying the bribe, I just kept coming back to the same office every day—day in and day out—until they at last got sick of seeing me and agreed to register SKS. That was step one.

Step two was transferring the $52,000 from the United States into India. The Indian government keeps close tabs on large sums of money that are transferred into and out of the country to ensure it isn't being used for terrorist activities or money laundering, so a fair amount of paperwork was required to make the transfer. Once again, an official asked me for a bribe to expedite getting permission, and once again I said no. This official was far more stubborn than the first. He knew how much money I was trying to bring in, so he knew the stakes were high. He had to assume that, with tens of thousands of dollars in the balance, I'd be willing to skim a little off the top to make things easier—that's just how things are done. But to his surprise, I refused to do it. And so, we found ourselves at a stalemate.

Weeks went by. I kept pushing for permission, and he kept denying it. We met periodically, though neither of us would budge even slightly in the other's direction. I couldn't believe this—here I was, trying to bring money into a country that needed all the help it could get to alleviate poverty, and I was being met by a stony "No, thank you." This was ludicrous! It wasn't like I was trying to come in and take money from Indians—just the opposite. After all the work I'd done already, it was incredibly frustrating to be sitting in Hyderabad, waiting for permission that might never come.

After six weeks of failed cajoling, my resolve began to break down. I set up yet another meeting with the official, which again ended in a stalemate. After the meeting, he and I ended up sharing a three-wheeled auto-rickshaw taxi, zooming through Hyderabad on our way to our respective destinations, when I began to think I had no other choice: If I wanted to work in India, I might have to pay this bribe, even though the thought of it made me sick.

It was January 30, 1998—the fiftieth anniversary of the death of Mahātmā Gandhi. In India, Gandhi's death is observed annually with two minutes of complete silence at 11 AM. Television stations go dark, radio programs go quiet, and people everywhere stop what they're doing to stand or sit quietly, remembering.

Sitting in the auto-rickshaw, just as I was thinking, "I actually might have to pay this bribe," all the traffic around us screeched to a halt. People got out of their cars, stepped out of shops, and stood utterly still on the sidewalks. "What's happening?" I asked, having forgotten, amid the day's frustration, about the commemoration. As we stepped out of our auto-rickshaw, the driver reminded me it was the remembrance of Gandhi's death anniversary.

If this were a scene in a movie, you wouldn't believe it. We had stopped just within view of Hyderabad's massive statue of Gandhi, near the State Assembly. I looked at the great man, sitting cross-legged with his eyes closed, his bald head gleaming in the sun. He looked like he was carrying the weight of the world on his thin shoulders. I thought, *I will never pay this bribe, or any bribe.*

The timing of this moment was nothing short of bizarre, but it jolted me into remembering what was truly important. I didn't offer the bribe, and I continued holding out for permission. And instead of sitting idly at my aunt and uncle's house and fretting about the delay, I decided to start working on how SKS would be set up, because I knew now that it might be months before permission came through.

I went to the district census bureau for statistics on poverty in nearby villages and began studying where we might start our lending. I borrowed money from relatives and rented jeeps so I could go into rural areas and start visiting villages. I began thinking about how to find good loan officers when the money finally did come through. Yet although I was keeping myself busy with important groundwork, I was frustrated beyond measure as the months rolled by and the official still refused permission to bring in my $52,000.

Finally, by the beginning of the Indian summer in April, I'd had enough. I began drafting an opinion-editorial for *The Hindu* newspaper, to shine a light on how corruption in India was driving me away. I didn't keep a copy of that essay, but the gist was this: Everyone complains that smart, ambitious Indians are leaving the country in droves. Well, I'm an Indian-American who wanted to come back and do something good for the country, but the government won't let me.

So, fine! I'll pack my bags and keep those funds in America, and do something there instead.

Biksham and I were still in touch, and I told him my plan. I really was prepared to leave, but not before telling everyone in India what their culture of corruption had wrought. Biksham listened patiently as I ranted, and then he made no pronouncement one way or the other. He simply listened, then went about his own business.

Which was why I was surprised when, very shortly after that, the permission was granted—thanks to Biksham's intervention. I hadn't asked him to do it, but after we spoke he had made a call over the official's head—to the secretary of the home ministry, the highest-ranking official in the ministry—and essentially said, "This kid wants to do something good. You should let him do it." And with that, the months of agonizing were over. It would take a few more months for the money transfer to happen, but I was finally free to start SKS. It was the summer of 1998, eight years since I'd first flown to Hyderabad with my gym bag of clothes and dreams of helping Indians. Now it was time to see what I could do. Unfortunately, from the very first step, I found out I had a lot more to learn about India.

CHAPTER 5

RANGOLI POWDER AND A HANDFUL OF SEEDS

It was a hot June day when I went out into the field with SKS's first employee, a young woman named Rama Laxmi, and suddenly realized just how unprepared I was.

I had hired Rama, a passionate community organizer, after placing an ad in a Hyderabad newspaper, and she was the perfect first employee. She had experience in microfinance and development, she had worked in rural villages, and she was unflappable. This last trait was probably the most important, as she met my bumbling start-up mistakes—and there would be many—with equanimity and poise.

We drove out to the countryside, to a remote town called Narayankhed, ready to start recruiting SKS's first members in the villages I'd identified through my census research. Once we'd gotten hundreds of miles outside Hyderabad, I had a flash of realization: There are no hotels out here, in the middle of nowhere! Rama and I had no place to stay, and it was too far to drive back to Hyderabad every night—we'd be on the road for eight hours a day, a colossal waste of precious time.

What to do? I was winging it, as usual, but of course that wouldn't do now that I was traveling with a colleague—an unmarried woman, no less. We began asking around, and I was relieved when a man in one of the towns told us he could help us out with a place to stay. But his solution turned out to be anything but conventional.

"I run a satellite TV business," he told us. "You can sleep at the building where I keep my dish."

As we soon found out, his "satellite TV business" consisted of splicing wires to provide illegal TV service to customers—a common practice in rural India ever since cable TV started penetrating the area in the late 1990s. The room he was offering us was part of the business. "You have your choice," he said. "You can stay in this room, where we keep the TV on all night to make sure the signal isn't disrupted. Or, if you want, you can sleep on the roof." We didn't want our sleep disturbed by endless all-night Bollywood movies, so we chose the roof. When I look back now, I can't believe I asked Rama to do this—sleep on the roof of a random building in her first week of work. To my immense relief and her great credit, she didn't question it at all.

Rama and I stayed on the roof of the satellite building for three nights, until we finally found a room we could rent in a small building nearby. We divided that single room into three parts: my sleeping area, Rama's sleeping area, and our office area. From the standpoint of cultural taboos in conservative rural India, this wasn't much better—but at least we now had a roof over our heads.

With our housing and office needs taken care of—after a fashion, anyway—we set about signing up our first SKS members. We enlisted the help of a couple of stringers for local newspapers, part-time journalists who knew the area very well, and asked them which villages were the poorest, where people would be most in need of loans. We then asked them to come along with us to those villages, to help make introductions.

Rama and I would walk into a village with a stringer, and, within a few minutes, the locals started approaching us. Who were we? What did we want? The stringer explained to them that we were starting a new lending program and wanted to meet with them. And soon enough, a group of interested villagers gathered around, ready to hear what we had to say.

When a big enough group had gathered, Rama would ask someone to draw a map of the village, using *rangoli* powder we'd brought. Rangoli powder, similar to chalk powder, is traditionally used for drawing decorative designs on the ground in front of villagers' houses. This was considered a woman's task, so right from the start, we were engaging with local women, one of whom would pick up the powder and start drawing the village.

Once she started drawing, we asked for the basics: Where's the village well? Where does the bus come? Where are the agricultural fields? As the watching crowd grew bigger, we asked more questions: How many small home-front convenience stores—called *kirana* stores—were there? How many tea stalls? Then we'd move into specifics about the villagers themselves. Which households were the poorest? Who needed work?

We also asked the women to diagram the seasonal cash flow. What time of year did the agricultural work pick up? How many days would people typically get work? Were they paid in cash or in kind? And if in cash, how much? In this way, we could quickly get an idea of how many people in a given village might be receptive to taking a loan, how much they would need, and when.

The techniques we were using were known as "participatory rural appraisal," which involved using highly visual group exercises to get villagers to talk about social and economic matters.[1] I had learned and used these techniques during my days at the nonprofit DDS, and I had picked up the philosophy behind participatory appraisal through my readings of Robert Chambers.

Normally, villagers would hesitate to answer such direct questions. This would be especially true if we wrote down their answers in notebooks, as most villagers were semiliterate, making them suspicious of whatever we might be recording. But by using the rangoli powder, we invited the villagers to actually take part in our mapping. They could see and understand what we were recording, and they even got caught up in the fun of it. In this way, we were able to get a true picture of village life, and we were learning from the best possible source—the villagers themselves. This allowed us to design loan and savings products and create a repayment schedule that would truly meet their needs.

The next step was to launch operations by inviting everyone to come back on an appointed evening for a public village meeting or, as we called it, a projection meeting. In every village, there's the equivalent of a town crier—a man who walks down the dirt roads and paths, banging on a drum and announcing events and news. We'd pay the town crier to announce our meeting, calling on people to meet in the village square. And when we got there, we were usually met by a hundred or so people.

We'd open the projection meeting with a role-play exercise, acting out scenarios explaining the need for microloans and how they work. By play-acting real scenarios—*The moneylenders charge too much! The banks are too far away!*—we showed how loans from SKS were the cheapest and most reliable option. At the end of the meeting, we'd invite the women to form themselves into groups of five, so we could start the training program for interested potential borrowers the next day. Though we appealed directly to women at these projection meetings, my staff and I would also informally chat with men—at the tea stalls or the bus stand—to get their buy-in as well. Typically, we could find five or so men who were open to having their wives join a group.

We decided on groups of five because that was the basic building block of Grameen's loan program, which we were emulating.

Five-member groups were small enough to enforce peer pressure if a member had the money but didn't make her payment, and large enough to easily cover a missed repayment in the case of genuine hardship. The only other stipulations were that members had to be poor, they couldn't be closely related, they had to live near one another, and they needed to trust each other. Once the women formed themselves into groups, we'd invite them to undergo a seven-day (which we subsequently streamlined to a five-day) training program, both to explain how the loan system worked and to reinforce their trust in each other.

The village women weren't stupid by any means, but they were semiliterate, so we needed to explain the concepts of credit, principal, and interest in a way they could understand and remember. We hit on the idea of using currency notes, coins, and marble-size seeds to illustrate these concepts visually. On day one of the program, we explained the concept of interest: If you get a 2,000-rupee loan, your weekly installment will be 55 rupees. Of that, 8 rupees is your interest payment, 7 goes into your savings, and the rest is paying off the loan principal.

We used marble-size seeds to explain how the five-woman groups would work—that if one borrower didn't pay her weekly installment, the other four would have to repay on her behalf. And if those four didn't repay, then the entire village lending center—as many as forty women—would not get new loans going until they made good on the missing payment.

This was the essence of the group lending idea pioneered by Grameen Bank. One of the main reasons regular banks won't lend to the poor is that they have no collateral, so the loan would be unsecured. Given that these are semiliterate borrowers, and given how small the loan sizes are, conventional banks simply don't think it's worth the risk or the high cost of appraising the loan. By having a group guarantee, we overcame that problem: Each group takes responsibility for any missed installment, and if the group isn't able to repay, the entire lending center is responsible. Such an ethic would also ensure that the entire lending center would carefully select new borrowers and that they would take care when approving each other's loans.

In new areas, some villagers didn't believe we would be firm on this rule. After all, the poor were used to seeing the government and nonprofits simply waive loans if they didn't repay. So, we structured our center meetings such that repayments would come first, then new loans would be disbursed.

Because we staggered the disbursement of loans, rather than giving them out to all members at once, there was strong incentive for whoever was supposed to receive a loan in a given week to make sure all repayments were made. Otherwise they wouldn't receive their loan. Weekly meetings were supposed to last an hour or so, but in the beginning they went a little longer, because if one borrower failed to make a payment, we would refuse to disburse new loans until the others managed to cobble together her share.

Often, when we started lending in a new village and no one happened to be waiting for a loan on a particular week, people decided to test us by willfully not paying. But we instructed our loan officers not to leave the meeting until the repayment came in. In some cases, a loan officer would have to wait for hours, occasionally even into the evening. If he or she had another meeting to attend, he would leave his collected cash and papers there and go to his next meeting. The borrowers would end up waiting, since it was not ethically acceptable to walk out if the meeting had not closed and the cash was lying there. This had a powerful social effect. The entire village would realize there was some issue, and they'd learn that everyone was waiting in the meeting because someone didn't repay. And that person would lose *izzath*, which means "respect." Colloquially, losing izzath meant losing face. Losing face is a fairly devastating thing in a village context, and people will do anything to avoid it. So as long as we showed our firmness from the start, we typically never had a repayment standoff again.

This is not to say that we insisted on a borrower repaying even if she was facing a hardship. Instead, we wanted to convey that while being a member gave you the benefit of receiving loans, one of the duties of being a member was to help others out in times of difficulty. We inculcated this sense of responsibility through a cooperation game, a technique that Rama had used in an earlier development job and then adapted for SKS.

We created a little cardboard hut for each woman and divided it into five pieces, like a jigsaw puzzle. Then, we mixed all the pieces from all the huts together, and gave each woman five random pieces. The task was for them to rebuild their little five-piece huts—without talking to each other.

The women made eye contact and passed their pieces around, helping each other and trying out combinations until everyone's hut was rebuilt correctly. "This is how group lending works," Rama told them. "You can't do it on your own. You have to help each other out." We continued to hone and refine the approach over time, but these basic tools would continue to serve us very well.

The second employee I hired was an idealistic young village woman named Nirmala Kambalimatam. Fresh out of high school, Nirmala brought something neither Rama nor I had: a local perspective. Because she'd grown up in a village, she had a much deeper understanding of village life and codes. Even simply hiring her was educational for me—I had to ask her parents for permission to hire her at SKS, and she initially told them that she was working at a bank so they wouldn't object.

Rama and I were outsiders in this rural world, and we were apt to make mistakes without even knowing it, so Nirmala was our guide. Once, for example, Rama and I started bringing fake cash to villages, to show how loans and interest work. I thought this approach was pretty clever, until Nirmala told us there was a counterfeiting ring known to be operating in the area. What kind of charlatans would waltz into a village with obviously fake cash? Clearly not the best way to build trust.

The days were long and intense. Poor people are generally available early in the morning, as they often work in the fields during the day, so we would get up before dawn and have our first village meetings at 7 AM. Then Rama, Nirmala, and I would come back to our little office and meet, to talk about what worked and what didn't. We were working from Grameen Bank replication manuals, but they were incomplete and in some cases unhelpful, so we were constantly making changes.

In the daytime, when villagers were unavailable, we spent hours meeting with government officials, gathering information, and taking care of accounts and loan documentation. And in the evenings, we'd conduct group trainings and projection meetings in new villages. We usually didn't finish until 11 PM, making the days incredibly long and draining.

It was all worth it, though, on the day we handed out our very first loan. Our first member was an older woman named Sathamma, who wanted the loan to start a vegetable vending business. She was a colorful character in her village—a woman who'd seen it all and wasn't afraid to speak her mind. "I'm not taking more than a thousand rupees," she snapped when we discussed her first loan. "I can only handle a thousand. So don't try to make me take more, and don't give me a hard time!" Laughing, I promised we wouldn't.

As it turned out, my father was in India the week we were finally ready to start disbursing loans. I invited him to come to the village for the first loan, on June 28, 1998, and he drove out from Hyderabad to join us in the lending circle. When the moment came, I asked my father to hand the cash to Sathamma. I hadn't really planned it, but it seemed the right thing to do, having our first loan come directly from my father's hand. At long last, after all the preparation, sweat, and headaches, SKS was in business.

It was a thrilling time. But the headaches weren't over yet—not by a long shot.

The rural area where we launched SKS operations, Narayankhed, was described locally as *khatarnak*, a word that translates roughly to "dangerous and nasty place." It's the backwater of all backwaters, a neglected, desolate, and poverty-stricken region where the hardships of life are etched in people's faces. Narayankhed is so unwelcoming that social workers, government employees, and others who are posted there are usually considered to be receiving a "punishment" posting.

I picked this region partly because it was so desperate, and partly because it was just a three-hour bus drive from the DDS compound, which meant that many villagers had at least heard of DDS. Being able to tell villagers I had worked for an organization they'd heard of brought us one step closer to establishing trust. And anything we could do to establish and maintain trust was critical, because without it we'd be doomed from the start. But trust could be elusive, as we soon discovered.

In our first village, the second loan we gave out was for a woman to buy a goat. This was a popular and easy way for villagers to make money: You could buy a goat and take it along with you to the agricultural fields, where it would graze while you worked, as a goat will eat just about anything. You could then breed the goat and sell its kids when you needed money.

In this case, we knew the borrower already had one goat, but she wanted to increase her business. The week after we gave the woman her loan, we came back to check on whether she'd actually bought a new goat. This was another principle I learned from Grameen: It was good to check on borrowers to make sure they were using loans for their stated purpose. Otherwise, the money would too often end up going for household expenses or other, non-income-generating purchases.

Rama and I drove to the village, and we met the woman at her house. "I bought the goat!" she said brightly. "Here it is!" With a flourish, she gestured to a skinny brown goat standing nearby.

"Great," I said and smiled at the woman.

"Wait!" said Rama. "This is not a new goat. This is the one we saw last week. It's the same color, with the same markings." I looked at Rama, amazed. How many goats had we seen, in how many villages? And she remembered that this goat was the same one she'd seen a week ago? How could she tell?

"No, it's not the old goat!" the woman protested. "I just bought it! The one you saw last week was black."

But Rama stood firm. "We're not stupid," she told the woman. "This is the same goat we saw last week."

It felt absurd to be standing in a dusty village in the middle of nowhere, arguing with a woman over the color of a goat. Was this what I'd spent all these years preparing to do? But we knew we had to make it absolutely clear, from the very beginning, that we wouldn't bend the rules for anyone. If SKS was going to establish not only trust, but also a culture of accountability, we had to be firm.

Rama wouldn't back down, and the woman finally confessed. Yes, she admitted, this was the old goat. She really wanted the loan, but she intended to use it to buy food. "You can't use it for that," Rama told her. "Buying food doesn't generate any income, so you'll be no closer to getting out of poverty that way. Either buy a new goat or give us back the loan money." The woman eventually agreed, and the next week when we checked in again, she had bought a new goat.

That situation ended well, but others did not. Sometimes, being firm with destitute, even desperate, people felt cruel rather than strategic. This was especially true when one person's carelessness resulted in hardship for another.

In one incident, a woman had made a partial deposit to lease a piece of land. She wanted to start an agricultural business, and she planned to use her SKS loan to pay the remainder of the deposit. Unfortunately, another woman in the group came late to the meeting—and our rules were clear: No one in a group could receive a loan if any member was late to that week's meeting.

"I'm sorry," I said to the woman. "But we can't give you your loan. You know the rules."

"But I'll lose my deposit!" she said, her voice rising. "It's not my fault she came late!"

Other women in the group nodded their heads—it didn't seem fair! But we had to stay firm, no matter how sick it made me feel in the pit of my stomach. For years, villagers had received subsidized credit from government programs and simply failed to pay back their loans. There was a culture of bad credit that the government couldn't—or wouldn't—do anything about, but if we fell into that same pattern, SKS wouldn't survive. So we had to be absolutely strict and consistent, even when it was painful to see.

We didn't give her the loan that week, but she devised a way to buy more time. In rural India, chicken is a precious commodity. She prepared a chicken dinner for the man she owed the money to, and asked him to give her one more week to pay him. He agreed, and the next week, everyone showed up at the meeting promptly. She got her loan, and her fellow borrowers got to see firsthand how important it was to support the group as a whole. We never had a problem with attendance or on-time repayment in that village again.

Even harder were situations when someone's luck simply turned bad. One borrower used her loan to purchase a plow bull—a sure-fire moneymaker in agricultural areas, and an investment that should have paid off for years to come. Unfortunately, just two weeks after the woman bought her bull, it up and died. Our policy in such cases was to waive the interest on her loan, but she still had to pay back the principal, week after week, with no foreseeable means of making that extra money. It was heart-wrenching, although she did manage to make those payments through her hard work and with the help of other group members.

There was a good reason we couldn't waive repayment of loans for animals that later died: Livestock fraud is a burgeoning industry in rural India, even today. Sometimes villagers would kill their goats to eat the meat, then try to make a claim for the dead animal. Other people even would cut off the ear of an animal and present it as proof it had died—then sell the one-eared animal to someone else. There just was no foolproof way to know if someone was telling the truth when they claimed an animal had died.

This is not to say that we insisted on a borrower repaying or a center taking responsibility even if the borrower was facing dire hardship. If there was a dire hardship, such as a fire or if a customer had to migrate to the city for work, we would write off the loan. Such cases made up the 2 percent of our defaults. But otherwise, we insisted on the center covering the individual and sorting it out after. Basically, we were sending the message that while being a member gave a person the benefit of receiving loans, one of the duties of being a member was to help others out in times of difficulty; that was the price of being in the center and having access to finance.

We took an equally firm approach to the rules of our seven-day training in each new village. If someone did not show up on time, we'd just pack up and leave. The latecomer would get an earful for inconveniencing the whole group, and invariably everyone would be on time the next day. From the very beginning, I knew that SKS could succeed only if we kept things running on time. Village life runs on a different schedule, and unless we insisted on punctuality, people would come late, meetings would drag on too long, and we'd have trouble serving all the villages we needed to in a given day.

We applied that same level of discipline to our field staff, many of whom were the first in their family to be educated, through affirmative action programs, and some who were working their first job ever. Unfortunately, some of them—especially those who'd worked somewhere else first—came to us with bad habits, such as showing up late.

To establish immediately that this wouldn't be tolerated, we adhered to deadlines and sent back potential recruits—even if they came from far away—if they were late. Likewise, we had strict cutoffs for recruitment tests, and even missing the cutoff by a single point meant that the candidate wouldn't get picked. This rule was painful to enforce, especially since some of our early candidates were sons and daughters of our newest members or, in some cases, children of villagers I had worked with at DDS. But we had to do it.

We also continued the same firm approach after a recruit joined SKS, especially when it came to money matters. In one case, a former field colleague of mine from DDS had "borrowed" from his training kit the handful of coins and currency notes we used to train borrowers—about 300 rupees, or $6. When we did a random check and found the money missing, I fired him on the spot. This might seem a draconian response, but we had to be a good steward of people's money—whether it belonged to our funders or our poor members.

As SKS grew, we hired more loan officers and expanded into more villages. Because cell phones weren't as prevalent in rural India in the late '90s, our employees didn't have them—so the only way to know a loan officer was having trouble collecting repayments was if he or she didn't come back to the branch office at the usual time. Whenever that happened, another loan officer would hop on a moped and head out to the village to find out what had happened, and relieve the first loan officer if needed.

We also encountered problems when our female loan officers began riding mopeds—the cheap and versatile transport of choice in rural India—to the villages. Mopeds had long been a popular way for Indian men to get around. But women didn't drive them, especially in conservative rural areas. If they rode them at all, they rode side-saddle, behind a male driver. It had always been that way. So, when our female loan officers started driving mopeds around, the reaction was swift and unequivocal. Men didn't like it, and they let the women know. Some of our employees were teased, but others experienced more serious harassment, even threats.

The first time Nirmala was scheduled to go alone to an evening meeting, I was concerned enough about her safety that I asked one of our male employees to surreptitiously follow her to the village. I didn't want Nirmala to know, as it might damage her self-confidence to know I was sending a "minder" to watch over her. I also wanted to hear from the male employee the extent of the harassment. "Stay behind her," I told him, "but not close enough anyone can tell you're following her."

That evening, as I heard Nirmala's moped putter back to the branch office, I was anxious to hear how things had gone. I had never seen Nirmala flustered, but she came running into the office with a look of terror on her face.

"Someone was following me!" she said, breathless with fear. "Every time I looked back, he was there!"

Oops. Not my most brilliant executive move. I had to confess that I'd secretly sent someone to follow her. So much for my attempts to protect my employees! I ended up terrorizing Nirmala more than anyone else ever had.

Meanwhile, back in the United States, a tech revolution was taking place. While I was living in primitive conditions in rural India, on the other side of the world Silicon Valley was aflame with creativity, entrepreneurialism—and money. The internet boom was in full swing, and venture capitalists were funding start-ups left and right. Not only was the boom changing the way the world communicated, it was also making a lot of young millionaires, many who happened to be Indian.

One of those newly minted millionaires was named Ravi Reddy. Ravi and his business partner Sandeep Tungare had cofounded a company called Think Systems, which created demand-management software for companies such as Nabisco and Dell. Ravi was in the right place at the right time with the right product, and in mid-1997, when he and Sandeep closed the sale of their company to i2 Technologies for $150 million, he was suddenly in a position to give money to causes he cared about.

I had known Ravi a long time—we're actually distantly related—and had hit him up for an initial donation in early 1997. At that point, he was interested in SKS, but he was not in a position to do anything substantial. On one of my trips back to the States, I heard he'd sold his company but didn't know the details. Then my mom told me he'd invited me to come by and visit while I was in the United States.

I drove to his home in New Jersey to see him, expecting little more than a friendly chat. But I got my first clue that things with Ravi were now very different the second I pulled up to his house. Before, he'd lived in a modest home in a nice neighborhood. When I arrived at the address he'd given me, I parked in front of a mansion.

Ravi greeted me warmly, then got right to business. He told me he and Sandeep wanted to put some of their money to work in India, but they didn't particularly like the nonprofit model. We talked about my belief that for-profit microfinance would allow for faster, broader, more sustainable growth than nonprofits. He knew I was planning to turn SKS into a for-profit company as soon as we were able, and he liked the notion of putting money into an entrepreneurial venture.

"I've been following your progress, Vikram," he told me. "We want to make a donation of fifty thousand dollars."

I was stunned. Our entire budget for the first year of operations was the original $52,000 I had raised. My salary was being paid by a two-year grant from the Echoing Green foundation, at $30,000 per year. With those two sources of money we had just scraped enough together to survive—but now, with this one check, Ravi and Sandeep were doubling our budget for operations. That initial funding—plus Ravi's ongoing financial support and business guidance over the years—would prove absolutely critical to our eventual success.

Ravi and Sandeep's vote of confidence made it easier to face the continuing hardships of starting up the business back in India. In those early days, our biggest problem was countering the lies of the local moneylenders. Before SKS—or BASIX, or Cashpor, or any other reputable microfinance provider—came on the scene, these moneylenders were often the only source of loans for villagers.

Local moneylenders charged exorbitant rates for their loans, usually 4 percent a month, but sometimes as much as 10 percent, which works out to an annual percentage rate of 48 to 120 percent. At such rates, anyone who fell behind on a payment could never expect to catch up—even just a couple of months in, your interest burden would already be so high that you'd simply enter an endless debt spiral. In some cases, moneylenders would demand that a male member of the household become "bonded labor," meaning he had to work for the moneylender at a low price to pay off the debt. In this way, moneylenders were able to solidify control in their villages.

At SKS, we started out charging 36 percent interest, which sounds incredibly high when compared to late-1990s Western loan rates of 10 to 12 percent. But there was no other option, given the very different circumstances surrounding loans to the poor. First, the cost of servicing these loans was much higher: In the West, your banker doesn't come to you each week to collect your loan payment face-to-face. But SKS loan officers traveled to every village, every week, to sit with the women and collect their payments. Second, because the average size of our loans was so small, it wasn't financially feasible to charge, say, 10 percent interest—those tiny repayments wouldn't even cover the cost of fuel for getting the loan officer to the villages. Finally, all the loans we were disbursing were handed out with no collateral whatsoever. We were going out on a limb, trying to be financially viable, and we had to have a small cushion in case borrowers didn't repay their loans.

The Grameen Bank charged lower interest than SKS, even in its early days. It was able to do so because it had received $175 million in subsidies between 1985 and 1996.[2] At SKS, my idea was to run things in a commercial way, without subsidies. Yes, we had received donations, but I converted those donations to equity that went to a philanthropic trust. In short, I was trying to prove that microfinance could be financially viable and scalable if it was run in a commercial manner—more scalable than if we accounted those donations as free money.

And while it may sound strange to Western ears, even at 36 percent interest the poor were able to run microbusinesses that enabled them to pay off their loans and still have a surplus. This was a radical idea at the time. Everyone, from fellow practitioners to development experts, said there was no way this would work. I was confident, however, because I had spent three years living and working in villages. I saw the micro-enterprises of thousands of women. They helped me understand the economics of their business. I knew it would work—or rather, I knew those women could make it work.

The truth is, we actually could have charged higher interest rates than we did, while still undercutting the moneylenders. But our goal was not to be extractive; it was to make enough profit to cover our costs and fund further growth. The latter was expensive: We had to rent branch office space, recruit and train new staff, equip them with mopeds, buy computers and supplies, and so on. Even charging 36 percent interest on microloans, we ran a deficit for several years before breaking even. Eventually, thanks to a greater volume of members and improved efficiency, we did break even. When that happened, SKS dropped its interest rates from 36 percent to 28 percent to 24 percent, and then to 19.75 percent in 2017, which was in line with unsecured loan rates for middle-class Indians with average credit scores.

Even at 2017's lower interest rates, some people may wonder if commercial microfinance can lead to an increase in income for borrowers. Indeed, there are recent influential studies that conclude that commercial microfinance does not increase incomes. I address one of those studies in the appendix of this book. For now, suffice it to say there is consensus that, at the level of the borrower as well as the larger community, access to and use of financial services, such as microcredit, is beneficial.[3] That is why, even at the earlier higher rates, there was always a demand from the poor for our loans.

There were numerous reasons why villagers preferred to borrow from us. Not only did we offer lower interest rates than the money-lenders, we also fostered a general sense of group support rather than leaving borrowers to struggle on their own. For all these reasons, moneylenders hated to see us come to town. We were stealing their business. They fought back, in a number of ways. First would be rumors: They'd tell villagers that SKS was from America and that we were really a front for a Christian evangelical group. Villagers would hear that we aimed to get them into debt, then forcibly convert them. Christian evangelists had been trickling into India for generations, but in recent years they had become more numerous and more active. Tagging SKS with that identity was an easy way to turn villagers away from us.

If that didn't work, other rumors soon followed. When male loan officers went into new villages, moneylenders would whisper, "Who's this guy, coming to your villages and asking for young women?" Stories circulated that we were trapping women into prostitution, or even that I had come back from America to steal money from Indians. And when our female loan officers went into new towns, they often heard veiled threats along the lines of: "You know this is very dangerous work for a woman, don't you?" For these reasons, we preferred to look for people to introduce us in each village. If we met someone who lived in a village where we weren't yet offering loans, we'd ask them to take us there and introduce us around. Unfortunately, this didn't always work out as planned.

On one memorable occasion, a young woman walked into a branch office to ask about our loans. She was from a village where we'd tried, and failed, to find an "in," so I was particularly excited she had shown up. She was young, progressive, and articulate—I couldn't believe our luck!

I went with her to the village, and we started walking around and chatting. This method had become our usual way of launching in a new village—just strolling around, starting conversations, and gauging interest. People in the village seemed intrigued, so we asked the town crier to call for a projection meeting the following evening.

When we arrived the next evening at the appointed time, no one was there. Not a single person had shown up, but a few were hovering around the edges, seemingly curious as to whether anyone else would come. What was going on? Usually we got at least a hundred people at these projection meetings. Everything had gone so well the day before, yet now we were getting the cold shoulder. We waited about a half hour, then returned to the branch office, disappointed and confused.

We learned later that the woman who had introduced us to the village was a local sex worker. At the time, I was embarrassed—here I'd been wandering around this town, saying, "Join our group! Come on and join our group!" To my regret, I didn't inquire further into her situation. To this day, I don't know whether she had come to us genuinely seeking a loan to improve her circumstances.

In the "Wild West" atmosphere of those first two years, there were only a few times when I felt truly, physically threatened. For the most part, the interference we got from moneylenders and meddlesome, bribe-seeking bureaucrats was more of a nuisance than anything else. But on a couple of occasions, I wondered whether I was going to be on the receiving end of an assault.

The first incident came after we repeatedly turned down a local politician who kept trying to extort us. He'd come to us and say, "I want you to hire these three people for SKS. They don't need to work; just put them on your payroll." Or, "I need to borrow one of your jeeps tomorrow. Make sure it's at my house." I kept saying no to everything, but still the requests kept coming.

Finally, he got tired of hearing "No." So he called me to his office for a little talk.

"New people who come to our region need to cooperate with local ways," he told me. He was absolutely calm, not thuggish or overtly threatening. He spoke with sophistication, but his message was primitive and clear. "Remember," he told me, "in Narayankhed, sometimes murders can even happen for such things."

I was scared and upset to have been so obviously threatened. Would this local politician really resort to violence? I had no way of knowing and didn't want to find out. I called a few of my relatives in Hyderabad, including one uncle who was well connected in this area. "What should I do?" I asked him. "I don't know how to handle this."

My uncle arranged a meeting for me with the chief minister of Andhra Pradesh. It was set up as simply an informational meeting, where I could tell the chief minister about SKS and our work—in fact, during our conversation, I never mentioned the local politician. But word spread that I had enough connections to have met with the chief minister, which was enough to get the other politician to back off. He knew this was a signal to him that I had a higher level of access to power, and I never heard another request from him.

This was the way I preferred to deal with most problems: I wanted to make them go away in the simplest, most direct way possible. All I cared about was the work, and anything that impeded it had to be dealt with quickly. Unfortunately, as the next incident shows, it wasn't always so easy to take care of such things.

At the end of 1998, six months after disbursing our first loan, we had 165 borrowers. We were operating in eight villages and had seven staff members—all loan officers. We had one branch office, where we took care of accounts and payroll matters, and we had expanded beyond that initial room that Rama and I had shared, taking more rooms on the same floor of that same two-story building in Narayankhed.

By mid-1999, we had grown to about ten employees, and managing them all, plus developing and sustaining the business, was becoming too big a task for me. So I hired my first executive: a polished, English-speaking, highly qualified chief operations officer. His name was Shyam Mohan.

We had recently purchased some land outside one of the villages, where we planned to build a DDS-style compound. This would become our new branch office, and eventually I envisioned having a kind of rural headquarters. Two small bungalows sat on our plot of land, and the plan was to use one as living quarters and the other as an office.

I wanted to show Shyam the site, so he, his wife, and I went there one night after wrapping up work in Hyderabad for the day. By the time we got there, it was late—maybe one or two o'clock in the morning, so our plan was to spend the night and look around in the morning. We parked and walked up to the door of one bungalow, and the first thing I noticed was that the electricity was off.

Now, this was not an unusual occurrence in rural India. Electricity was, and still is, an unpredictable luxury rather than a given. I assumed it was a typical temporary power failure and didn't think anymore about it. Shyam and his wife went into the bungalow they'd be sharing, and I went into mine, right next to it. We said good night and shut our doors.

A couple of hours later, in the absolute dead of night, I was awakened by the clacking of someone locking my door from the outside. Rural Indian doors had external metal handles that could be padlocked. I jumped out of bed and rushed to push the door open, but it wouldn't budge. I was trapped in my bungalow!

I started yelling just as I heard the pounding on Shyam's door. I looked out through the bars of the window, and though it was pitch black, I could make out the forms of five or six men, some of whom were carrying crowbars. They were beating on Shyam's door, which was locked from the inside. I could hear Shyam yelling, too—both of us were screaming at the top of our lungs, trying to get someone's attention before these men broke Shyam's door down and did who knows what.

These men were on the attack: They pounded savagely at Shyam's door, whacking it with their crowbars. I felt completely helpless, trapped in my little room while a gang of thugs was threatening my COO and his wife. Even if I could get out, what could I do? There were six of them and one of me, and they were armed. So I just yelled and yelled, desperately hoping someone from the nearby village would hear and come save us.

The men pounded on Shyam's door for what felt like an hour, before finally giving up and leaving as quickly as they'd come. When it seemed the danger had passed, Shyam and his wife opened their door, unlocked mine, and we stayed together in my bungalow. We stayed awake the rest of the night, holding makeshift weapons in case the thugs returned. Shyam and his wife were, not surprisingly, completely terrorized.

To this day, I don't know who was behind the attack. It might have been ordered by a local moneylender who didn't like that SKS was operating in his territory. It might have been an intimidation tactic from a local politician. The one thing we did learn was that the power outage was anything but routine: Someone had cut the electrical wires to the buildings. The attack was premeditated, and it worked. The next morning a traumatized Shyam told me, "I can't do this, Vikram. I quit."

I had certainly been afraid the night before, but deep down I never really believed anything truly terrible could happen to us. Would thugs really attack and beat an American for working in their village? Wouldn't that just cause more trouble than it was worth for them? I still don't know what those attackers' ultimate goal was, but I suspect it was to frighten us away from the work we were doing. Instead it just left me more determined to press on.

CHAPTER 6

MCDONALD'S OF MICROFINANCE

By the end of March 2000, the end of our second full fiscal year, SKS was serving 695 members and had disbursed about $20,000 in loans. We'd started slowly because we had to—but now it was time to begin ramping up our numbers. If the first two years were about creating a solid, stable base for operations, the next two would be about streamlining our systems and increasing our growth rate. We were off to the races.

Unfortunately, as I soon discovered, it was still hard to get others in the field to take us seriously. In 2000, I went to a dinner in Seattle hosted by the Grameen Foundation USA. The foundation had decided to focus on the three largest MFIs in India: Cashpor, Share Microfin, and ASA. I had managed to finagle an invitation, but SKS was still the skinny kid on the playground, waiting to be picked.

I ended up in a conversation with Steve Rockefeller, a grandson of Nelson Rockefeller who was an executive at Deutsche Bank and a Grameen Foundation USA board member. We talked about SKS, and I told him about our plans for expansion. Either I didn't explain it well or he didn't quite believe me, because in response he said, "Maybe you could become a franchisee of one of these other MFIs."

He meant well, no doubt. But I had no intention of becoming a franchisee of anyone, and I found the notion vaguely insulting. I'll admit that I have an ego, and this comment provoked it. I realized that the only way to convince people we were serious about our business model—growing faster and serving more poor people than any MFI in history—was to just knuckle down and do it. No one had ever come close to growing at the pace I envisioned for us, and no one seemed to believe it was possible. But I believed I could find a way.

It started with a bottle of Coca-Cola. One dust-choked afternoon in rural India, I bought a Coke at a roadside stand. As I gratefully gulped it down, I found myself wondering, *How did that company manage to scale globally at such a rapid pace?* A few years earlier, you couldn't buy a Coke anywhere in India—the company ceased operations between 1977 and 1993 due to a fight with the Indian government over revealing its secret formula.

But in 1993, the Coca-Cola Company returned to India and expanded at a breathtaking pace, and soon you could find that familiar red logo in the remotest corners of the country. The same was true of other aggressive companies in other parts of the world. For example, when Starbucks and McDonald's decided to expand, they were instantly everywhere. How did they do it? And what lessons could we take from them to help SKS do the same?

All of a sudden, it came to me. A Coke is a Coke is a Coke, no matter where you buy it. It's a single, standardized product that is made, shipped, and sold in the same way everywhere. Coke was able to scale so rapidly because it had a very simple product in a recognizable, standardized package. Why couldn't we create similar products, loan and insurance products for the poor that were standardized across the board, no matter where we offered them, and to whom?

The answer was, we could. And so we did.

We had already taken the first step by offering loans only in pre-set amounts. We realized from the start that if we offered different loan amounts for different borrowers, we'd end up with a confusing jumble of numbers for the loan officers. And because we were tracking all of our numbers by hand, the potential for mistakes was just too high. If a loan officer had 500 borrowers, each of whom had a weekly loan repayment as well as an insurance payment, that loan officer would be making more than 150,000 individual entries per year—on cardboard passbooks, paper collection sheets, and thick dusty branch ledgers—all by hand. But with standardized amounts and an unchanging interest rate, the loan officers would have to note only variations, not every individual entry. That was the first step.

The next step was to eliminate coins. We set the loan repayments at round numbers, so loan officers wouldn't have to count and carry coins, a simple enough fix that made their work that much easier. We also required borrowers to hand over their weekly payments with the bills flattened, stacked face up, and divided into denominations, so the loan officer could count them quickly. Before, they'd bring bills that had been crumpled and stuffed into the folds of saris, and the loan officers had to smooth the bills out before they could even begin to count them.

These sound like obvious, minor fixes—but they made a tremendous difference in time management. Before I launched SKS, I'd watched a number of meetings run by other MFIs; invariably, their loan officers spent large amounts of time counting coins and painstakingly recording differing numbers in passbooks. These simple changes helped our loan officers shave significant time off their meetings, which in turn allowed them to schedule more meetings per day, further cutting our administrative and staff costs.

I became obsessed with the idea of cutting meeting times down to the absolute minimum required. My model for this was McDonald's: As just about everyone knows, at any McDonald's in the world, a customer can walk in and get food served within minutes. I had even seen little timers by the cashiers showing "average time to serve," with forty-five to sixty seconds being a typical average. The transactions at our borrowers' meetings were certainly no more complex than those at McDonald's, so why couldn't our loan officers function just as quickly?

I began taking a stopwatch out to the villages, to time our loan officers in action. We looked at every possible place to shave even a couple of minutes off the meetings, and over time they became tighter and tighter; if you'd sat in on an SKS borrowers' meeting, you would have seen a completely streamlined, assembly line–style process, with loan officers and borrowers moving smoothly and quickly through their scheduled tasks. We also made sure each loan officer's daily meetings were scheduled in villages that lay along a single road, so the employee could travel quickly between them. As a result, our loan officers were able to run more meetings per week than those of other MFIs doing comparable, rural-based loan work.

With these improvements in place, we'd taken care of the second of the three *C*s: capacity. We knew the problem of capital would be solved when SKS converted into a for-profit entity and we were able to solicit investors. But that couldn't happen until we solved the other *C* problem: cost.

How could we lower the very high transaction costs of offering microloans? Very simply, we needed to cut down on the number of staff hours it took to log and maintain records of our loans. The only way to do that was by trying something very few other MFIs were doing at the time—something, in fact, that many in the field thought was an expensive folly. We needed to develop an easy, scalable, cheap software system that our loan officers, many of whom had only high school educations and no computer experience, could use.

Ever since I'd seen that Grameen Bank employee hand-copy ten years' worth of a member's loan information, I knew we had to find a way to automate the business of tracking loans. Most MFIs recorded their transactions in three places—borrowers' passbooks, collection sheets, and, finally, back-office ledgers. There was simply no way we could grow at the rate I wanted while recording all those transactions by hand.

So, two years after we launched, I committed about $250,000 to developing an easy-to-use software suite, specially designed for our needs. At the time, our entire loan portfolio was only about $25,000, so this was a huge—some even called it reckless—leap. Undaunted, I recruited the help of a friend I knew from Chicago, Bala Krishnamurti.

Bala was a brilliant developer who took his job very seriously. He, Rama, and I started working together to figure out exactly what we needed, which right away turned out to be more difficult than expected.

"I need to know what exactly the loan officers do," Bala told us, "so I can design the software to address those needs most efficiently."

I started to answer him, but he interrupted me. "No," he said. "Let me hear it from a front-line loan officer."

Bala and I traveled to one of our branches to talk to Nirmala, our first loan officer. As she began to describe the process to Bala, I was surprised—she was already doing certain things a little differently than I thought. So much for standardization! If we couldn't keep all our loan officers on the same tasks when we were small, could we really do it when we started growing exponentially? We needed this software more than ever, as having a single software suite that everyone used would help solve that problem.

We needed something easy to use, flexible, and as cheap as possible to develop. Of course, you almost always have to sacrifice one of those factors to get the other two. So Bala, Rama, and I began heated debates about what to sacrifice—or, more correctly, Bala and Rama debated and I played the arbiter. Rama would say, "We must have the ability to set up three different repayment schedules—biweekly, weekly, and monthly!" Bala would pipe back, "But that will significantly increase our costs!" All I could hope was that despite the disagreements, Rama's input from the field and Bala's creativity with software code would lead us to a design for an efficient and cost-effective system.

Once we agreed on the deliverables, Bala recruited two local developers. After twelve months of work, our fledgling IT team created a software product that did absolutely everything we needed: It had a simple, logical interface that worked on a point-and-click basis, with language fonts that could be adjusted to match local languages and dialects, and it integrated portfolio tracking with accounts. It was incredibly easy to use, so much so that one of our loan officers later told the *Wall Street Journal* she had two skills: "I know sewing and I know the SKS system."[1]

Because we had standardized the loan repayments, loan officers could prepopulate the blanks in the online forms with those amounts, drastically cutting down on the hours needed to update records. Bala did such an excellent job that we used essentially the same system for nearly a decade—and even when we invested in a $2 million overhaul of the system in 2008, it was only to accommodate more products on the back end of the software. The interface and front end remained virtually the same during the life of SKS.

With that initial investment in software, we had solved the final *C*—cost—and could begin ramping up in earnest. But I wanted to push the technological barrier even further, after an experience I had during another visit back in the United States.

I was living full-time in India, so on periodic trips back home I needed to rent a car. One afternoon, while turning in my rental before catching a flight back, I noticed that the Hertz attendant used a handheld device right at the car to process my account and print a bill. It was quick and elegant, and far more efficient than having everyone walk into the Hertz office and stand in line. When I returned to India, I began telling people about the handheld. Why couldn't SKS do the same thing?

Would it be possible for our loan officers to use handhelds in the field, rather than logging loan repayments by hand and then automating them once they got back to the branch office? Even though our new software had improved our efficiency tremendously, we'd be even better off if we could eliminate that first step of hand-copying the repayment amounts.

In 2000, when we first began exploring the use of handhelds, not many companies were using them. A few rental car companies, as well as Federal Express and other package-delivery services, were the only ones I'd seen employing this new technology—mostly because it was expensive. Like any new technology, the price would drop after initial adopters started using it, but these types of handhelds hadn't reached that point yet.

With that in mind, when we started experimenting with handhelds for SKS, I looked for the cheapest hardware I could find. We bought several refurbished Palm Pilots from Overstock.com and designed an application that involved using smart cards that could be inserted in them. Rather than having a paper passbook for recording loans and repayments, each borrower would have a smart card—basically an electronic passbook—that could be inserted into the loan officer's Palm Pilot to transfer the information digitally. The loan officer could then transfer all of the group's information directly from the Palm Pilot into the computer at the branch office.

We ran this pilot project for one year, and from a technology perspective it was a great success. But there was one problem: We could only justify a full roll-out of the program, with its costly investment in hardware and training, if borrowers could also use the smart cards as cash substitutes.

At the time we launched the Palm/smart card project, regulators, bankers, and payment providers were pushing for the creation of a payment infrastructure—ATMs and points-of-sale—in rural areas. Unfortunately, the regulation to do so never emerged, making it impossible to use the smart cards as cash substitutes. So, even if we rolled out the use of handhelds, our loan officers would still have to deal with two tasks: handling cash payments and inputting amounts. This wasn't efficient enough to justify the cost, so we shelved the program. Interestingly, it took fifteen years for the Indian government to finally create a new category of banks, called "payment banks." By 2017, many MFIs were finally trying to use digital money as cash substitutes, similar to our experiments back in 2000.

Despite the setback of not being able to use smart cards, by 2002 we had our software and our "Coke-ified" standard practices, and we were poised to begin explosive growth. As mentioned, at the end of our fiscal year 1999–2000, we had 695 members and had disbursed around $20,000 in loans. At the end of fiscal year 2000–01, we had 1,922 members and had disbursed $117,243 in loans. Then, the numbers began shooting up: 5,819 members and $543,285 in loans disbursed in 2000–02; and by the end of 2002–03, we had 13,519 members and cumulatively disbursed more than $2.4 million in loans. We also were able to maintain a 98 percent repayment rate throughout this period of growth.

Despite all the streamlining and growth, unexpected hurdles kept popping up to threaten our work—some that were very personal for me, and others that bordered on the bizarre.

Two years after founding SKS, I had gotten married to a woman I first met in graduate school. Malini and I first started dating back in 1996. I met her when I volunteered for Apna Ghar, a shelter in Chicago for South Asian women who were victims of domestic violence. Malini was a staff member at the time.

Soon after we met, I saw Malini speak on a panel discussion on feminism at my university. She was passionate, eloquent, and attractive. I was hooked. I was also drawn to Malini because, like me, she wanted to live a meaningful life and not pursue a conventional career path. And like me, within the Indian-American community, she was viewed as odd for having that desire. There was a spiritual underpinning to her desires, in the same way that my own spiritual inclinations drew me to study theology at Harvard Divinity School and to hitchhike around America. She had even spent a summer volunteering at an orphanage in south India.

We had a lot of common ground. I had found a kindred spirit.

After a few months of dating, however, we parted ways because she knew I planned to move to India, and she wanted to stay in the States. The breakup was amicable, and when we ran into each other again in September 1999, during an extended visit home, we reconnected. When Malini—who had been born in India—said that she was ready to live in India, I was ecstatic. We started dating again, and very quickly, after just a few weeks, we decided to get married. Honestly, I did not want to get married that quickly, but her parents—who were very traditional—encouraged it, especially because Malini had planned to come to India during her winter break. Her father understandably felt it would be shameful for her to travel with me in India without being married. So I agreed to get married within a few months.

I know that sounds hasty, but in rural India, I had been living in a very traditional culture, where being unmarried at age twenty-nine was considered odd. The first few times villagers expressed surprise on learning I was single, I didn't mind. But by the hundredth time, it had really started to wear on me. I began to wonder if they were right—if there was something wrong with being unmarried and so focused on my work. The other sentiment in play was that I had become lonely working in rural Indian villages. The work was exciting, meaningful, and very busy, but it was also isolating. Even though I was around people all day, it was difficult to connect to them on a personal level because our lives were so different. I missed relationships with people who shared my background and were familiar with American culture. Some days I felt like a missionary of sorts, out in the hinterlands doing the most fulfilling work I could imagine—yet feeling very lonely at the same time. Modern amenities such as cable TV were entering rural India in the late 1990s, but I still missed a range of American experiences—from going home for Thanksgiving to everyday pleasures like playing basketball and watching sitcoms and eating hot dogs and hamburgers. I couldn't even enjoy the simple fun of peppering conversations with jokes because my overseas wit was often lost in translation—and, believe me, I'm a funny guy.

I was a jittery, delighted groom when Malini and I married in December 1999. Although I went back to India right afterward, she stayed in the States to finish law school. For the first year or so we had a long-distance marriage. Malini spent school breaks in India, and I would get to Chicago when I could. She did, however, spend the entire summer of 2000 with me in India. We lived in a small one-bedroom guesthouse on a farm outside the village of Anthwar, near SKS's first branch office. There was a neem tree in front of the guest house, where we would have tea together in the morning, and at day's end, we would go up on the roof and watch the sunset. That village is where I had thought Malini and I would make a life together.

At the end of the summer, she went back to school. Then, in February 2001, our son was born.

Now I was more anxious than ever for her—and our son—to join me in India. But Malini told me she no longer wanted to live in India, that especially with a new baby, she wanted to stay in the comfortable suburbs of Chicago. I was devastated, but there seemed to be no middle ground. Eventually, we could not reconcile our differences, and in October 2001, we separated.

The marriage had lasted eighteen months, and the divorce, which grew increasingly acrimonious, took almost as long. By December 2002, when everything was finalized, I was not only emotionally spent, I was financially tapped out from attorneys' fees. And now I had a young son who was living in Chicago with his mother while I was in India full time. I couldn't stand the thought of being away from him so much.

Financially and personally, this was one of the worst periods of my life. SKS was doing great—growing just as I'd hoped and planned. But I was crushed under a $90,000 graduate school debt plus astronomical divorce fees—around $100,000. Under Illinois law the primary income earner must pay the attorneys' fees for both spouses and our divorce proceedings had dragged on. When our divorce was finalized Malini had just completed law school (she specialized in family law and became a divorce attorney).

In the nonprofit sector I'd been earning a minimal salary for my entire working life, averaging about $40,000 a year for my first six years at SKS; there was no way I could even start to dig out from under my mountain of debt, and I had no savings at all. In fact, to pay the divorce attorneys' fees, I was forced to borrow from family and run up credit cards—and I was already carrying another $45,000 in personal credit card debt from taking cash advances over the years to help fund SKS deficits.

Eventually, I realized I had no choice: I would have to resign as CEO of SKS to get my life back in order. I informed the board, while telling them I wanted to stay actively involved as chair.

After a transition period, I had a tearful farewell with our staff in India. I couldn't quite believe that my tenure as CEO was ending like this, but I just didn't see any way around it. The sole comforting factor was that in Chicago, I would get to see my son more often. Meanwhile, on the SKS front, my worry was assuaged by the fact that, by now, our processes were all in place, so what SKS needed most was a steady hand on the plough. I asked Sitaram Rao, a passionate and dedicated SKS board member, who passed away in 2009, to take my place. Sitaram, to whom this book is dedicated, was a seasoned finance professional who had made a career shift to development. Aptly dubbed by the press as the "Mentor of Indian Microfinance," he was a treasured friend and role model to me. He was the right person to hold down the fort while I reluctantly settled into Chicago to try to get my personal and financial life back on track.

Starting in January 2004, I worked full-time on writing up my dissertation; I had done my field research in India while working with SKS. With no income during this time, I began juggling credit card balances just to survive—I literally had an Excel spreadsheet showing how much debt I carried on each card and when I needed to transfer balances. I even seriously considered filing for personal bankruptcy, but I just couldn't reconcile it with the message of fiscal discipline I'd been preaching to our borrowers in India.

Worse yet, my former wife and I could not reach an equitable agreement on parenting time. I was relegated to having my son every other weekend and one weeknight a week. I rented an apartment across the street from my son's daycare center. That way, from my window, I was able to see him when his teachers took the children outside to the playground.

CHAPTER 7

BALANCING THE PROFESSIONAL AND THE PERSONAL

One cold day in March 2004, I went to the home of Malini's parents, where she was living, to pick up our son for one of our regular visits. I was particularly looking forward to the visit because my mother had flown in from New York. She did not get to see my son very often because she and my father lived so far away.

When we arrived to pick up my son, Malini was not there. Her parents were home with my son. So my mother and I waited in the driveway. And waited. And waited. Finally, I asked her father if I could just take my son, since Malini was running so late. He agreed, and I took my son's bag to the car and then got my son.

That's when Malini drove up and became angry that I was planning to leave with our son before she arrived. She and I exchanged heated words. As I was getting in my car to leave, she ran up and opened the back door to take our son back. She was very emotional, and as she reached for him, I stepped in front of her and took him out of his car seat. I carried him, running, to the front door of the house and rang the doorbell, hoping Malini's father could help calm her down. From experience, I knew he was the best person to ask for help.

As I stood ringing the doorbell, Malini came up behind me and attempted to grab our son out of my arms. I turned abruptly to shield him, and in doing so my elbow grazed Malini. Furious, she called the police and told them that I had intentionally hit her.

At the time, I didn't think about the implications of what was happening. Malini's parents invited me and my mother to sit and wait for the police, and so we did. A police car pulled up—sirens blaring—and two cops ran in the door. One of the officers saw us sitting there quietly and asked, "Where is he?"

"Well," I replied. "I think I'm the guy you're looking for."

I never imagined this episode would lead to any serious repercussions; I just figured it was the latest in a series of emotionally difficult moments between two people who'd experienced an acrimonious divorce. Soon I was handcuffed and put in the back of the police car. The cop blared heavy metal music and left me there while he went back into the house. I sat for a long time, perhaps an hour. My mother was still inside. It was hard to know what was going on. Then the cop came over to my car, finally turned off the blaring music, and sped me away to the police station.

For a few hours, I had no idea what had happened to my mother, but I used my one phone call to check on her. The police had eventually taken her back to my apartment. Meanwhile, I was photographed and processed and spent a night in jail, waiting for a bail hearing. I sat in a windowless six-by-eight-foot cell with a barred door. The lights were left on all night, and I couldn't sleep. I just kept reading and rereading the few sentences on the Rights of Prisoner signs that were posted on the wall in English and Spanish. In the morning, I was taken to court, where I learned I had been charged with a misdemeanor for domestic battery.

I scraped together money for an attorney, and he told me I could accept a plea bargain for a lesser charge of simple battery, which would then be expunged from my record after one year. This option sounded better than having a potential conviction for domestic battery, which would be permanent—but on the other hand, it required me to plead guilty to intentionally hitting Malini. I was unwilling to make a false guilty plea. Also, I didn't believe I could actually be convicted of domestic battery for incidental contact when all I had done was to try to shield my son. I told my lawyer I preferred to go to trial. I had faith in the American justice system.

I soon learned that domestic violence laws had become stringent in the United States. Any physical contact was considered a crime. I knew this was good policy, since so many genuine domestic violence victims had suffered in the court system due to weak or unenforceable laws. But these tougher laws ensured that I was caught in the broader net as well.

At the end of a day-long trial, I was found guilty. I sat in the courtroom, stunned. Malini had also filed a petition the morning after the arrest to terminate my parenting time with our son. Now, not only would I have a conviction on my record, but I would also have to fight—and pay more lawyers' fees—to re-establish parenting time with our son.

So here I was: I had a criminal record. I hadn't finished my dissertation. I had no job. I had huge debt that was growing by the day. And now I was borrowing more money for attorneys to fight in family court just so I could see my son, which was the reason I'd left SKS and India to return to Chicago in the first place. This was truly the lowest moment of my life.

I eventually was able to re-establish my parenting time with my son. Meanwhile, I tried unsuccessfully to appeal the conviction. A few months later, the law firm Mayer Brown started doing pro bono work for SKS (which changed to a paid engagement after the company became a for-profit). When one of their partners, Marc Kadish, found out about my criminal conviction, he had the firm take up my appeal pro bono. Kadish explained that both my initial lawyer and my appellate lawyer had made errors. The former had failed to present the argument that I had been trying to protect my son, which led to the contact. My appellate lawyer had simply delayed getting my appellate filing in on time, and that is why it was rejected. After Mayer Brown got involved and pursued the appeal again, the firm was able to secure an appellate court hearing for me. Mayer Brown assigned one of their star attorneys, a Rhodes Scholar, to argue my case. I could not ask for a better second chance.

On the day of the hearing in the Illinois Appellate Court, I could tell from the questions from the three-judge bench that it did not look good. I remember one of the judges making a statement like, "It does not matter if there is actual innocence. The appellant has no standing."

By "standing," he meant that my first appeal had been filed too late. Sure enough, I was denied on a technicality. The Illinois Appellate Court didn't budge, and I was stuck with the criminal conviction. In India, I was skilled at navigating the complex nuances of doing business in outlying villages, including managing thousands of customers and millions of transactions. On my home turf, I'd been caught off guard. I bear no ill will toward the mother of my son, but to this day, my stomach churns at the thought that I will have a life-long criminal record as a domestic batterer.

I deeply regret my actions on that day. When Malini took our son out of the car, I should have just closed the door and left. I didn't. And my inability to walk away led to events that have a lasting impact.

Years later, both Malini and her parents wrote a letter to the governor of Illinois requesting that I be pardoned. Malini wrote, "I, in fact, do not believe that Vikram's actions on that day were premeditated or intentional but rather almost involuntary, as everyone was seeking to console, protect, and grab hold of my son . . . I respectfully ask that you grant Vikram the clemency that he so richly deserves and expunge his April 21, 2004, conviction from any and all records." It was heartening to see her write that, but the request for a pardon was denied.

After the conviction, I had no choice but to put one foot in front of the other, hoping things would get better. The first step was to chip away at finishing my dissertation. Once I finished, I knew I'd be in a better position to find work. I also knew that, given my financial position, I couldn't afford to take a teaching or a development job, which would have been my first choice. For the first time in my life, I'd have to take a job not for reasons of personal or professional commitment, but for the money. I sought out the highest-paying job I could find in Chicago: an entry-level position at the management consulting firm McKinsey & Company. I didn't know much about management consulting, but, if nothing else, I could learn firsthand about Fortune 500 companies and how they run their businesses while digging my way out of debt.

I applied and made it through one written test and three rounds of interviews, and in August 2004, just after submitting my dissertation, I started work. Slowly, I began getting my life back on track.

It was surreal to be an entry-level employee in a giant firm after having launched my own start-up, especially since many of my colleagues were freshly minted MBA graduates several years younger than me. Most were typical hustling young business types, competing to see who could log the most hours at the office, but I was just trying to do enough at the firm to survive; my heart was still with SKS. I'd start at McKinsey around 8 AM, work all day long, then jump into SKS business starting around 10 PM—just as my colleagues in Chicago were packing up and the business day in India was getting started.

It was an insane schedule, but I wanted to stay as involved as possible with SKS even from afar. And, of course, I was already used to working crazy hours from the first seven years of getting SKS off the ground. The saving grace of spending all those hours toiling at McKinsey was the salary: I was making about $150,000 a year, typical for an entry-level MBA, but far higher than anything I'd ever earned before. Slowly and painfully, I began to pull myself out of debt.

Meanwhile, on the other side of the world, SKS continued having to deal with unexpected and occasionally bizarre hurdles to its expansion. Even as I was spending my days in the antiseptic corporate environment of McKinsey, I was reminded in my nightly phone calls and periodic visits to India that it was a whole different world out there.

In late September 2004, local gangsters in the town of Nizamabad began attacking our loan officers. First, they tried to extort us, demanding to be paid a small amount of cash in exchange for a guarantee of safety in their district. When we refused to pay, they launched a campaign of threats and intimidation: Bands of thugs wielding broken bottles started attacking our loan officers, sometimes stealing their backpacks.

After a few such assaults, the gang approached our district manager again for a cash payment, obviously expecting us to accept their offer in exchange for our loan officers' safety. But to their surprise, we once again refused to give in. They tried another tack, launching a campaign of rumors and lies to try to discredit us.

Nizamabad is a largely Muslim area, so the gang began spreading rumors that SKS was a secret Christian organization, trying to convert borrowers. This rumor was not a new tactic. We had seen moneylenders who wanted to get rid of us try to do the same. But the Nizamabad gang took it to another level. They falsely claimed to have found a Bible in one loan officer's backpack. In India, there's a grave sensitivity around religious issues, particularly as it relates to Muslims, who are a minority group. The sensitivities go back as far as the 1947 partition of India, which created Pakistan as a separate Muslim state. There was a bloody and long conflict that ultimately claimed as many as a million lives. After partition, millions of Muslims continued to live in India, but raw feelings persisted, and even today, perceived attacks on the Muslim faith—from any source—arouse an instant and visceral reaction in India. This is especially true around Ramadan, the holiest period of the Muslim calendar. Unfortunately for us, the Nizamabad gang spread these rumors during Ramadan or, as it's known in India, Ramzan.

The more we resisted, the more the rumors, threats, and attacks intensified. One loan officer was forced to humiliate himself by stripping down to his underwear in a public square. Others were chased with machetes. We stopped sending loan officers to the hottest spots, but our members wanted their loans, so they started coming to our branch office to make repayments. They'd pool their money and send one member in an auto-rickshaw to deliver it to us.

At this point, we had the local members on our side, even though they were Muslims, too: They wanted their loans to continue, and they were resisting anti-SKS pressure as much as we were. We should have held a mass rally with our members then, to show others in the district that we had their support. But our local team was cowed by the continued threats and unsure whether they could gather the momentum they needed. We hesitated, and the gang seized its opportunity. They stepped up their intimidation even further, directly turning their attention to the members.

They threatened to forcibly cut our members' hair—a severe disgrace for any Indian woman, but especially for Muslim women, who traditionally wear their hair long. This was too much for most of our members, many of whom gave in to the pressure, stopping their involvement and making no more repayments. We were hanging on by a thread, hoping to get things back on track, when the thugs launched their final blow—the one that would eventually make the newspapers back in the United States.

The gang went to the local Muslim leaders, re-voicing the claim that SKS was a secret Christian evangelical group. They also complained about the fact that Muslims were taking loans for interest from us. Technically, it was correct that *sharia*, Islamic law rooted in the Koran, prohibits interest paid on loans. But in reality Muslims in India were fully involved with lending; for years, banks, MFIs, and local moneylenders, including Muslim ones, had been offering loans in Muslim communities—even Bangladesh, where Professor Yunus started Grameen Bank, is a predominantly Muslim country.

It was a technicality, but a compelling one for the Muslim clerics of Nizamabad. They issued a *fatwa*, or religious ruling, against SKS.

That was the final straw. With a fatwa hanging over our heads, SKS was now the organizational equivalent of persona non grata in Nizamabad, and any remaining support among our members vanished completely. We had no choice but to close that branch and walk away from the portfolio—nearly $250,000 in loans. This was an incredibly painful development, and not just financially for us; our borrowers would suffer too, and we couldn't do anything to help them. I was still determined not to give in to extortion demands, but this was the perfect example of how taking that stand could, and did, harm us.

If the fatwa felt surreal, our confrontations with armed leftist rebels were even more so. In all the planning I'd done in the early days, figuring out how SKS would run and what our potential problems might be, I never anticipated having to face down shadowy groups of leftist guerrillas sending threatening messages from deep in the forests.

The early 2000s were the height of the leftist guerilla movements in parts of rural India. The movement has waned as of 2017, but back then there were many small bands of armed rebels engaged in warfare against the Indian government. They were conducting what they believed was a revolution on behalf of the people of India, engaging in acts of violence and intimidation in an effort to destabilize the Indian government. In 2000, for example, the People's War Group of Naxalites assassinated a state minister of home affairs with a landmine blast. Other groups kidnapped corporate executives. In 2003, a Maoist group tried to kill the ruling chief minister with a bomb. The government considered them to be terrorists, and their groups have been outlawed in several Indian states. For this reason, they had retreated to secluded places, usually deep in forested areas where they had cover and isolation while planning their campaigns of violence.

Not surprisingly, the leftist rebels didn't take kindly to a capitalist organization like SKS spreading through rural India. Almost from the beginning, we saw signs that they were taking notice of our work, as they had ways of making their presence known. They started with indirect intimidation, such as stopping a loan officer and inquiring about his business, or popping up at a public meeting to say we were exploiting the villagers. But soon enough, they began employing more direct tactics, such as sending letters with block printing telling us to stop, or making threatening calls to our branch offices.

On one occasion, before I had left for Chicago in 2004, one group sent word that they wanted me to come to their hideaway in a dank back alley of Hyderabad. I was wary of going, but also, in my typically optimistic way, I thought I might actually be able to convince them that what we did was good for the same people whose cause they had taken up. We were giving poor Indians the tools to help themselves, after all—giving them a way to get out from under the thumb of exploitative landlords and moneylenders. Wasn't this at least partially in line with the goals of a revolution for the people?

I agreed to the meeting, and the guerrillas sent instructions to meet at a certain street corner at a certain time. I took two SKS employees with me—a local area manager and an older employee who functioned as our designated troubleshooter. At the corner, we were met by a man who walked us down a maze of alleys to a non-descript house, and then showed us into a bare-bones upstairs room with just a table and chairs. A couple of guerrillas were waiting for us there, and they got right to business.

They demanded extortion payments—everything from money to jeeps to AK-47 assault rifles. These weren't like the demands from local politicians, who could be dissuaded by appeals to higher-level public officials. The men sitting across from us were desperados, lawless types who fully expected to kill—and die—for what they believed. I could hardly believe this was even happening, but I told them the same thing I'd told the politicians: We would never make a payment to them, not even a rupee.

The leader leaned toward me, anger flashing across his face. With a sneer he told me all the ways his guerillas could harm me if we didn't do as they said. There would be mayhem, he told me, and no one would ever find the bodies. Did I really want to take that chance?

By now, I was shaking, though I tried not to let him see that. I was convinced he meant what he said, and I was afraid not just for my own safety, but for the safety of my employees. This was completely out of hand—these men were not kidding around, and I was the one who'd ultimately have to answer for putting SKS employees' lives at risk.

"Look," I told the man, "we're not going to give you anything. But if you're going to do something violent in retaliation, please make sure you do it to me." I took a piece of paper out of my bag and started scribbling on it. "Here's my address, and here's the license plate of my vehicle. Please leave everyone else, our staff members and borrowers, alone."

I pushed the paper across the table, and we stood to leave. My legs were trembling, but I managed to make it downstairs and out the door. I was convinced I was a dead man, and even told the two employees with me where I wanted to be buried—under a tree on the grounds of our first SKS branch—if the rebels killed me.

They didn't, of course. But I was filled with fear. Yet, in all honesty, despite being frightened, I think I still never believed real harm would come to me in any of these threatening confrontations. Somehow, I had this optimism, a spiritual faith almost, that since I was doing good work and had good intentions, I would be protected—in the same way I'd felt protected when I was hitchhiking in the States during my college days.

My standing up to these rebels was nothing compared to what a group of our borrowers did a couple of years later. Guerrillas had threatened to harm an SKS loan officer, telling him they'd kill him if he didn't accede to their demands to stop all SKS activity in the areas they controlled. At the next weekly meeting, the loan officer told his borrowers about the threat—and the women proceeded to do something truly extraordinary. One by one, they took a stand at the meeting and declared that they would defend him. Then, in an act of remarkable bravery, several of the women actually went to meet the guerillas at their camp in the forest. They told the guerrillas that before ever laying a hand on the loan officer, they would have to "take us first."

When I heard this story, I was incredibly moved. These women showed the kind of courage you rarely see in life. And they showed remarkable loyalty to SKS, which also touched me deeply. Yes, we were forced to face strange and sometimes frightening circumstances to grow our business. But as the bad times showed, we were doing so with extraordinary members and employees.

Despite the peaceful resolution of these two significant confrontations, the larger issue of making peace with the leftist rebels continued throughout the life of SKS. The rebels, like us, adhered to strong, principled stands—it's just that their principles were very different from ours. Learning how to peacefully coexist in light of those differences was an ongoing challenge that was never fully resolved.

In late 2004, while still in Chicago and working for McKinsey, I began putting together an initial group of investors for a first round of investment in SKS. Six years after our launch, with more than 40,000 members and $10 million in cumulative loans disbursed, we had finally broken even. At last, it was time for SKS to make the switch from nonprofit to for-profit. And that meant we could finally begin raising much larger sums from investors, rather than scrambling for donations. The first step was incorporating a for-profit company, which I did in late 2004. Then I applied for a license from the Reserve Bank of India to become a non-bank finance company under the name SKS Microfinance Pvt. Ltd. While that was in process, I started fundraising.

The first person I called was Ravi Reddy, the tech entrepreneur who had surprised me with a $50,000 donation back in 1998, and who had continued to support SKS in the years since. Ravi had always been drawn to our for-profit vision for SKS, and he, along with his business partner Sandeep Tungare, were eager to become angel investors. He also helped me identify other investors who might be interested in stepping up.

I flew to San Francisco and made my way down Interstate 101 to Silicon Valley, the hub of venture capital in America. Once there, I made pitch after pitch to potential investors, telling them all the same thing: "The poor are entrepreneurial, and their businesses earn extraordinarily high returns. If you invest in SKS, we can invest in them—and fortunes will come to both of you." I put together a PowerPoint presentation and walked the venture capitalists through an explanation of how SKS worked. And I told them we had a 98 percent payback rate among our borrowers.

At that time, microfinance was just beginning to make news— but it was still a little-understood business taking place a world away. Also, VCs had been burned badly when the dot-com bubble burst a few years earlier, so they weren't as free with their money as they once had been. Even though a number of potential investors were intrigued, several told me the same thing: "We're interested, but only if you return to the helm as CEO." The idea was that an early stage venture investment was primarily a bet on the drive and the passion of an entrepreneur. The formula wouldn't work if I wasn't in India.

Ever since moving back to Chicago, I had had the typical visitation schedule for divorced dads: every other weekend and one evening a week. Since going to work for McKinsey, I had been relegated to seeing my son only every other weekend, since I was traveling during the work week. Given those circumstances, I came up with another possible scenario: I would move back to India as CEO of SKS, but as part of my new contract, the company would fly me back to Chicago every fourth week. My ex-wife could have our son three weeks in a row, but then I'd have him the fourth. I'd work twenty-one days straight but then have seven days with my son, so I'd actually get to see him more each month than if I stayed in Chicago.

I'd been in the nonprofit mind-set for so long, this felt like an audacious thing to ask. But in a for-profit company, this wasn't an unreasonable request. Similarly, I knew I couldn't continue to survive on a nonprofit salary—my legal debts weren't paid off, and now I had a son to support—so I realized I needed to ask for a more corporate salary. With trepidation, I asked for an annual salary of $100,000. This was a huge pay cut from my McKinsey salary, but, on the other hand, it was the largest salary for any head of an Indian microfinance institution.

My requests caused consternation among some of our initial investors. But another of our first-round investors was Vinod Khosla, a cofounder of Sun Microsystems who had made billions with the sale of Sun and become a partner at Kleiner, Perkins, Caufield & Byers, one of the most successful venture capital firms in the world. And he had something to say to the others about my salary request.

Vinod was probably the most influential Indian tech entrepreneur in America. Sun Microsystems, which he had cofounded with Scott McNealy, Andy Bechtolsheim, and Bill Joy, had changed the face of computing with its software, hardware, and IT services. I had spent two years trying to convince him to invest in SKS, but his answer had always been the same: "In principle, this is interesting," he'd tell me. "But I don't have the time to devote to it, and I don't like to put money into something I can't give time to."

"Well," I'd reply, "we've spent an hour together—what do you think that's worth?" Vinod would just smile wryly and shake his head. Eventually, I had worn him down with constant appeals and growing evidence that SKS was a good bet. At last, in 2005, he agreed to become an investor—with the caveat that I had to return as CEO.

But now I had to convince my first-round investors about my salary needs. I laid out my financial position and the situation with my son, and I explained that I felt like this was the only solution. Various investors and I went back and forth over two weeks, until a phone conversation with Vinod finally tipped the balance.

I was in Washington, D.C., on McKinsey business, staying at the posh St. Regis Hotel near the White House. Vinod and I were on the phone, discussing the salary issue, when he asked me point-blank what my monthly expenses were in Chicago. I told him about child support, paying off debt, and the other general expenses I had. Finally, after a pause, he said, "Okay. We'll do it."

I was so relieved I wanted to cry. As we had gone back and forth over the past few weeks, I'd felt my whole life was in the balance. I wanted nothing more than to be able to return to SKS—and this would allow me to do it, while still being able to see my son regularly as well as acting in a fiscally responsible way toward him.

With Vinod's coaxing, the other investors got on board, and the deal was sealed. Our first-round investment—from Vinod Khosla, Ravi Reddy, Sandeep Tungare, Unitus, and the Small Industries Development Bank of India (SIDBI)—totaled $2.5 million. The parent nonprofit organization, Swayam Krishi Sangam, received significant sweat equity for having created the microfinance portfolio, which I allocated to a set of philanthropic trusts since nonprofits were not permitted to hold equity in a finance company. I did not take any sweat equity for myself because I felt that if a nonprofit creates value with donor funds, that value should go to an entity with the same philosophical leanings.

This was not the norm. Founders typically get sweat equity for having created the value that provides the foundation for investment. Some of my business friends were shocked that I did not take sweat equity, since I'd created SKS and that was the way it worked in the for-profit world. But, even though it may have been unusual, I felt it would have been unethical for me to personally take any.

While I was comfortable with my decision, that choice also meant that I did not have any ownership of the new for-profit SKS Microfinance Pvt. Ltd. Instead, the new investors created an employee stock option pool in which I participated. That program would commence when the for-profit SKS Microfinance Pvt. Ltd. started operations. Stock options are the right to purchase shares in the future at the current value of the underlying shares, but these rights do not come with the voting rights that other shareholders have. I was not worried, however, because our investors believed in my vision for SKS Microfinance Pvt. Ltd. Besides, I was on the board of the trusts, so I was able to influence the direction of SKS through that shareholding, which was 48 percent of the shareholding after the first-round investments were made.

From my position on the board of the trusts, I nominated Sitaram Rao as the trusts' nominee director for the board of SKS Microfinance Pvt. Ltd. As I mentioned, Sitaram was the board member who had taken my place as CEO when I was in Chicago. I asked Gurcharan Das to become chairperson of the board of SKS. I did not know Das, but I had read his book *India Unbound*, which provides an economic history of India from independence to the new millennium. I loved how Das weaved together memoir and history, criticism of India yet also optimism about the country. I found his contact information, called him, met him, told him about SKS's mission, and asked him to serve as chairperson. He agreed. With him and Sitaram on the SKS board, I had kindred spirits to help me in the journey to blend capitalism and philanthropy in SKS's new avatar.

In inviting Das to become chairperson, I was separating the roles of CEO and chairperson. At the time in India, it was common to combine these roles; a typical designation in India was "CMD," meaning chairperson and managing director (the term equivalent to CEO). I felt it important to separate these roles to create good governance by not having excess power consolidated in one board role.

Similarly, I wanted to do something uncommon with stock options. Following trends in the tech sector in the United States in the 1990s, stock options were typically given mainly to senior management of start-up companies. At SKS, I wanted to go one step further. Since our field staff were from the same social strata as our members—often sons and daughters of our members—I wanted them to have stock options as well. So I created a stock option pool in which every single employee received stock options. I knew many of the field staff did not fully understand the concept of stock options, but I wanted them to have stock options because I wanted SKS to be able to help make a difference not only in the lives of our members but also in the lives of the staff.

With all the negotiating completed, finally, to my relief and excitement, after nearly a year and half away, I could now head back to India to become the CEO of SKS Microfinance Pvt. Ltd., the now for-profit finance company.

CHAPTER 8

GOAT ECONOMICS

In October 2005, two months after I returned to India and SKS, I
drove to the airport in Hyderabad to greet a VIP. Rahul Gandhi, son
of the late prime minister Rajiv Gandhi and the current Congress
Party president Sonia Gandhi, was coming to Andhra Pradesh to pay
SKS a visit. He had recently been elected to Parliament, and this was
his first trip to our state since the election.

As a scion of the Nehru–Gandhi family, thirty-six-year-old
Rahul was a big deal in India. An up-and-coming young politician
who was trailed by a pack of news cameras everywhere he went,
he was expected to become a serious contender for prime minister.
About a month earlier, his chief of staff had called to say that Rahul
wanted to see firsthand how microfinance worked, so we had made
arrangements to take him out into the villages.

I got my first hint of how significant this was when the calls
started coming in. Rahul's team had asked me to keep the visit
confidential for security reasons—but slowly, word leaked out, and
before long I was getting calls from government officials, the media,
and senior politicians asking for details. I always refused, but when
Rahul's arrival date came, the secret was out: More than 10,000 people came to the airport to see him.

I arrived at the airport and was escorted into the VIP lounge, where I was to receive Rahul before taking him out to the villages. As I entered the lounge, I walked past a line of politicians who were being made to wait behind a glass barrier. They couldn't quite believe I was being allowed in while they had to wait, and a couple of them began complaining, saying things like, "I'm a minister—who is he?" Eventually, the security head asked me to leave the lounge because of the growing ruckus, and I was escorted directly out to the tarmac to receive Rahul, who came off the plane in jeans and a short-sleeved shirt, and greeted me warmly. To my great satisfaction, I was then able to walk with Rahul right back past that same line of politicians, enjoying their surprised stares all the way.

I sat with Rahul in the backseat of his bulletproof black SUV, and we left the airport sandwiched between a cavalcade of security vehicles. Because his grandmother, Indira Gandhi, and his father had both been assassinated, Rahul was always kept in a tight security bubble—and there was even more concern today, as the road we were taking was the same one where Maoist guerrillas had assassinated a senior minister of the state just a few years earlier. Which is why what happened next was even more astounding: Just after we reached the outskirts of the city, Rahul told his driver to stop. "Everyone will recognize me if we drive up in this thing," he said to me. "Let's get into your vehicle instead." The security guards tensed up immediately, but Rahul just strolled from his bulletproof SUV over to my jeep and climbed in. I followed him, and told my driver to start driving.

Rahul and I had a wide-ranging discussion during the two-hour drive to the villages. I explained our work using a PowerPoint presentation on my laptop, and he listened intently, asked thoughtful questions, and didn't have the usual stunned reaction when I mentioned our interest rates—he clearly had the sophistication to understand our approach. We also talked about poverty. What do the poor want? What are the challenges they face? What are their dreams and aspirations? Rahul seemed genuinely eager to learn.

As we neared the first village, Rahul's team told him that huge crowds and media had gathered—somehow, even the details of where we were going had leaked. But Rahul was unperturbed. He simply turned to me and asked if we could go to a different village, explaining that if there were crowds and press, he wouldn't be able to see how things really were, which was the whole point.

I was amazed. I have to admit that when Rahul's chief of staff first asked about a village visit, I thought it would be little more than an attempt at building his image. But with this request, it was obvious that, for Rahul, this trip wasn't about image. He wasn't seeking out press coverage—he wanted to truly understand what was going on in the country, from the ground up.

Eventually, we ended up staying at the first village, as the police were able to cordon off the crowds and press so Rahul could interact just with the villagers. He sat in on a center meeting, asked questions of our members, and even handed out a loan. After the meeting, we visited one borrower's hut, where she explained how she made money from her microenterprise, a milk-producing buffalo. She also told Rahul about her husband, who was in bonded labor—a form of illegal debt bondage (in which compulsion into servitude is derived from debt) that still exists in India even now.

As the woman explained her husband's predicament of working essentially without pay, Rahul started asking more questions. Which landlord was he working for? How long had he been a bonded laborer? Where was he now? As he talked, I realized Rahul wanted to go to the farm where this laborer was bonded and perhaps try to get him released. By this time, though, it was dusk, and the head of security was giving me alarmed looks, as he'd also realized what Rahul had in mind.

Once darkness fell, it would be easier for leftist guerillas to launch an attack, so the security head urged Rahul to return to Hyderabad in his bulletproof SUV. He relented, and as we pulled out of the village, he saw the thousands of people still standing outside the security cordon, hoping to catch a glimpse of him. "Stop the vehicle," he said, then turned to me. "Give me a second. You've shown me your work; now I will show you mine." He jumped up on the roof of the SUV and began waving, as people in the crowd wildly screamed. After a few seconds, he hopped down and got back into the SUV, and we were off.

On the way back to Hyderabad, Rahul wanted to talk further, about everything from politics to economics to philosophy. At one point, he spoke of the need for people in the social sector to get more engaged with politics. "We have to get good people into politics," he said, looking straight at me. "Otherwise, we'll never have real change." As he spoke, I found myself intrigued by the idea of entering politics—but just as quickly, the feeling left me. The kind of political empowerment of the poor I had in mind would surely face resistance from vested political interests, and I just didn't have the stomach for engaging in the necessary compromises of Indian politics. Better, I thought, to build on relationships with progressive politicians like Rahul Gandhi, to influence government policies from the outside in.

As we approached the city, Rahul asked whether I had dinner plans. I took him to Paradise, a restaurant that specialized in the famous Hyderabad biryani, and we talked through a long dinner. I finally dropped him off at 11:30 that night.

Images from Rahul's visit to Andhra Pradesh dominated India's news cycle the next day, accompanied by front-page articles on SKS—who we were, what we did, how our program worked. For the first time, ordinary Indians across the country were hearing about us. We were already making a name for ourselves in the rural areas we served, but this was the beginning of much wider recognition. And as we now moved into a period of hyper-growth, SKS was positioning itself for the next leap: becoming a household name.

When I resigned as CEO in January 2004, we had about 25,000 members. By the time I returned in August 2005, we had grown to

120,000. This was a phenomenal growth rate by any measure, and there were certainly challenges along the way, but SKS was on pace to scale. A big reason for our growth was the stellar leadership of Sitaram Rao and the passion of Praseeda Kunam, a young, driven firebrand who really stepped up at SKS during my absence. But while we'd grown rapidly, we hadn't yet reached the exponential growth we'd need to achieve my vision of scaling microfinance beyond what anyone had ever done before.

I knew that one big challenge to adding so many new members would be finding—and training—enough managers to serve them all. At the time, the typical microfinance model of recruiting and training field staff was an apprentice model, where new loan officers would work for four to five months and then be deployed to the field. But if we wanted to grow at the pace we envisioned, that training period was far too long.

How could we accelerate the process? Here again I looked to the example of franchise companies such as McDonald's and Burger King, because of their great success in quickly training and deploying large, unskilled workforces. We enlisted the help of a British franchising consultant, and the top field staff and I sequestered ourselves for a week, writing up a step-by-step manual that would describe in painstaking detail every single process our loan officers would use.

At the end of the week, we emerged with an extremely detailed manual and a streamlined two-month training process for loan officers—tools that would help us train up to a thousand new loan officers a month, many of whom came to us with little experience handling money and numbers. We modeled our process on Hamburger University, the renowned McDonald's training facility where new franchisees learn everything about how to run a fast-food restaurant the McDonald's way.

Under our eight-week program, each fresh SKS recruit—typically a recent high school graduate—attended a weekly theory class, then spent five days a week in the field shadowing a loan officer.

Initially, the recruits learned by watching, but they gradually took on responsibilities themselves, learning by doing. By the end of the training, they already had hands-on experience and could seamlessly transition to work as loan officers—thereby solving the problem of how to add hundreds of new loan officers quickly.

From this rapidly growing pool, we could promote and train the next two levels: branch managers and district managers. But there was still one more problem to solve. How could we quickly find and train area managers, the higher-level employees who would each supervise twenty-five branches, with a member base of more than 100,000? These positions required recruits with much more advanced skill sets.

At this point, the conventional thinking in microfinance was to bring in managers with ten or more years of work experience, then train them for six months or more. But bringing in such experienced staff was costly, and seasoned people sometimes come with baggage—stubbornly conventional thinking about how things should be done, based on their "experience." Also, even though an area manager's work was more complex than that of a loan officer, we couldn't afford to take six months to train them. Our plans called for an aggressive expansion from Andhra Pradesh into multiple Indian states, so we needed new area managers immediately. But how could we quickly identify, hire, and train highly capable people, and at a low cost?

The answer to the first problem solved the second one as well. Rather than hiring older, more experienced recruits, I decided to go in the opposite direction. A couple of months before returning as CEO, I asked Praseeda to hire four recent management graduates, the Indian equivalent of MBAs. In India, such students study management right after their undergraduate work, so we basically had four "kids"—all in their early twenties, and all eager to start their first jobs.

People were surprised and a little dubious about this approach, with one MFI leader even saying point-blank that those types of recruits couldn't cut it. But I had reasons of my own for believing that relatively inexperienced young people could do such high-level work. "Just because they're young doesn't mean they can't do it," I told my colleague. "I was young at DDS, too, but I just needed some guidance and trust."

The four young people Praseeda had hired began their training in May 2005, but three months later, when I arrived in India to resume the CEO role, all four were still working in Andhra Pradesh. "This wasn't the idea," I told Praseeda. "We need to send them out to the new states." She knew that had been my intention, but while I was away, she just couldn't bring herself to send these inexperienced kids out to run multiple branches in brand-new territories. It felt like too great a risk—one Praseeda wasn't willing to take.

But I was. I immediately called the four young people into a meeting and said, "You're each going to run an area, and you're going to do it in different states. We're expanding, and you're going to lead the way." I unfurled a map of India and laid it on the table in front of them. "Okay," I said. "So, who wants to work in which state? Anyone?" The four faces before me looked absolutely blank.

"Come on," I said. "Speak up! Don't be shy!" I pointed to a young man in the front. "Where do you want to go?"

"Really?" he asked. "Just pick one? Just like that?"

"Yes," I said, growing impatient. "Look, do you want to be an apprentice for the rest of your life? Didn't you study management so you could be a CEO one day?" I looked around at the four of them; they seemed a bit shell-shocked. "Now's your chance to actually run something," I said. "So, let's go! Pick your state."

One by one, the four chose their states, and within a few weeks they had all relocated.

Yes, this was risky—but we didn't have time to second-guess ourselves. And at this point, my experience at McKinsey came into play: Before spending that year at McKinsey, I had never spent time with executives of Fortune 500 companies. I'd had this vague notion that there was some kind of magic to what they did, because they were so large and successful, and I considered myself a novice in comparison. But the more time I spent with them, the more I realized that we really *did* know what we were doing at SKS. And in some cases, we were functioning at a higher and more efficient level than these big, global companies. Seeing that gave me a lot more confidence in my own abilities when I returned as CEO.

The simple truth was that we had to expand quickly, and this was the most efficient way to do it. I knew that if we could find young people as determined and eager as I had been in my days at DDS, it would work. I had faith in these young people, even if they didn't yet have it in themselves. My hunch was rewarded. Very quickly, SKS became one of the leading MFIs in every one of the states where we'd sent our new young area managers: Odisha, Karnataka, Maharashtra, Madhya Pradesh.

While my recruitment of entry-level managers went well, recruitment of senior executives did not. Soon after I had returned to India to steer the now for-profit SKS Microfinance Pvt. Ltd., I recruited a chief operating officer. I knew that, with our expansion, we would need someone with experience handling large-scale financial services sales teams.

In 2005, I had met M. R. Rao, then national head of alternative channels for ING Vysya Life Insurance. He had approached SKS to explore being a partner to sell insurance in areas where we worked. But first he wanted to see if the SKS brand was strong enough—whether members would buy insurance policies from us. He started out by asking villagers if they would consider buying insurance products. Then, he asked them which they'd prefer—insurance from SKS, ING, or the well-known state-run Life Insurance Corporation of India (LIC). In villages where SKS was active, our members responded that they preferred an SKS product to the others. Rao wasn't surprised, as our members might be expected to show brand loyalty. But then he asked villagers who *weren't* SKS members—and they said the same thing. Of the three offered, villagers overwhelmingly preferred an SKS product, whether they were our members or not. When Rao realized the extent to which SKS had penetrated the rural market, he didn't simply forge a partnership between ING and SKS. He decided to leave ING and join SKS.

I was intrigued. Rao had broad experience in finance. He had previously handled vehicle financing, and he was managing insurance products at ING—an area I wanted SKS to get into. Besides, it would have been hard to recruit any other senior executive in an established firm because microfinance was still seen as a second-class citizen within financial services, something that was nice to do but not serious finance. Rao, on the other hand, had a different view because he had been given an inside look at the potential of SKS. So, I made an offer to Rao to join as our chief operating officer.

My second-in-command at the time, Praseeda Kunam, however, refused to work with Rao, saying that she would not work under a "car salesman." Thinking it was best for the company to bring in a seasoned banker, I went with Rao, and Praseeda left SKS. We were all set to move forward when I received a call from Rao in September 2005. He was no longer coming aboard. ING had made a counteroffer that was too good for him to pass up, so he remained with ING, putting me (and SKS) in a great bind. Praseeda had already left to join the ABN AMRO Foundation, and Rao now was not joining us. I was left doing the work of two C-level executives in what was arguably our most critical year. We had just converted to a for-profit and just received investments of $2.5 million led by Vinod Khosla (a man who expected results). I had just sent our new MBA recruits to four new states, and the media was starting to pay attention. There was no room for error.

I had no choice but to hunker down and single-handedly charge ahead. With our recruitment and training up to speed, our software streamlining our recordkeeping, and $2.5 million of equity solving our capital needs, I had to focus on my primary goal for SKS: to grow,

grow, grow, as fast as we could. In all honesty, I'd been aiming toward this moment all these years: It was time to prove to everyone—other MFIs, investors, bureaucrats, nonprofits—that we could practice microfinance in a way that would serve more poor people than anyone had ever thought possible.

I had never worked so hard in my life, consistently clocking 100-hour work weeks. By the end of fiscal year 2005–06, we had 80 branches and more than 200,000 members, had disbursed $34 million in that fiscal year, and were profitable. Our repayment rate continued to be high at 98 percent.

In a *Forbes* cover story about me, Vineet Rai—head of the Indian impact investment firm Aavishkaar—was quoted and described the moment well. He said, "The Vikram who went away was a soft-spoken almost naïve, nice human being. The one who returned from McKinsey was a clear visionary who knew how to build a large company. It's the difference between saying 'I want to go to the top of Mount Everest,' versus 'I know exactly how to get there.'"[1] It meant a lot to hear that compliment from Vineet, as he had known me in the early days of SKS.

In late 2006, I received a call from Rao. Now that we were profitable and getting recognition, he wanted to join the team. I was reluctant. He had damaged our ability to scale with his last-minute renege on my 2005 offer, putting me in an impossible situation. How could I trust him to follow through this time? But my mentor Sitaram Rao—who was not related to M. R. Rao, though they had the same last name—put in a good word on his behalf, and I desperately needed a number two. I was at a personal breaking point. So I hired him.

When Rao joined in October 2006, we were poised for further growth. Our systems were in place. Our core product had been perfected. I had trained and groomed our first batch of MBA recruits who were leading SKS field operations in different states. Rao just had to hit the accelerator while I was at the helm to ensure quality; my foot was hovering over the brake in case we went too fast.

He hit the accelerator, and SKS went into full speed. In the fall of 2006, we increased our MBA hires from four to twenty. This time around, I designed an accelerated two-month training for the MBA hires, like the one I had created for loan officers, so SKS could get them into the field even more quickly. The program was so successful that, in the years to come, we steadily increased our numbers of young people hired to be area managers, topping out at recruiting 100 a year.

During the two-year period between October 2006 and October 2008, we grew fast. The numbers show that the combination of my focus on quality and Rao's aggressive approach to sales worked well. The year 2006 brought a perfect confluence: a sharp spike in our growth, plus increased worldwide awareness of microfinance, plus the rising profile of SKS that had accelerated following the Rahul Gandhi visit all led to an explosion of attention. If 2004 had been the most difficult year of my life, 2006 soon became the most rewarding.

In March, SKS signed up its 200,000th member, with a total of 400,000 people—members and their spouses—covered by our life insurance product. I set an ambitious goal of "7 by 7"—700,000 members by March 2007—and announced it publicly, which turned a lot of heads in the microfinance world. For years, SKS had been the aggressive young upstart that talked a big game but had yet to reach it. Now, we were reaching it—and beyond.

A couple of weeks later, I received an invitation to the TIME 100 Gala. Each spring, the magazine named its list of the "100 People Who Shape Our World," and I thought at first I was simply being invited to the cocktail party. But when I got a call from a reporter soon afterward, I realized with a shock that I was being included on the list. This was beyond my wildest imaginings—SKS was still only the third-largest MFI in India, but the *TIME* editors had chosen me.

When the issue hit the newsstands on May 8, 2006, I was one of two Indians on the list—the other was the cofounder of the technology giant Infosys, Nandan Nilekani. We joined such luminaries as Pope Benedict XVI, Chief Justice John Roberts, U.S. President George W. Bush, the Irish singer-songwriter Bono, the incomparable Oprah Winfrey, and then Chinese Premier Wen Jiabao. I could hardly believe it was true until I bought the magazine in a shop and flipped through to see my photo. No one else seemed to believe it either—throughout the day, Indian TV stations flashed photos of Nandan and me, most often accompanied by the caption, "Who is Vikram Akula?"

The night of the gala, I walked onto the red carpet at the Time Warner Center in New York and smiled sheepishly at the dizzying barrage of camera flashes. The whirr of shutter clicks was nonstop.

Not surprisingly, a photographer yelled out, "Who are you?"

I was "influential" but not well known, and certainly not in the United States. I yelled back my name and watched her scribble in a notebook.

"What do you do?" she wanted to know.

"Microfinance."

"What's that?"

I was unused to this kind of celebrity attention, but I was used to the question. While the microfinance movement was now widespread in various parts of the developing world, most Americans had not yet heard of it. That evening, I found myself answering that same question from others who were on the list. Some, such as politicians Condoleezza Rice and Michael Bloomberg, were aware of microfinance but not aware of the headway I and others were making in India and elsewhere. But others—from entertainers Jennifer Lopez and Will Smith to fashion magnate Ralph Lauren—were not, though they were all gracious and supportively listened to me.

As I milled around the reception that evening, I thought of the millions of women SKS worked with in India. I was there to represent them. My job was to make sure that their voices, their dreams, their aspirations were part of the global conversation that would take place that night. I needed to explain to the other ninety-nine "most influential people in the world" what microfinance was and why it was so important. My job got somewhat easier one week later when the *Wall Street Journal* ran a front-page story about me in its May 15, 2006, issue. It detailed how and why I started SKS and what we were aiming to accomplish, reaching a whole new constituency of people, further raising our profile, and arousing even more interest in the idea of for-profit microfinance. Suddenly, everyone wanted to learn about microfinance and how we practiced it. And that included two of the richest people in the world, with whom I met that very week.

The Gates Foundation was considering launching its own microfinance funding program, and Bill and Melinda Gates, as was their habit when entering a new sector, were trying to learn everything possible about it. Melinda Gates had come to India six months earlier to see microfinance in action, visiting villages and holding discussions with Indian microloan providers, including me. The next step after her field visits was convening a global roundtable: The Foundation invited eight MFI practitioners from all over the world to fly in and meet with Bill and Melinda at their offices in Seattle.

The eight of us were shown into a plain conference room in a nondescript (but, as I was later told, bulletproof) building. We'd been told that Melinda and Bill would be joined by his father, Bill Gates Sr., as well as a "friend" of theirs. That friend turned out to be business magnate Warren Buffett. When the four of them walked into the room, we all stood as if on cue. Nobody planned it, but I think we all felt a bit overwhelmed with meeting some of the most powerful business and philanthropic minds in the world. And they were here to learn from us.

I had an even more surreal feeling when Melinda introduced everyone around the table. When she got to me, she had barely gotten out the words "this is Vikram Akula" before Warren Buffett jumped in, saying, "I know who you are. I just read about you in the *Journal.*" I smiled and nodded, incredulous that the most influential investor in the world had just read about *me* in the famed publication.

We launched into a wide-ranging discussion, explaining the basics of microfinance, the differences in how it's practiced in various parts of the world, and the structure developed by Professor Yunus back in the 1970s. Melinda was the facilitator, as she'd met all of us already, but Buffett and Bill Gates took active parts, too. At one point, Bill leaned back in his chair, his brow furrowed.

"But hold on," he said. "There's one thing I don't get." He peered through his glasses, looking straight at me. "What are people possibly doing," he asked, "where they can pay twenty-eight percent interest on a loan and still make money?" I had answered this question many times before, but never to the world's richest man. I pulled myself up in my chair, took a deep breath, and responded with an example: "Say you have a landless agricultural laborer," I began. "Even though she owns absolutely nothing, she can take a loan of, say, two thousand rupees—about forty dollars. She can use that money to buy a goat. She can then take that goat with her to work when she goes to the fields. The goat eats virtually anything along the way, so there's no investment from her side to feed it—she just takes it to the fields, ties it up while she's working, and then walks it back home when she's done."

As Bill Gates scribbled notes on the pad in front of him, I went on. "A goat typically gives birth twice a year—usually two kids per birth, but sometimes only one. So, even in the conservative scenario, if the goat gives birth twice and gives only one kid each time, you've got two offspring," I said. "And the value of each offspring is usually about fifty percent of that of the mother goat.

"So, by the end of the year, you've got one hundred–percent return. You've got the mother goat, worth two thousand rupees, and two kids, worth a thousand each. Even if you took out the cost of capital at twenty-eight percent of the loan, you're making in the range of seventy-plus percent return on invested capital." Bill looked up from his pad. "The laborer can pay the weekly loan installment from her work in the fields, or if needed she can sell the goat kids for cash and still have a significant asset—a mother goat worth two thousand rupees—that she can sell later."

This standard explanation of what I call "goat economics" seemed to impress him, but I wasn't finished yet. I went on to explain that this is a typical scenario with microenterprises—they tend to yield extraordinarily high returns, for four reasons. First, and most important, they most often use family labor, which is far more productive than hiring wage laborers. Think of your classic immigrant-owned grocery store in the United States, with sons and daughters providing the bulk of the labor. It's both more productive and cheaper than hiring others to do your work for you.

Second, in the "informal economy," micro-entrepreneurs don't have to pay any legal fees or taxes—making it much easier, and quicker, to turn a profit. Third, poor entrepreneurs have very few infrastructure costs. A village grocery, for example, is a home-front store, not a separate place that requires extra infrastructure costs. And fourth, for the preceding three reasons, capital represents only a small percentage of the new venture's overall input. Capital is a catalyst, no doubt, but the fundamental economics of microbusiness really aren't significantly impacted by the interest rates. What's far more important is timely access to capital.

For all these reasons, the poor are able to make good money, even with high-interest-rate loans. "Though twenty-eight percent might seem high," I said, "the demand among poor Indians for our loans has exploded, and we have almost no defaults among borrowers. At SKS, we have a ninety-eight percent payback rate—much higher than the rate of Western loan paybacks." The conclusion was obvious: The system was working for the poor. And there was no reason it couldn't continue to work, for borrowers, investors, and lenders.

As I finished my explanation of goat economics, I watched Bill Gates scribble a few more notes on his pad. A thought popped into my head: "I'm explaining to the world's richest man how the world's poorest people make money on goats." It was an amazing moment, one that pretty well summed up that year.

But of all the attention we got in 2006, the most important wasn't from newspapers or magazines or even Bill Gates. The most important was from investors, who suddenly began to see SKS not just as an interesting play in the microfinance world but as a solid, rapidly growing business with a tremendous profit potential.

The calls started coming in May, just after the *TIME* and *Wall Street Journal* articles put SKS on the map. Bankers and venture capitalists began reaching out, asking for meetings and field visits, and saying things like, "Don't go anywhere else for money, Vikram. We'll give you whatever you need."

This was brand new territory for me. After years of having to convince donors and investors to take a chance on us, we suddenly had an influx of wealthy suitors. I didn't really know the language of venture investing, and I didn't even know who some of the major players were. In August 2006, when we got a call from Sequoia Capital—one of the largest venture capital firms in Silicon Valley—one of our board members had to tell me to meet with them. Sequoia had been an early investor in Apple and Google.

I was pretty naive about how venture investing worked at this level, so I just went with the flow, trying not to let on whenever I was confused about something. In one meeting with Citibank in Mumbai about raising debt, I listened patiently as one of their people talked about "dirty paper" and "clean paper"—financial terms that everyone in the room seemed to know but meant nothing to me. I just nodded my head, looking serious and attentive, wondering what in the world those terms could mean.

In other ways, my naiveté actually helped. Once word got out that Sequoia was interested, other firms came calling, and soon we had about a dozen potential suitors. This was perfect, I thought—we could hold a bake-off, see who would offer us the best deal, and pick and choose as we pleased. I didn't realize this wasn't how things were done in the world of venture capital, so I just happily forged ahead, essentially asking these investors to impress us, rather than the other way around.

When the Sequoia team came to India for a field visit, I scheduled an unnecessarily early time for heading out into the villages. "We'll come pick you up at six AM!" I told the team, thinking to myself that their level of enthusiasm for getting up so early would show me how enthusiastic they were about the business—and the investment. I wanted to test them, to see how dedicated they were to our mission. On the other hand, I didn't really worry about impressing them, as I knew our business model was solid and our growth potential huge. To my mind, it would be obvious to everyone why they'd want to invest with us.

My hunch was correct: At the end of the field visit, Sumir Chadha of Sequoia turned to me and said, "We'd like to make an investment." He rattled off a "pre-money valuation figure," and once again I didn't know exactly what that meant, so I just nodded sagely and said nothing. I couldn't wait to find out what that offer actually represented.

As it turned out, figuring out our valuation was the biggest question we had to answer. Whoever ultimately invested in SKS would receive a percentage of the company's stock in return, so to figure out that percentage we had to determine how much the company was worth overall. How could we possibly assess that number accurately? In the fiscal year ending March 2006, we had only $100,000 in profits—but we were also growing at a breakneck pace. By August 2006, we had about 300,000 members and nearly $75 million in loans disbursed, and we were on track to more than double the number of borrowers when the fiscal year ended in March 2007, and reach beyond two million the year after that.

Much of the value of the company lay in its potential for growth, and no other MFIs were aiming to grow as fast as we were. How do you put a figure on that? There really wasn't any other model with which to compare us. In fact, Harvard Business School wrote up a case study on that question for use in its classes.

With all the attention swirling around, we decided to invite bids from ten of the VC firms, banks, and private equity groups that had expressed interest. We sent financial statements and a business plan to each of them, giving them seven days to respond in writing with a proposal. This method, too, was incredibly unorthodox, but it worked: Eight of the ten responded, and their pre-money valuations of the company ranged from $10 million to $18 million.

It would have been easy to simply choose the investor who gave SKS the highest valuation, but there were other factors to consider. Which group could best give us strategic guidance on hyper-growth? Who could open up doors to different kinds of debt financing, or connect us with vendors and business partners? In the end, we liked Sequoia very much—but their valuation wasn't the highest. Not wanting to leave money on the table, I decided to go back to Sequoia and ask them to meet the highest valuation. The way I saw it, if we could get them to match the numbers we wanted, we'd be all set.

A few of my friends and advisers thought this was, finally, pushing it too far. Entrepreneurs just didn't treat VCs as the supplicants! I was doing everything backward, and this, they feared, could be the last straw. But I was determined to get the number I wanted from the investor I wanted. We set up a meeting, and I essentially said to Sequoia, "This is the deal we want." They didn't hesitate, matching our number on the spot.

I finalized the deal with a handshake in December 2006: Sequoia would be the lead investor for an $11.5 million round of financing for a 23 percent ownership stake.[2] The holding of the trusts went down to 27 percent. I still had no ownership, though I had stock options. Sumir also joined the SKS board of directors.

I might not have entirely known what I was doing, but I had done it. SKS was attracting the big money now, which would further fuel our growth, leading to more investments and more growth, and eventually an initial public offering. My for-profit business plan was working, and we'd be able to help more poor people than ever.

But within the microfinance community, not everyone was so thrilled. Muhammad Yunus, who won the Nobel Peace Prize that year for his pioneering work in microfinance, had long been a vocal critic of for-profit MFIs such as ours. With his new platform as a Nobel Laureate, he ramped up his criticism. And with SKS's new visibility, we were a natural target—although Professor Yunus never criticized me personally, at least not in the initial years. Suddenly, the debate about nonprofit microfinance versus for-profit microfinance turned hotter than ever.

This great debate hinged on one question: Was making a profit from lending to the poor the equivalent of exploiting the poor? In the view of Professor Yunus and others, it was. They believed the only ethical way to lend to the poor was to charge interest rates that just covered expenses. Inviting investments from large venture capitalists, as SKS was doing, and promising investors healthy returns—that was considered exploitation. In a 2006 *New Yorker* article, Professor Yunus had this to say about the idea of making profits off lending to the poor: "When they have enough flesh and blood in their bodies, go and suck them, no problem. But until then, don't do that."[3]

One reason there was so much unease about for-profit microfinance is that some MFIs, notably in Latin America, had been charging extremely high interest rates—sometimes over 100 percent, according to the Washington, D.C.–based multilateral institution CGAP.[4] One, Compartamos Bank, routinely charged around 105 percent at that time, and reportedly gave its field agents bonuses for disbursing larger loans and maintaining high repayment rates—something SKS had never done and would never do, at least not as long as I was in charge. When Compartamos had an IPO in April 2007, raising $467 million for 30 percent of the company and enriching several private investors, critics on all sides assailed the company for predatory lending practices. As Professor Yunus put it in *Bloomberg Businessweek*, "When you discuss microcredit, don't bring Compartamos into it. Microcredit was created to fight the moneylender, not to become the moneylender."[5]

Professor Yunus argued that MFIs should seek their capital from either donors or social investors, who would be content with just getting their principal back—and thus not requiring MFIs to charge high interest rates. This concept is intriguing, but by Professor Yunus's own account, the pool of donor funds and social capital is quite limited. The pool of such funds that was allocated to microfinance in the mid- to late 2000s was far short of the $250 billion or so equity and debt needed to provide finance for the world's poor. Moreover, it was the well-established, high-profile MFIs that received the lion's share of donor funds. For example, as mentioned, Grameen Bank had received $175 million in subsidies between 1985 and 1996,[6] and presumably received more donations after that.

Clearly, the huge quantum of donor capital needed to truly scale microfinance did not exist back then—and still doesn't. But what about other sources? Was there any other pool of cash that would be sufficient to meet the MFIs' needs, while allowing them to charge minimal interest rates? There was—but the catch was, we were not allowed to use it.

If MFIs could have accessed savings deposits from the poor, we'd have had no need for external commercial capital (while also providing the poor with an important financial tool). But unfortunately, most countries, including India, did not allow MFIs to take deposits from the poor. The Reserve Bank of India was likely wary of the potential for money laundering as well as the potential for fraud. Grameen Bank overcame this problem by becoming a bank for the poor through a special act of Bangladesh's parliament. So, it had both plenty of donor funds and access to savings deposits.

But for most MFIs in most countries, there was no way to mobilize savings deposits. Eventually, the Reserve Bank of India established a category of small finance banks in 2015. Today, the situation has finally changed. India has licensed ten small finance banks, and one MFI was even given a universal banking license. But back then, before small finance banks were permitted, the hard truth was this: The only place where MFIs could get enough capital to loan to borrowers was through commercial banks, and banks would only lend based on the amount of equity—investment—an MFI had. Typically commercial banks lent three to four times the amount of equity an MFI could demonstrate. And the only way to get equity was by offering high profits in return. Investors were not ready to invest unless they saw a very large upside potential, because they saw microfinance as risky; they balked at the idea of giving unsecured loans to poor women who had no credit history and who were often illiterate. Small profits, in their view, just weren't worth the risk involved.

If all MFIs took the route Professor Yunus prescribed, they'd never get the capital needed to achieve the exponential growth required to serve all the poor who need loans. Achieving that scale was the single most pressing need back then—nothing else came even close. I believed in this because I felt back then—and even now—that every day that we couldn't afford to offer a loan to a poor person was a day that person remained unnecessarily mired in poverty.

This view surprised some people. Once, in a meeting with a group of senior bureaucrats, one accosted me, asking with great indignation, "We've heard you are charging twenty-four percent interest on your loans! What do you have to say to that?"

He clearly expected me to backpedal or apologize, but instead I drew myself up with equal indignation. "Sir," I barked back. "You are absolutely wrong. We do *not* charge twenty-four percent interest. Absolutely not. In fact, we charge *twenty-eight* percent," I declared. "And let me explain why."

The bureaucrat's expression changed from smug to startled, but I was happy to take this opportunity to explain how our rate structure worked.

I explained that because we weren't allowed to take savings deposits, we had to borrow money from commercial banks at around 11 percent. Furthermore, it was extremely costly to use a vast network of field officers to deliver tiny loans to members in tens of thousands of remote villages across India—about 12 percent of the loan amount. Finally, we set aside 2 percent for defaults, leaving us about a 3 percent profit margin—the minimum needed to attract commercial investors in a new sector that was perceived to be risky.

I went on to explain that, even at 28 percent interest, ours was the lowest-cost financing available to the poor. Loan sharks charged more; private sector commercial banks didn't serve customers in rural India; and going to a government bank would mean several trips for borrowers—each one involving bus fares, lost wages, food expenses, fees for the broker who would assist with the application, and even bribes that had to be paid to the bankers. A World Bank survey of India's poor during that time period indicated that the poor paid bribes as high as 20 percent of their government bank loans.[7]

By the time I finished, most—though not all—in the room were convinced. The fact is, some people will never feel comfortable discussing poor people and profit in the same sentence, no matter how much sense it makes.

I believe that a commercial approach was the best way to give the most poor people access to finance. My early days at DDS taught me a crucial lesson: The poor are really no different from you or me. They're not stupid or slow, and they aren't looking for us to rescue them or teach them anything. The relationship between SKS and our members was mutually beneficial. Our members were receiving tools that had long been denied them, and were using them to do things they were naturally skilled at doing. In return, SKS was building an enormous customer base, establishing a brand, raising money in investments, and continuing to expand the number of poor members served. It was a perfect circle, one that benefited everyone.

The notion that it's somehow unethical to enter into a profitable business working with the poor is insulting to the poor. They are not children who need our protection. They're working women and men who can and were thriving under a system that allowed them to take their economic lives into their own hands. Treating them as anything less is unjust.

Did that mean it was okay to charge extremely high interest rates such as those of Compartamos? No. There's a big difference between charging the highest interest rate you think the market will bear, as Compartamos seemed to be doing in 2007, and charging rates that allow for continued expansion without pushing the market to its limit. The truth is, SKS could have charged far higher interest rates than we did back then, and still have overwhelming demand. Remember, the alternatives for most poor Indians were moneylenders and loan sharks—or not being able to get loans at all and falling into either landless labor or unemployment.

I did not believe in either the Grameen approach or the Compartamos approach. Instead, I was promoting a third way. It was not simply a middle ground of moderate rates and moderate profits; it was something entirely different. It was an approach that simultaneously would yield both low interest rates and profits for investors. How would we do that? The answer lay in what I called Amazon territory.

CHAPTER 9

AMAZON TERRITORY

An Indian folktale called "One Grain of Rice" tells the story of Rani, a girl who lives in a village of rice farmers. The *raja*, or king, decrees that everyone should deliver all their rice to be kept in the royal storehouses, in case of famine. When times are good, all is well—the raja metes out enough rice for everyone and keeps the rest in reserve. But when famine strikes the land, the greedy raja goes back on his promise, refusing to feed the villagers.

The raja keeps all the rice for himself, even as the villagers grow hungrier and hungrier. One day, he even makes plans for a great feast for himself, although the villagers are starving. He orders a servant to transport rice from the storehouses to the palace, and along the way the servant drops a few grains—which a young girl named Rani quickly picks up.

Instead of keeping the rice for herself, Rani delivers it to the raja, saying, "This belongs to you." Touched by her display of loyalty, the raja says he will give her whatever she asks in return.

"Please, just give me one grain of rice today," Rani replies. "One today, and two tomorrow, and four the next day." The raja nods, and she goes on. "For thirty days, sir, that is all I ask. Just double the number of grains each day for thirty days." The raja consents.

Rani knew what he did not: Doubling the number of grains may not seem much in the beginning, but by the thirtieth day, the raja would have to give her more than a billion grains of rice—the entire contents of the storehouses.

I like that folktale because it shows the power of numbers. And the power of numbers is what made the incredible scale SKS achieved not simply a great microfinance business, but a different kind of business altogether. It's what allowed us to reach what I call Amazon territory.

If a company makes a penny or two on a product it sells to a small number of people, it will never make much money. But if a company makes a few pennies on each product, and it sells fifteen to twenty products to tens of millions of people—that's when it starts to make real money. This is how Amazon.com has become so huge: by making small fees, a little bit of money, from multiple products—books, retail goods, video streaming, music, and so on—targeted to huge numbers of customers.

When SKS achieved a critical mass of more than a million members across India in 2007, with channels for product distribution already in place, we opened up a whole new world of possible revenue streams. And, just as important, we opened up new opportunities for our members: great deals on goods and services, increased political power, and social initiatives that would have been impossible to undertake with smaller numbers.

Historically, India's rural markets have been very hard to reach. The country's infrastructure is underdeveloped, so roadways are poor. It has never been cost-effective for companies to travel deep into rural areas to sell their products or services, as the cost of doing so invariably exceeds the revenue produced.

But within a decade after I founded SKS, we had already established highly functioning distribution channels. Our loan officers were traveling to remote villages every single week, regularly meeting with members, and developing relationships. With those channels firmly in place, my idea was to use them for distributing other goods and services. There really is a "fortune at the bottom of the pyramid," as the late author and professor C. K. Prahalad wrote in his influential 2004 book of that title—and I felt SKS was perfectly poised to tap into it.

This is why our "third way"—somewhere between the Grameen and Compartamos extremes—would work. Because our member base was so large, we were able to source goods and services for them at a very low cost. We were also able to offer suppliers our channels to market and distribute those goods and services, making it cost-effective for them to do so. With the savings on both ends, the costs to members would be extremely low, even after we added a small financing charge for purchases. The supplier would get a small margin on a large number of goods sold, and SKS could earn a small margin on its finance charge—ultimately resulting in high profits because of the size of SKS's member base. Everybody could win.

Here's an example: By 2008, more than a half million of our members had used their loans to open or expand small home-front groceries, or *kirana* stores, where they sold things like toothpaste, soap, shampoo, and food items. The store owners made money from their businesses, and their fellow villagers benefited by having greater access to goods.

So far, so good. But here's the problem: The poor still pay disproportionately more than the rest of the world for their goods. If you buy a gallon jug of laundry detergent at your local grocery store, you're paying far less per wash than a poor person who buys little foil packets, called sachets, with individual servings of detergent. Buying in bulk always results in savings, but the poor don't have the cash flow to pay for so much of an item all at once. Additionally, by the time those single-serving sachets make it from the supplier through multiple middlemen, the price has been marked up several times over. The resulting high per-unit price of such goods is one reason why the poor have a harder time pulling themselves out of poverty.

But with more than a half million of these SKS-funded kirana stores operating across the country, why not create a de facto national chain, increasing the storeowners' power and giving them access to cheaper bulk goods, direct from the supplier? Why not, in other words, create the equivalent of a grassroots Walmart across India?

In the fall of 2008, I found myself sitting in front of a well-coiffed, pinstripe-suited man with a British accent who could help us achieve this goal. His name was James Scott, and he was the Asia region head of Metro Cash & Carry, the European equivalent of the wholesaler Costco. His company had been trying to get into India for years, but they'd faced numerous obstacles, bureaucratic and otherwise. He'd come to realize that, while Metro might be able to directly serve some of the high-end customers, they couldn't break into the vast potential of small kirana stores on their own—they'd need to partner with someone who already had a foothold among the tens of millions of potential customers.

James was a captain of industry, but his eyes lit up as I started telling him about our members' tiny village kiosk grocery stores. "We have a half million stores across India," I said, and you could practically see him doing mental calculations. It was a funny scene—James in his fine suit, representing a giant German conglomerate, and me in my kurta pajama shirt and sandals, making a business deal on behalf of a half million poor women.

Under our pilot program with Metro, launched in 2008, SKS members with kirana stores bought goods directly from the wholesaler. Instead of paying a high commission to a middleman in the local town, who might be selling whatever he could get his hands on, the kirana store owners now had standard, high-quality, branded goods—at a much cheaper price than they had been paying. And Metro had found a way into the gigantic market that had eluded them. All this was possible only because of the number of members we had—numbers we never could have reached operating as a non-profit MFI.

Similarly, through a deal with Nokia and Airtel, in 2008 we started financing cell phones for our members at rates cheaper than those normally available. The demand for cell phones in rural areas is extremely high, but the market had reached a saturation point: middle-class people who wanted phones already had them. And the poor who wanted them couldn't afford them. The cell phone companies knew there was a giant unfulfilled market out there—but there was no way to access those customers without incurring costs that exceeded the potential revenue.

We approached Nokia and Airtel with a proposal, offering to use SKS branches and loan officers to take orders and hand-deliver phones. A huge opportunity for these companies, our proposal eliminated the costs that had kept them from expanding into this market. In return for this distribution, Nokia offered our members handsets at a steep discount, and Airtel offered a significant reduction on the cost of minutes. SKS financed the purchase, and, just like that, millions of rural poor got access to cell phones they couldn't previously afford, while the phone companies got a whole new client base. Once again, we brokered a deal in which everybody could win.

In some cases, reaching the vast market of the rural poor involves more than just taking advantage of distribution channels. Because the needs of the poor are different from the needs of the middle and upper classes, entire product lines must be reconsidered. This was another lesson I learned from my earliest days at DDS: We needed to directly ask the poor what worked for them, rather than trying to force them into buying existing products that were designed for people in completely different circumstances.

The best example of this need for input was our search for a whole-life insurance product for the poor. Historically, poor Indians have been almost entirely uninsured—clearly a real impediment to moving up the economic ladder. At SKS we wanted to change this, to offer products that would protect borrowers and their families in the event of illness or death. This venture was actually our first step in exploring what other products we could distribute—when you're already offering loans, it's easy enough to prepare another kind of paperwork for another kind of product, which the loan officers could then offer to our borrowers in their weekly meetings. We started with term life insurance, then health insurance, and then explored a whole-life insurance product, with the standard attributes of paying a benefit on the death of the insured and also accumulating a cash value that could be withdrawn.

Our experience with whole-life insurance was telling. Almost immediately, we ran into the first problem: Existing insurance products didn't really work for the poor, who have different needs than more economically and socially stable groups. One insurer I met with asked me flat out, "How do you sell insurance to poor people?" But he was asking the wrong question. We didn't need to convince the poor to buy insurance products. After all, given their vulnerability to calamities such as drought or illness, the poor are extremely attuned to risk. Instead, we needed to ask a different question: What kind of product can we design that will meet the needs of the poor?

Our loan officers began asking members what they needed and wanted in an insurance policy. For one thing, they told us that typical monthly premium rates were too high for them. Another big problem was that they were often scammed by insurers who canceled policies after missed payments. If you've been putting money into a policy for months, or even years, and the whole thing gets canceled upon a few missed payments, you've just thrown your money—hard-earned, desperately needed money—down a hole.

Our loan officers saw poor women pull out tattered old policy documents, asking if we could do anything about their lapsed policies. But it was too late for them. Crooked insurance agents, who knew the poor were very likely to miss payments now and then, had simply absconded with their money. So, the insurance industry, in the experience of many poor Indians, was nothing but a scam.

We set about trying to come up with a product that suited the needs of the poor: We needed a policy that would be cheap, no more than 20 rupees (about 50 cents) per week, and that would never lapse—even if members missed payments. These were strict demands for an insurer to meet, but on the other hand, marketing and distribution were already taken care of, which would take a huge burden off the insurance company.

Still, most insurers laughed us out of their offices when we proposed our model. But one, Bajaj Allianz, was visionary enough to say yes. This company leapt into these untested waters with us—and its whole-life insurance product for the poor became one of the most profitable parts of its business.

As SKS expanded to more villages and offered more products, we became one of the best-known brands in rural India. Kids in villages mimicked our role-playing games, offering imaginary loans to each other. Potential loan officer recruits would call when they heard we were starting in a new place. And potential members came to our branch offices, asking us to start up in their villages. SKS was earning its place as a trusted brand in rural India.

The power of the SKS brand drew many companies seeking to leverage it. Airtel, Nokia, Bajaj Allianz, and others paid for advertising space in our member passbooks, while CavinKare, a consumer packaged-goods company, paid us for providing free product samples and coupons to our members. Other companies were attracted by the wealth of data we captured about our members, which included everything from demographic information to household assets. For example, we launched a housing loan product with one of India's biggest banks, HDFC, which was delighted by the fact that we had detailed housing data for all our members—everything from the current size of their house to the roof quality to the wall material. These details made it easy to target housing loans with great precision.

In those years, many companies approached us wanting to part-ner with us and expand into rural India. We were always very careful about making sure the products we offered were appropriate for the poor—not just cell phones, groceries, and insurance, but also prod-ucts such as solar lights and water purifiers. The products had to appeal to a large percentage of our members, while simultaneously being of low cost and very high quality. The results were that our suppliers found new market segments, our members got high-quality goods for cheap, and we took a small percentage of the transactions.

As of October 2017, SKS had distributed 2.6 million phones, 2.1 million solar lamps, 2.3 million sewing machines, 1.7 million cycles, 70,000 cooking stoves, 40,000 water purifiers, 23,000 blenders, and 4,000 mopeds and motorcycles. That's more than 8.8 million prod-ucts in total, not including insurance products.

Above and beyond the economic benefits to having such large numbers, SKS was also able to offer our members social, educational, and health benefits—another sphere where microfinance was able to effect lasting, positive change in the lives of poor people. Take, for example, sanitary napkins. I realized that poor rural women didn't have the necessary access to sanitary products, a fact I discovered in a rather odd way. As I walked around villages, I'd often see piles of cow manure with pieces of cloth in them. I asked what they were for, and one of my field staff explained that poor women used the cloth instead of disposable sanitary napkins. After several uses, they'd throw them away in the manure pile.

When cloth used for this purpose isn't washed properly, it can lead to health problems. This situation was made worse by the fact that rural India was increasingly seeing factory-made synthetic cloth instead of the traditional handwoven cotton cloth. The latter allows air in, making it more hygienic when used as a sanitary napkin. But the synthetics don't allow air, which leads to even more potential for infection.

I realized that if SKS could introduce access to low-cost sanitary napkins, we could potentially stem a serious health problem. In addition, we would simultaneously create and capture a brand-new market among a brand-new customer segment.

I also had ideas for pure social initiatives that would not generate any profits at all. These were social initiatives for which we were uniquely positioned, thanks to our distribution channels, to provide a social good. Our deworming program was a perfect example.

Worm-borne diseases affect millions of poor Indians, particularly children, every year. When these parasites enter a person's body through contact with contaminated soil or water, the results are horrific: diarrhea, stomach cramps, lethargy, vomiting, and even internal bleeding. Yet for all the agony these diseases can cause, they are relatively simple to prevent—often a single tablet can protect a person from the parasite's effects.

UNICEF donated these tablets, but they would often sit unused in rural health care centers. The Indian government wasn't distributing them, in part because of government inefficiencies, and in part because there was—and still is—great mistrust among Indians for any government health initiatives involving children, so villagers probably wouldn't have accepted them anyway.

Even if the rural poor did not trust the government, they had grown to trust SKS. We volunteered to have our loan officers take time from doing regular business at their meetings to help distribute these tablets. Under a pilot program in 2010 to deworm children, our loan officers carried these tablets into the field, explaining to borrowers why they should take them, and answering any and all questions. In this way, we helped provide deworming tablets to 135,583 children in a one-week pilot program. We were trying to do our part in the global initiative to "Deworm the World," a program launched by the World Economic Forum's Young Global Leaders network, of which I'm a member.

Likewise, when there were floods or cyclones, we suspended our loan repayments and mobilized for disaster relief. During the 2008 Bihar flood, one of the worst floods in India's history, our loan officers delivered blankets and food to affected communities. We were even included in the country's national disaster management planning discussions.

Another example of using our microfinance channel for social initiatives was our Ultra Poor Program. For-profit microfinance isn't a realistic option for the absolute poorest Indians, who lack the stability to start businesses and meet regular payment schedules. These are the people who struggle simply to survive on a day-to-day basis, who spend their lives in a constant battle against chronic hunger, persistent disease, and illiteracy. Their ranks often include widows, the elderly, the disabled, and other marginalized groups who are far out of the mainstream and have many basic unfulfilled needs.

SKS's nonprofit foundation, or "society" as it is called in India, in collaboration with the Bangladesh Rural Advancement Committee (BRAC), started an Ultra Poor Program—a three-pronged program that aimed to bring the ultra-poor up to minimal standards of health, economic, and social stability. For economic stability, the program offered members a free "asset basket" of their choice—anything from a buffalo to chickens to sheep or other assets such as groceries to sell or the necessities for a small teashop.

The recipients had no obligation to pay us anything in return, as the assets were intended to help lift them to the next economic rung. We also assisted the ultra-poor in accessing government entitlements, such as food-for-work programs. For health, the program offered monthly visits from a medical assistant, information sessions, and health screenings. And for social development, we offered group meetings, where the normally isolated ultra-poor could meet together to discuss problems and issues, and spend time building relationships.

In addition to these social initiatives, the strength of our numbers also provided political influence—an area where our members, most from backward and scheduled castes, had never had much power. When we lobbied government central bank policy makers on banking reform, for example, we could inform them that we represented more than eight million members. Assuming there were five people per household, that was about forty million people—a number that made policy makers sit up and take notice, giving us an instant voice.

Our numbers caught the attention of leading politicians. The Congress Party—the party of Jawaharlal Nehru and Indira Gandhi—invited my input on their election manifesto before the 2009 elections, asking what policies would best help the rural poor. Likewise, the leader of the national Bharatiya Janata Party (BJP), L. K. Advani, met with me prior to their election campaign, while the then BJP chief minister of the state of Rajasthan, Vasundara Raje, as well as the BJP deputy chief minister of Bihar, Sushil Modi, both reached out to us, asking us to expand our work in their states and offering their full support. These politicians knew that, with so many members across the country, our numbers could even sway elections—though we would never have purposefully done so. But numbers do matter, and they gave our members clout.

Finally, SKS membership brought everyday forms of political empowerment. For one thing, we extended loans to women, giving them additional bargaining strength in the home. We held our meetings in public places—a first for many scheduled caste members, who for generations weren't allowed to gather in public spaces. And in local elections, SKS members have even run for office and won, due in part to the leadership roles they learned through their association with us.

Reaching Amazon territory gave our members all these benefits, and more. And we never could have gotten there if not for our for-profit system. SKS represented the best of both the nonprofit and the for-profit worlds: It was the ultimate expression of "doing well by doing good."

The financial world agreed, even in spite of the biggest economic meltdown since the Great Depression of the 1930s. In October 2008, after Lehman Brothers collapsed and after the U.S. stock market plunged, we finalized our 2008 round of investment: a stunning $75 million from Sandstone Capital, Silicon Valley Bank, and Kismet Capital—the largest investment in microfinance as of 2008. With that investment in place, our next step was to continue to expand in India, to fully develop the "Amazon territory" distribution channel, and to expand to other countries. In 2008, in fact, we were approached by potential partner MFIs and some governments from a diverse list of countries: Sri Lanka, Nepal, China, Vietnam, Mali, Nigeria, Morocco, Egypt, Afghanistan, Peru, Colombia, and Belize. I personally visited rural China a half dozen times, and we had planned to launch there.

However, I wasn't able to personally lead our international expansion because, after our pioneering investment of $75 million in October 2008, I handed over the reins of SKS. I stayed on as the nonexecutive chairperson of the board but left the CEO role in December 2008, eleven years after founding SKS.

CHAPTER 10

BRINGING IN THE BANKERS

I left the CEO role of SKS because, at the time, I felt that we would benefit from the experience of seasoned banking professionals who were familiar with running a financial institution serving millions and employing tens of thousands. I also thought that having venture capitalists on the board would better enable SKS to raise the funds it needed for continued growth. Besides, those venture capitalists had invested significant funds, so they had the right to nominate board members. Paresh Patel of Sandstone Capital joined the board as did Ashish Lakhanpal, who had managed the funds of tech entrepreneurs Ravi Reddy (my relative) and Sandeep Tungare (his business partner), early SKS supporters. Ravi and Sandeep assigned their investment rights to Kismet Capital, which was set up by Ashish.[1] Sumir Chadha of Sequoia had been on the board since Sequoia's investment in 2007. Ashish and Paresh happened to be former classmates at Harvard Business School. Sumir was also an HBS alumnus. Their various investments in SKS led them to own 59 percent of SKS. The trusts' ownership went down to 17 percent; I still had no ownership, though I had my stock options. Incidentally, Sumir had said we needed someone with an academic background on the board. He suggested Tarun Khanna, who had been his professor at HBS.

There were also reasons beyond the professional why I wanted to step down. While the company had been growing and expanding, my young son was still in Chicago with his mother. Though I was traveling frequently to see him, it was painful not to be more present in his life. I missed him deeply. Personal family matters—which I understandably won't air, to protect my family's privacy—also made it imperative I relocate to Chicago as soon as possible. In addition, the international travel had taken its toll on me. I had been traveling back and forth to see my son virtually every month for more than three years.

In short, I felt I had created an institution that was ready to grow without me, and I was excited to return to Chicago and find some life balance. Ever since graduating from college but particularly since launching SKS, I had been working at almost breakneck speed. I was looking forward to spending more time with my son, delving into new ventures, and proceeding into the second act of my life. I bought my first car (a Honda Civic) and my first home (in Palatine, a suburb of Chicago), became the coach of my son's seven-and-under soccer team (The Incredibles), and got a gym membership (at Lifetime Fitness). I finally wanted to enjoy being middle class in America.

Before I left India, SKS hired a new CEO from the banking industry. I was torn about whether to recommend my second-in-command, our COO M. R. Rao. We had been a great team; my focus on quality and his aggressive approach to growth were a perfect combination. I also liked him. He was personable and had invited me home for dinner several times. I enjoyed talking to his wife and children. I helped his daughter with her college application essay and chatted about basketball with his son.

I was also endeared by the fact that Rao and his wife had adopted their son. It was rare to see Indians adopting children who were not related to them in some way. In addition, Rao and his family showed they cared about me. Rao would occasionally bring home-cooked food to the office for me for lunch, and he told me his parents were on the lookout for a new bride for me. In a country where arranged marriages were the norm, this gesture made me smile.

But I also hesitated to recommend Rao for CEO because I felt we needed someone who would pay a great deal of attention to the quality of field processes; otherwise, the high-speed vehicle that was SKS could veer off the road. My concern was that this next phase of growth would not be simply scaling the existing core lending products but also developing new products and using our distribution channel to market and sell these new products. Creating new products requires a different skill set than scaling a well-tested product. The former requires an entrepreneurial mind-set—being able to make decisions in uncertainty, an appetite for risks, strong instincts, and a solid feel for the environment. Scaling, on the other hand, requires being able to take an existing system and push it. I don't want to make too much of a judgment about the relative merits of these different skill sets. Both activities are difficult. But, clearly, finding people with an entrepreneurial mind-set is more difficult than finding people who can push the accelerator in order to grow.

I discussed the issue with Sumir Chadha, the managing director of Sequoia, who had become the key player on the SKS board since leading Sequoia's initial investment in March 2007. By the end of that year, Sequoia had invested more funds and owned the single largest shareholding with 30 percent. I relied on Sumir's guidance in areas that were outside of my expertise. That is, I knew microfinance—inside and out—but I readily admitted that I had no experience in raising capital or in commercial finance. After all, my education was in the humanities and social sciences. The bulk of my career had been in rural India. Sumir, on the other hand, lived in those other worlds. After his schooling at HBS, he had worked at Goldman Sachs before founding WestBridge Capital, which then merged with Sequoia.

I shared my ambivalence about Rao, and Sumir agreed that we should seek outside candidates. He recommended a search firm, the same firm he had engaged in late 2007 when we were recruiting our CFO. At that time, Sumir worked with the firm to select S. Dilli Raj. I deferred to Sumir on the CFO recruitment because, as mentioned, commercial finance was not my expertise. After Raj joined, Sumir worked closely with him on various financial transactions.

For my replacement as CEO in 2008, Sumir and the firm selected Suresh Gurumani, who had been heading the retail banking division of Barclays in India. I had a say, of course, and I liked Gurumani as well—for two reasons. The first was that, even before the search started, Gurumani and I had been exploring a mobile banking pilot between Barclays and SKS, so he and I were already thinking along the same lines about the next generation of microfinance. He seemed to have that entrepreneurial spirit I felt the CEO needed. The second reason was that Barclays is a staid, systematic English bank with a reputation for valuing quality in the banking process. If I was not going to be present to ensure that we had strong processes, having someone from a quality-oriented bank would be important. Gurumani seemed to satisfy that second criterion of mine.

I have to admit that there were also a few negative things about Rao that clinched my decision not to recommend him for the CEO role. One was how he handled team members who disagreed with him. While Rao was always cordial, even deferential, with me, I knew he could be intimidating to others. I had once seen him publicly berate a junior manager. The young man looked like he was about to cry. Such an authoritarian streak did not entirely shock me, as it is not uncommon for Indian executives to have a very brazen approach. Rao may well have picked that up in his previous executive roles at mainstream Indian companies. It certainly wasn't my style and it wasn't the culture I wanted for SKS, so I counseled him against it. But I also understood that I would not be able to undo twenty-five years of imbibing mainstream Indian corporate culture.

There were, however, some things that I probably let go too far. Two stellar performers had left SKS after butting heads with Rao.

One was Anna Somos Krishnan, who headed our housing loan initiative and our data analytics department; the other was Paul Breloff, who headed our business development group. They happened to be foreigners, so perhaps they pushed back against Rao (whereas Indian employees were hesitant to do so). As a result, the conflict came to my attention.

In both cases, I had long discussions to try to resolve issues, but when it looked like differences were irreconcilable, Krishnan and, later, Breloff decided to leave SKS. I agreed it was for the best. Both went on to do other great work in the field. Krishnan went on to head Planet Finance in India and now leads LongWealth, which promotes purpose-led businesses. Breloff went on to found and lead Accion Venture Lab, a financial inclusion investment fund, and founded Shortlist, a Mumbai-based tech-driven recruiting firm.

These issues were on my mind when we were recruiting a new CEO. I could not look past them to recommend Rao.

One additional thing I liked about Gurumani was that he had worked with Rao before (as his manager). In fact, Gurumani had fired Rao. I had not known about the past dismissal at the time Rao joined SKS and only learned the details when we were recruiting Gurumani. Since the circumstances of the termination are personal, I won't share them here. For me, what was important is that Gurumani had shown the ability to address Rao's issues. Gurumani seemed to have everything SKS needed. It looked like bringing him in as the new CEO would enable a smooth transition as I headed to Chicago to deal with the urgent family issues I was facing. And, despite his history with Gurumani, Rao also seemed to have a good personal rapport with him. In fact, before a formal offer was extended to Gurumani, I felt I owed it to Rao to let him know that I was not recommending him for the position and that the board was selecting Gurumani. I met with Rao and explained what I felt were his numerous strengths but also areas where I felt he needed improvement. As was my style, I was honest, perhaps too honest. I thought frank feedback would help make team members become even better. Rao seemed to take my comments well. He did not express any significant disappointment in not being recommended for the CEO role. In fact, he had commented that he would rather have Gurumani as CEO than someone else. Rao said, tongue in cheek, "Better the known devil than the unknown angel."

Gurumani started as the new CEO on December 9, 2008.

CHAPTER 11

AKULA VERSUS THE
U.S. STATE DEPARTMENT

After I left India, SKS continued to grow at a remarkable rate. The numbers of our borrowers, the amount of our portfolio, and our employee base all doubled in one year. And the repayment rates remained high. I figured that I had left SKS with the right combination for success—Rao as the driver of growth and Gurumani to keep an eye on quality.

Things were going so well that in our June 2009 SKS board meeting, the board—led by the trio of Sumir, Ashish, and Paresh—decided SKS would pursue an initial public offering the following year, in 2010. As nonexecutive chairperson, I had a say. I was also in favor of an IPO, since my vision had been to tap capital markets to be able to provide loans to more poor borrowers.

It had been about six months since I left SKS. The board asked me to return to India and lead the IPO. No other MFI in India had gone public, so there was very little experience in or knowledge of how best to proceed when opening a microfinance institution to public trading. Normally, the board would ask its CEO to lead an IPO, but the board thought, who better to lead the company into these uncharted waters than the person who had founded it? I knew the story, I believed passionately in the story, and I could sell the story.

I said no.

I was not interested in returning to India for the same reason I had left it in the first place—my son. Now that I was back on the same continent as him, I was not about to leave him again. The board persisted and persisted. The more I thought about this opportunity, the more I realized I could not turn it down. It would be the capstone of my twenty-year development career. Even if I looked at it exclusively from the perspective of a father, a successful IPO would enable me to provide my son financial security because of the stock options that I held. Those options were currently valuable on paper, but a successful IPO would make them valuable literally.

So, I made an offer to my ex-wife. In 2008, I had exercised and sold some stock options of SKS. I used those funds to offer her a financial arrangement to move to India with our son, so I could lead the IPO without having to be away from him. I would provide her a house in Hyderabad, living expenses, and those funds over the course of four years. I needed four years because it would take a year to prepare and complete the IPO, and then my stock options would be locked in for three years after that. It wasn't a perfect arrangement, of course. The money I offered her was all of my savings, but I knew that, if the IPO was successful, there would be more money, soon enough. Most importantly, if I was going back to India, I was not going without our son. I could no longer bear not being a daily part of his life, and it was too exhausting to make the monthly trips between Hyderabad and Chicago.

Malini agreed. Six months after I had left SKS as the CEO, I was back in India in mid-2009 to begin orchestrating one of the world's first IPOs of a microfinance institution. My life became a juggling act between the daily interests of SKS and the needs of my son and his mother. Admittedly, it was a stressful time, but I couldn't have been happier to be able to do the work I love and spend daily time with my son.

A few months after we were all back in India, events occurred that prompted me to consult with one of Malini's close friends as well as with our son's guardian ad litem, a lawyer and social worker who had been appointed by the county court in Chicago to represent our son's interests. On their advice, I filed for custody of our son. While not my plan upon arriving in India, that difficult choice became necessary for me, a father doing what I believed would protect the well-being of our son. To protect my family's privacy, I won't convey the details that led to my decision to request custody. Since we were living in Hyderabad, the guardian ad litem advised me to file in Hyderabad and not in Chicago. The Hyderabad court granted me temporary custody in October, with a trial date set for November.

Malini engaged lawyers who responded by filing petitions both in Hyderabad and in Chicago, arguing that India did not have jurisdiction because, they claimed, Malini and our son had never actually relocated to Hyderabad but were only on a visit. Therefore Hyderabad did not have jurisdiction. The Hyderabad court had a trial on the jurisdiction question and determined that Malini and our son had relocated; we were all "ordinarily residing" in Hyderabad. The court cited evidence such as the fact that Malini had signed a four-year lease, had taken a foreign residency permit from the Indian government, and had enrolled our son in school, which had been in session since August, for two months when I filed for custody.

Meanwhile, the Chicago court considered the Uniform Child Custody Jurisdiction and Enforcement Act. That statute provides that the "home state" is defined by a number of criteria, ranging from where the child is currently residing, to "significant connections" to a particular state, to where a child has lived with a parent for six consecutive months prior to the commencement of a change of custody proceeding. Since we had not lived in India for more than six months and there were significant connections to both Chicago and to Hyderabad, the determination was not straightforward. In situations where there is this lack of clarity with regard to two states of the United States, the two judges would speak to each other. This requirement to communicate is replicated in the Hague Convention on the Civil Aspects of International Child Abduction, which requires that judges in two different countries communicate to resolve the question of jurisdiction.

The United States is a signatory to the Hague convention. India is not. So there was no scope for the two judges to speak. From the Hyderabad court's perspective, jurisdiction was clear; it was with India, because that was where we all resided. Now the Chicago court would need to wrestle with the question of jurisdiction on its own. Until it did, however, the U.S. State Department viewed this as an abduction, and, in fact, the U.S. Embassy actually tried to help Malini leave India with our son. I figured all of this out in dramatic fashion.

Initially, after the Hyderabad court gave me temporary custody, Malini had visitation provisions. On her first overnight weekend visit, she had planned—with the assistance of embassy staff—to leave India with our son. She needed the help of the embassy because I had our son's passport, and the embassy would have to issue a new passport (something they were not supposed to do without the permission of both parents). Moreover, under the Indian court order, our son was not to be removed from India. In fact, there was even a Chicago court order requiring us not to remove our son from school until the issue of jurisdiction was resolved. Nevertheless, the State Department did not heed the Chicago court order.

On a Friday night in October, I dropped our son off at his mother's house. Later that night, I got a call from one of her close friends in Chicago who told me that Malini was planning to leave for the United States. I was not sure what to do. By 11:30 PM, Malini's friend in Chicago had provided enough information—such as flight details—to make me realize that Malini indeed was planning to sneak away with our child. In desperation, and of course not realizing that she was coordinating with the embassy, I called the U.S. consulate emergency number. I was hesitant, so when an official answered, I paused a few seconds. Before I could speak, the official on the other end said, "Malini, is that you?"

My heart skipped a beat. I hung up, panicked. Even though the jurisdiction question had not been resolved by the Chicago court, if Malini returned to the States with our son now, I most likely would lose custody. The jurisdiction question would simply become irrelevant. Custody would revert to what had been the status quo before we left for India.

I went to the police, who said they could not do anything because nothing had happened yet. I would have to wait until she made her move.

Because her friend from the United States had told me the time of Malini's morning flight, I was able to get to her house early enough to see her leave. I arrived around 6:00 AM and parked at a distance. Soon after that, she made her move. She loaded suitcases in a car and drove to the airport, our son in tow. I raced to the local police to make a formal complaint while my lawyer sped to the airport to alert the airport police. My son subsequently told me what happened. Malini and he made it to the airport by about 7 AM, but as they were pulling up to the airport entrance, my son saw a friend of mine, whom he recognized; he told his mother. My friend was standing with a police officer. When Malini realized this, she turned her car around and went back to her house.

That afternoon, Malini returned our son to me as per the visitation schedule. My lawyers informed both the Indian and Chicago courts of what happened, and Malini was no longer allowed overnight visitation with our son.

She left Hyderabad and went to Chicago to work on her case with her lawyers, traveling back and forth as the cases went on in

India and Chicago, having parenting time with our son whenever she was in Hyderabad.

By November, the full custody trial was completed in Hyderabad, and the court reaffirmed its ruling that India had jurisdiction, and it also made my temporary custody order a permanent custody order. Malini's lawyers appealed this ruling to the High Court in Hyderabad, the equivalent of an appellate court, and eventually to the Supreme Court of India. It took several months, but both courts upheld the jurisdiction and custody ruling of the Hyderabad court.

Now it was up to the U.S. court to make a decision on jurisdiction. There was a trial in Chicago, which took a long time because there was a change of judges. Finally, in March 2010, the Chicago court ruled—against me.

The Chicago court held, in its order issued on March 30, 2010, that it "believes that Malini and Tejas continue to reside in Illinois and not in India." The Chicago court order explained: "The Indian court did not make the requisite finding under Section 201 (a)(2) because (1) 'ordinarily residing' under the totality of the factual circumstances does not meet the requirements and (2) the Indian court failed to find that the parties and the child are not presently residing in Illinois." In short, the Chicago court judge felt that the Indian court's determination of "ordinarily residing" in Hyderabad was not the same as "not presently residing in Illinois." The implication was that the United States, not India, had jurisdiction. So, according to the Chicago court, I had abducted my son. Law enforcement was activated. The local police in Illinois contacted Interpol, which issued a notice against me. Thankfully, it was not an arrest warrant, just a lookout notice. Meanwhile, my Chicago lawyer appealed to the Illinois Appellate Court. But unless and until that appeal was heard and the Chicago court ruling was overturned, the U.S. State Department stood firm in its determination that I had abducted my son.

Malini met with the press, and the press loved it—and covered her extensively. I could not understand how she was able to garner so much press attention, particularly in India. It was just a custody case, albeit one with international dimensions. Perhaps part of the attention had to do with SKS's success and the imminent IPO. And part of it was the tabloid-ish nature of the story. The press, which had built up the profile of SKS (and me) over the years, now seemed to relish tearing me down. Some news outlets published my former wife's full-length interviews or letters without any editing, let alone any fact-checking.[1]

In the midst of the barrage of negative press, I declined to defend myself. It was a tough decision, but my son was still young—only eight years old—and I wanted to protect his privacy. So, I would respond, "No comment." Malini's interviews ended up running without any countervailing view.

Still, the attention seemed excessive. Why was this happening? How was she able to organize and pay for press conferences? Why did reporters find her credible? I could only watch as the number of stories against me proliferated—first in the vernacular Indian media, then in the English language media, with a headlining story even appearing on the major Indian national news channel, NDTV.[2]

Because of the Indian news coverage, the news outlets in the United States picked up the thread. In March, Chicago's *Daily Herald* ran two stories: "Hoffman Estates Mom Fighting to Bring Son Home from India," followed by front-page story "Where Does Tejas Belong?"[3] NBC News in Chicago followed with a lead story on their evening news, including the tagline, "Malini Byanna Can't Get Her Son, Tejas, Back from India."[4] I had friends from the United States calling me, asking what was going on.

Meanwhile, in India, the press would stand outside the entrance to our gated community, trying to get photos and videos of my son. The head of our neighborhood security, however, was savvy and kept a close watch on the gaggle of media to ensure that none of them got in. Meanwhile, thankfully, the press had no access to my son's school because it was on a vast campus that was part of an international agriculture research center under the purview of the United Nations. I nevertheless hired an armed security guard for my son. The guard was there not just to ward off the media but also because of threatening letters from leftist guerilla groups that had been sent to our office. My son made the best of it. He and his friends had the security guard play goalkeeper for their neighborhood soccer games.

SKS was, of course, also affected. I was getting skewered in the media and said nothing in my defense. This bad press was coming just as SKS's IPO was being planned. Investors raised the issue of my ex-wife's allegations. Our IPO prospectus contained a full two pages of disclosures of all the various legal cases related to litigation with my former wife. And because of the Interpol notice, during the IPO road shows when I traveled to Hong Kong, Singapore, London, and New York, I had to have lawyers on standby at each immigration post in case I was detained. Thankfully, that never happened.

Because of SKS's wide national presence, I often had to meet CEOs of our banks as well as senior politicians, bureaucrats, and regulators in various states of India. When I met an official for the first time, they would often say, "Your ex-wife came to meet me." Unbeknownst to me, she had been meeting with various officials, even the head of the stock exchange—something I found out years later, after the individual had left the stock exchange and we sat next to each other at a dinner at a conference in China.

In April 2010, the then U.S. Treasury Secretary, Timothy Geithner, was making his first visit to India in that role and was scheduled to meet me. The Treasury Department advance team had set up the meeting. But apparently, the U.S. State Department objected because they deemed me an unlawful abductor; the Chicago county court had ruled just a week earlier that the United States had jurisdiction in my son's custody case. In the end, the Treasury Department vetoed the State Department, and the meeting took place.

Perhaps the most devastating coverage of the custody case was from the *New York Times*. Though it was by no means the harshest of the numerous articles against me, it was the one that crushed me. You see, in high school, my tenth-grade social studies teacher introduced me to the *New York Times*. And I fell in love. I loved the news stories, the op-eds, the week in review, the Sunday magazine, the book review, the sports page. I knew the reporting had a liberal orientation, but that fit with my worldview. I loved the look and feel of the paper. I even used to deliver the newspaper on a paper route as a teen.

When we had our IPO, and the *New York Times* said they would be running a business section cover story on our IPO and a profile of me, I was, of course, delighted. When published, the profile had nothing to do my life's work or SKS or the IPO; it was all about the custody battle over my son. "Amid Celebrity, a Long Legal Battle Over a Child" read the headline.[5] The night before the story ran, I came to realize it would be a negative article when I received a call from the *New York Times* reporter in India for a comment. I knew the reporter, as he had come to an SKS press conference, and we'd had a few one-on-one conversations. He was always polite and professional. But not now. He accused me of being involved in the abduction of my son. I replied, "A parental abduction of a child is tragic, but that's not what this case is about." I ended up staying up throughout the night, as the story was going to press. I pleaded and tried to explain the facts to the reporter and eventually escalated it to the *New York Times* business section editor. But the story ran as it was originally framed.

A U.S. State Department spokesperson was quoted, saying the case was an "international parental child abduction." The spokesperson added, "A child is still being retained abroad, and Ms. Byanna, who has sole legal and physical custody of him, as determined by an Illinois court, is still unable to exercise her custodial and parental rights."[6]

Though I still love my *New York Times*, these days I read it alongside other print media to ensure I am getting a broader perspective. The *New York Times* article was not inaccurate, but I felt the focus on a personal matter, which did not relate to SKS's IPO, was not warranted.

A few weeks after the *New York Times* story was published, the Illinois Appellate Court finally issued its ruling on jurisdiction. It held that the Chicago Court had erred. Jurisdiction was with India; it had always been with India. There was no kidnapping. No abduction. I had rightly received custody of my son, back in October of the previous year. Illinois law enforcement requested that the Interpol notice be withdrawn.

For the press, however, the story had been completed. They had written their copy with their colorful headlines. A follow-up story with a correction or retraction was not newsworthy. Everyone had moved on to the next "scandal." A Google search of my name (or my son's name) calls up old media stories as well as my ex-wife's old allegations. To this day, I continue to get questions about my divorce and custody proceedings from nearly a decade ago.

The questions prove to me the significance of the "right to be forgotten," the often-discussed principle against online search engines spewing out old news that indefinitely remain a prominent part of a person's internet footprint. In the matter of my divorce and the custody dispute for my son—who has lived with me since 2009—he and I would like to be forgotten.

CHAPTER 12

BIG BANG IPO

Once Suresh Gurumani started as CEO in December 2008, I became the nonexecutive chairman of the SKS board. As such, I had no role in the daily operations of the company, so I was able to focus on preparations for the IPO when I returned from Chicago in June 2009. It was a genuine intellectual exercise to weave the SKS story into a 319-page document. I worked closely with a team of our investment bankers and lawyers. As for the microfinance parts, we researched and wrote everything from scratch. After all, there was no model, nothing we could pull off the shelf. The work was grueling and unglamorous, filled with paper, research, and the stuffy confines of offices and conference rooms. When we finished the prospectus, however, we were ready—ready to sell the company and the concept that had become my life's work.

I should say *almost ready*. To do an IPO, SKS needed permission from the government's Securities Exchange Board of India (SEBI). That was still pending. So I met personally with the then-chairperson of SEBI. I walked him through the SKS model and explained my philosophy of trying to tap capital markets for the poor. It appeared that I had addressed any concerns that SEBI may have had because SKS received permission soon after.

I started attending global conferences to garner wider attention for SKS. One of those conferences was the World Economic Forum Annual Meeting in Davos, Switzerland. I had been going to Davos since 2006, ever since being named Social Entrepreneur of the Year by the Schwab Foundation. In 2010, I was invited to appear on the plenary stage. The topic was whether the world was meeting the U.N.'s Millennium Development Goals, and I was on a panel with Bill Gates, the prime minister of Zimbabwe, and the former prime minister of New Zealand, among others. I arrived at 8:45 AM, a bit early for the 9 AM panel discussion, and was led into the green room. I was sure I was going to be the first panelist to arrive, but there in the room was Bill Gates. By this time, we had met a couple of times before, and we engaged in small talk for a bit. The other panelists started to arrive, the last being Morgan Tsvangirai, the prime minister of Zimbabwe, who passed away in 2018. He walked around the room and gave his card to everyone present, and, when he came to me, he deferentially handed me his card and said, "My name is Morgan Tsvangirai." It was such an act of humility on his part, and I was touched by the warmth of the action.

As for the actual plenary stage talk, I focused on the theme of using market-based approaches to advance the Millennium Development Goals. It was a heady feeling to be on the plenary stage, knowing that the audience was among the world's most powerful people, and they were there to hear from me. The moderator, former United Nations Deputy Secretary-General Mark Malloch Brown, introduced me first. "We have got Vikram Akula, one of the lesser known panelists," he said. "But when you look at the size of what he has done, he is one of the superstars of microfinance, and I think we will be seeing him on panels like this a lot more in the coming years."

I was able to speak with confidence—and with a demonstrated track record of having scaled SKS Microfinance. I felt I had found a way to tap capital markets in a manner that worked for the poor.

That Davos talk gave me the momentum I needed as I started a series of road shows for the SKS Microfinance IPO planned for later that year. Road shows are, of course, a standard practice for any company in the lead-up to an IPO. It is a way for the company's management to present the company to possible investors, analysts, and fund managers. Over the years I had done literally hundreds of such presentations for SKS to drum up investor interest and support—from the tea and samosa parties in the early days to presentations to venture capital firms that had funded us since we converted to a for-profit.

Before the IPO was launched, we decided to sell some shares to a group of pre-IPO investors, meaning investors who buy at a discount to the IPO price but who are locked in and cannot sell their shares until thirty days after the IPO. We had a targeted plan for approaching these pre-IPO investors, but there were times when a particularly important investor called out of the blue and said he or she was ready to hear our pitch.

One such moment happened with George Soros, one of the greatest investors in contemporary history. I happened to be in Mexico, visiting a borrower group of the only other pure microfinance company to have gone public, Compartamos, when I received a call from one of our board members saying that George Soros would like to meet with me. In New York. Tomorrow. I was in a remote rural Mexican village, but when George Soros beckons, you do not say no. I told the Compartamos staff that I needed a taxi right away to the Mexico City airport, and they found a driver willing to take me. It was him and me—me with no Spanish, him with no English, and, at some point, he suddenly stopped at a house without any explanation. He got out of the car and left me in the back seat. I looked around my unfamiliar surroundings and took stock. No one really knew where I was. I didn't even know where I was. *What the hell is going on*, I thought after the driver's absence continued, and

I started remembering stories of ransom kidnappings by Mexican cartels. Finally, the driver came out and gestured to switch cars. Later, I came to understand that he simply wanted a faster car. "*Rápido, rápido,*" he explained. It was a good thing he made the switch, as when I got to the airport, I was the last one to board the day's last flight to New York.

The next morning, I showed up at George Soros's New York office in Central Park South in my traditional kurta, a little weary from the previous day's travel but excited to meet Soros. I walked up to the receptionist, and—without looking up—she asked, "Who's the delivery for?"

"No, no, I have a meeting," I said.

"With who?" she asked.

"George Soros."

She let out a little laugh.

"No, seriously," I said. "I am here to meet with George Soros."

She called up and realized that I did have a meeting and profusely apologized. When it was my turn to go into the conference room, I walked into a room with a spectacular view of Central Park and the handshakes of a half-dozen investment managers and other executives with whom Soros worked. And, of course, George Soros himself. I started my pitch and felt I was doing great, hitting all my notes, selling the company I had created. But Soros didn't seem convinced. He looked strained, and I thought I was failing until I was informed he was hard-of-hearing and that I needed to speak up. I raised my voice and could sense his enthusiasm also rising. Like most accomplished, successful investors, Soros has many different funds, and SKS was pitching for an investment from his Quantum Fund. Ideally, we wanted Quantum to invest $50 million.

After I finished, Soros shook my hand and left the room. I sat with his investment managers, and they told me I had done a good job. Still, the reality was that even if Soros loved the presentation, decisions were not always up to him but to the managers now sitting with me. I was staring out at beautiful Central Park, trying to gauge their interest, when the door to the conference room opened up again. The familiar shock of healthy white hair peeked from behind the door and Soros reappeared.

He walked up to me and touched my arm. "If Quantum doesn't do it," he said to me, "I'll do it personally." I will never forget that moment. It was a grandfatherly gesture—from perhaps the world's most influential investor—that affirmed my life's goal of making capital markets work for the poor.

Quantum did end up being an anchor investor. After all, by our fiscal year of 2009–10, we had expanded to 7.2 million clients and maintained a loan portfolio of close to $1 billion.

Finally, the day of our IPO arrived. August is the monsoon season in India, when it rains on an almost daily basis. For Indians, the monsoon is sacred, and it has come to represent so many of our hopes. And our fears. The water is absolutely necessary for the agricultural season, for our crops to grow and for our people to get fed and to thrive economically. Yet, the monsoon can be dangerous. If there is too much rain there can be flooding, leading not only to crop damage but to the deaths of people and livestock.

The day of the IPO, a Monday, I walked onto the stage at the Bombay Stock Exchange in a burnt orange kurta, the color of the earth. With me were our CEO Gurumani, our CFO Raj, and, most important, five women who were clients from the different regions SKS Microfinance operated in across the country. For the occasion, and as always, we stressed the five-member group model; it was what had made SKS successful. It was what identified us as a company. It was our essence.

The New York Stock Exchange has the bell; the Bombay Stock Exchange has a gong. Dressed in colorful, resplendent saris, the women together took hold of two gavels and hit the gong to mark the opening of the first microfinance company to sell publicly on the Indian open market. There is a wonderful photograph from that moment. I have a bright smile and am standing to the right of the gong, to the right of the women, and I am in mid-clap. All the hard work, the years of being in the field, the meetings with villagers to design products, the work with staff to refine processes, and then writing the lengthy prospectus, the hundreds of road shows—all of this led to the IPO. In the coming days, all of that hard work would literally pay off. Our IPO raised $350 million, $165 million of which was new funding. Our IPO opened at an initial market capitalization of $1.5 billion and, within a few weeks, it reached a market capitalization of $2.2 billion.

As mentioned, I had created a stock option program that covered all the staff. So when our IPO took place, our field staff—many of whom were sons and daughters of borrowers—all of a sudden earned a lot of money. In fact, on the day of the IPO itself, many employees sold shares, and more than sixty employees made more than 1 million rupees each.[1] Some of those staff actually withdrew the funds in cash to bring home to show their family because their families did not believe them. One woman—from a very poor background—came to my house a few days later to thank me. She broke down crying. This type of wealth—albeit only about $22,000—was beyond what she could have imagined. I was happy for her and for all the others who had worked so hard to achieve our mission.

But for me, what was most exciting was not the fact that SKS staff had made a lot of money, nor the $2.2 billion market cap. What excited me was that I had finally succeeded in creating a model of microfinance that could answer that question posed to me by the woman in the faded purple sari many years ago—"Am I not poor, too?" Now, with our IPO, with having created a model of microfinance that could tap global capital markets, I could say to that woman, or any poor woman anywhere in India: "Yes, you too can have an opportunity. How much do you need to start your small business?"

PART II
THE FALL

CHAPTER 13

THE BACKLASH

During the IPO ceremony at the Bombay Stock Exchange,[1] Gurumani, Raj, and I had been on stage. Our COO Rao was not. We did not plan to exclude him. It just happened. Gurumani was the CEO; he needed to be on stage. The IPO was under the purview of the CFO, so Raj had his rightful place. As founder, I had my seat, alongside the managing director of the investment banking group of Citibank and the head of the Bombay Stock Exchange. Once we were on stage, I noticed the oversight and called Rao to join us. He refused.

Rao did not say anything to me at the IPO, but a few weeks after we returned to Hyderabad, he laid down an ultimatum. He threatened that he would resign if Gurumani was not fired. Worse yet, Raj stood with Rao in this surprising demand. And Rao said that the senior management team would also leave.

Their animosity toward Gurumani stemmed from a list of grievances. For starters, they said that he was getting credit for steering SKS in the two years leading up to the IPO when in fact they were the ones doing all the work. In their opinion, Gurumani was actually hindering operations. The pair voiced some other grievances, including allegations of financial impropriety, which the board investigated and deemed false. More than anything, Rao and Raj seemed extraordinarily emotional in their antipathy for Gurumani.

Perhaps if I had remained more closely involved in day-to-day company affairs, I might have seen early warnings of the management clash. But I had made a commitment not to interfere in the daily operations of the company when I left the CEO role because, ironically, so it now seemed, I'd wanted to give Gurumani a platform to establish himself. Having read literature on successful transitions of founders, I knew that if I remained involved in day-to-day affairs, I would be viewed as a decision-making center by employees. So I stayed out and stayed away—which was easy enough because, initially, I had moved to Chicago, and when I returned to India, I was focused on the preparations for the IPO. In fact, my sole window into the company was through reports at board meetings. And those reports suggested things had been going well—very well.

Though I knew that you don't fire your CEO shortly after the launch of an IPO, Rao and Raj held their ground. *It is him or us*, they insisted. I had no choice but to bring this ultimatum to the board. Naturally, the board resisted. Our board members had expertise in public companies and knew that there would be public perception problems if we dismissed our CEO so soon after our IPO. Once they heard from Rao and Raj, however, the board realized the intensity of their animosity. Still, the board was hesitant. They asked me to talk to Gurumani and see if I could get him to amicably resign.

I tried. I met with Gurumani at the ITC Sheraton Hotel, near our SKS headquarters in Hyderabad. Initially, Gurumani agreed to resign. We worked out a severance package that would give him half of his stock options, which were to have vested by the end of the year. But the next day, he changed his mind. Now the board had a dilemma: Should we side with Rao and Raj, who—by all accounts—seemed to have the support of the broader management team and, as such, were more critical to the ongoing success of the company? Or should we support Gurumani, whom the public may have perceived as the real driver of performance? In my mind, it was clear. If I were to weigh Rao and Raj (and presumably the rest of management team en masse) versus Gurumani, we had to keep the management team intact. But the board was divided, with one independent director arguing fiercely in favor of Gurumani while another director argued just as fiercely in favor of Rao and Raj. It was a stalemate.

On my end, I was anxious to get this resolved as soon as possible. I was aware of rumblings from the field that SKS was going to face some major challenges because of events outside of the current power struggle. I did not know the full extent of what was about to hit us, but my reading of local-language newspapers and interactions with the press made me aware that something was coming. It was going to be big. We had to be ready. I knew that we had to get the management issues sorted out before that onslaught came. If not, there was no way the company could survive.

I had to bring about a resolution to the issue, so at a board meeting in Mumbai, I kept the meeting going until the board came to a consensus. By around 8 PM, we finally decided to fire Gurumani. Rao and Raj had won.

When the media reported Gurumani's firing, the story was that I had wanted to wrest control over SKS. People thought that I was tossing Gurumani aside after a successful IPO because I wanted more power. That couldn't have been further from the truth. Rao became the CEO, and I remained on the sidelines as the nonexecutive chairperson of the board; I had no interest in running SKS again. I could not understand how the papers came up with such an incorrect spin. The negative press about me, however, was not my focus. Instead, my attention was preoccupied with something far more alarming.

The stories first appeared in the Telugu press. The articles were small pieces, a few column inches in the back pages of local newspapers, and were only in newspapers of one state, Andhra Pradesh (AP).

The topic was the suicides of microfinance borrowers due to over-indebtedness. In the weeks following SKS's successful IPO, the suicide stories became longer and moved from the back pages to the middle pages to the front page, from the local-language media to the English media, from newspaper to television. It was alleged that there were tens of, perhaps more than 200, suicides of microfinance borrowers in the months before and after our IPO.[2]

As the stories gained traction, opposition political parties upped the ante. Politicians told borrowers not to repay their microfinance loans and demanded that the state government ban microfinance. Some politicians even called for attacking microfinance field staff. Fearful of the heated political climate, borrowers grew hesitant to repay loans. Often, they would come to the weekly meetings with repayment in hand, but local political thugs would disrupt microfinance meetings, or loan officers—scared for their lives—would simply not show up.

The ruling party in Andhra Pradesh, however, would not be out-done by opposition parties. The AP government hurriedly passed the Microfinance Ordinance on October 14, 2010, which required MFIs to obtain government permission for each new loan. This effectively stopped MFI lending because the government machinery simply did not give permission, and even if it did, the cost of seeking governmental approval for each microloan would be prohibitive. Prior to the ordinance, MFIs in AP had been disbursing about 500,000 loans a month. The Microfinance Ordinance ended that. Borrowers, who had already been scared to repay loans, now saw that MFIs were not giving any new loans, and they began to lose confidence. Repayment rates plunged.

The news reports were confined to one state, Andhra Pradesh, but it happened to be the largest microfinance market of any state in the country. SKS had 25 percent of its loans in AP, and other MFIs—including the second and third largest in the country—had even greater percentages of their loan portfolio in AP because they also had initially started in that state.

What really happened? Were there suicides caused by MFIs? There are widely divergent answers to that question.

Some blame MFIs. Author and economic consultant Milford Bateman wrote in an op-ed piece published by the blog *India Microfinance*:

> What is happening in AP today is an economic, social and humanitarian disaster. Mounting individual indebtedness in the poorest communities (largely thanks to the ease in obtaining multiple loans), artificially inflated and distorted local economies (many inflated into nothing more than giant bazaars and permanent street sales), spectacular levels of profiteering by the CEOs and key private investors attached to the main MFIs, increasingly aggressive loan recovery techniques, and growing numbers of reports claiming multiple cases of suicide that apparently directly followed on from such aggressive loan recovery techniques.[3]

Others maintain that the collective event was an attack orchestrated by the Andhra Pradesh government and without a factual basis. In 2012 Legatum Ventures reported:

> The AP Government stated that the goal of the AP Act was to protect the poor, but from the evidence it is now clear that it was primarily directed towards stifling the operations of private sector MFIs. The AP Act specifically excluded the Self Help Groups (SHGs) that are run by the Society for Eradication of Rural Poverty (SERP), an Andhra Pradesh government-backed microfinance business, which has historically received significant support from organisations such as the World Bank, and which directly competes with private sector MFIs. The AP Act does not try to hide its anti-competitive aims: the text of the Act declares that its goal is "to [protect] the interests of the SHGs" . . .
>
> The AP Government's claims that private sector MFIs have exploited India's poor by charging usurious interest rates and practicing coercive recovery techniques cannot be substantiated. Recently, old allegations of increased suicide rates among MFI borrowers resurfaced, but based on data from SERP itself, it appears that the

actual rate is lower than the statistical average in the state of Andhra Pradesh, meaning that people who receive private sector loans are less likely to commit suicide than those who do not—an inconvenient truth for those opposed to private sector involvement in microfinance in AP.[4]

The truth about the suicide stories, as I will unravel in the next few chapters, lay somewhere in between these two extremes. I know, because, after all, I had arguably the best view of things. It was not a ringside seat; I was actually in the ring.

CHAPTER 14

CULPRIT NUMBER ONE: THE MICROFINANCE INDUSTRY

At the outset, let me say that even a single suicide caused by microfinance is tragic and unacceptable. For this reason, then and now, I was and am compelled to thoroughly delve into the question of any possible link between self-inflicted deaths and the practice of microfinance institutions in Andhra Pradesh. My research of reports and other evidence indicate that at a statewide level, there was no link between microfinance and suicide; the number of suicides of borrowers in AP did not rise beyond the statistical average of other regions of India. It's equally true that some suicides can be directly attributed to microfinance. I know this pair of statements is seemingly contradictory, so let me explain.

In 2015, Dr. Arvind Ashta, of the Burgundy School of Business, and coauthors published their findings on the topic and counted fifty-four distinct suicides in AP reported by the media in the month of October 2010. Ashta's research team noted the following:

> We checked if the 54 suicides reported by the media in October 2010 could be expected on average in a country the size of India with a billion people—where the average suicide rate is 10 per 100,000 inhabitants

per year. After controlling for the population of Andhra Pradesh, an average family size of five individuals per household, each with three or four loans and the size of Self-Help Groups, we found that 54 suicides should theoretically not be the cause for unjust alert or be unilaterally blamed on an increased borrower stress due to microfinance.[1]

According to the federal government National Crime Records Bureau of India, poverty or bankruptcy cause less than 5 percent of Indian suicides. An illness, family dispute, marital conflict, or fractured romance is a more likely cause of self-inflicted death.[2]

Moreover, this research finding was not just known after the fact. Even as events were unfolding, Eric Bellman of the *Wall Street Journal* reported:

> With more than six million borrowers in Andhra Pradesh alone, it is statistically practically inevitable that there will be some suicidal microborrowers. If the number of suicides in the populace of tiny borrowers is in line with the average for India, there will be more than 600 that will choose to take their own lives this year in Andhra Pradesh. Still, correlation is not causation, even though it makes good political speeches.[3]

Indeed, there were no accusations of MFIs causing borrower suicides in 2009, the year before the SKS IPO, or the year before that or the year before that. In 2010, however, the year of our IPO, and immediately after our IPO but not before it, there was a groundswell of reports of suicides allegedly caused by MFIs.

The question of whether suicides were caused by microfinance is made even more complex when noting that in 2009 and 2010 there was an unusual spike in suicides in south India, including in Andhra Pradesh. The *New York Times* reported: "Suicide has become something of a phenomenon in India, especially in the south, which now has one of the highest suicide rates in the world—a fact that has both puzzled and alarmed public health experts."[4] The reporter went on to explain that after the then AP Chief Minister Yeduguri Sandinti

Rajasekhara died in late 2009, there were allegedly dozens of suicides. And that during the peak of the 2009 through 2010 struggle for Telangana to become separated from Andhra Pradesh as a new state, there were estimates of 200 or more suicides.

I am not in a position to speculate whether political events motivated suicides or whether the deaths that occurred after Rajasekhara's death and during the Telangana struggle were in fact suicides. I mention these cases here to lend context. In south India, at that time, there seemed to be, tragically, a spike in suicides or at least a spike in deaths attributed to suicide for political reasons—with the attribution often made by political leaders. Was there a similar phenomenon at play when politicians attributed suicides to microfinance in October 2010? If, indeed, this was the scenario, in the case of microfinance, the numbers reported may have been elevated by the fact that families may have thought they would financially benefit (including receiving a waiver of the loan and government ex gratia) by claiming a death was suicide resulting from pressure from MFIs.

It is plausible that false attributions emerged.

This all said, there was an evident problem in the MFI industry. When Sequoia Capital invested $11.5 million in SKS in 2007, the investment made headlines across the world. No venture capital firm had ever invested that much money in a microfinance institution—and it was Sequoia doing the investing. Sequoia had a sterling reputation in venture capital circles. The firm had been an early investor in tech giants such as Google and Apple, investments that had returned a multitude of riches. When Sequoia invested in SKS, venture capitalists across the world turned their heads, and their investment portfolios, to this new frontier industry of for-profit microfinance. And along with these new investors came new practitioners and a new ethos in the microfinance field.

These practitioners were different from the original breed of MFI leaders, stalwarts such as BASIX founder Vijay Mahajan and Cashpor founder David Gibbons, who had dedicated their careers to development and who were now trying—as I was—to use market forces to enhance development. The new entrants to microfinance comprised mid-level bankers who had spent the bulk of their careers in mainstream commercial banks. Perhaps they left banking to try to do something more meaningful; perhaps they entered microfinance attracted by the profits. I am not sure, but I am certain that the profits in the sector also attracted what I termed "rogue MFIs"— traditional moneylenders who took on the garb of microfinance but were actually just loan sharks. I would sometimes hear about local financiers who put up signboards displaying the SKS name and logo, even though they had no connection to us. There was not much we could do about these fly-by-night rogue operators, although it's reasonable to assume that their strong-arm tactics may have contributed to borrower distress and debt-driven suicides.

Rogue operators aside, the new MFIs led by former bankers tended to view everything through a financial lens, which meant questioning any aspect of the business that was high cost. And the costliest aspect of microfinance was forming and training groups. Long-time practitioners of microfinance—particularly the predominant Grameen Bank model—knew how important group formation and group training were. After all, we were providing unsecured (that is, collateral-free) loans to poor women whom we did not know and who had no financial records, let alone credit scores. The member-chosen, supportive groups were the key element in ensuring that borrowers used their loans to generate income, and not for personal consumption, and therefore had the capacity to make repayments.

Such strong group support did not just magically happen. It was cultivated. Proper and systematic group training created high-functioning group support. As described in the early chapters of this book, SKS devoted considerable time and effort to the development of the group system, including developing detailed field manuals that guided each step of group formation and group training. Our field staff were equipped with and trained to use our curriculum verbatim.

Consequently, the women in the SKS-guided groups were careful when approving loans and would draw on their knowledge of the loan applicant and the local market conditions. In a rural context, where people live and work together for years and where financial information is, relatively, transparent, this knowledge is quite significant. Fellow group members were aware of each loan applicant and her family and the overall debt of a particular borrower's family and would take that into consideration when approving new loans.[5]

The chart on the next page shows that groups would typically make the loan size commensurate with the repayment capacity of a loan applicant; that is, they would "right-size" the loan. The chart data shows loans distributed in fiscal year 2008–09. The dark shaded bar represents the loan amounts for which borrowers were eligible, depending on their tenure. The light shaded bar represents the average loan amount that was approved by groups for borrowers of various tenures. From the data collected, it is clear that groups were thoughtful about approving loans and determining appropriate loan sizes.

Moreover, there were other checks and balances at SKS. To briefly recap, the Grameen system required that loans be used for income-generating activities. In addition, lending groups were composed of five members, which meant the groups were small enough that the members had to genuinely think about the capacity of potential fellow borrowers and the loan activities those loan applicants proposed (they could not just be a free-rider in discussions and let others handle it). Yet the group was large enough that if a member didn't make her payment and others had to cover for her on a particular week, the burden would be spread across four members, making it manageable. Since repayments were weekly, they were small—small enough that other group members could easily help out with any missed installment. Even in our early years, when our interests were relatively high, typical weekly installments were about ₹240 (about $6) for a typical ₹10,000 (about $230) first-year loan; that meant guarantor members would need to pay ₹60 (about $1.40)

"RIGHT-SIZED" LOANS

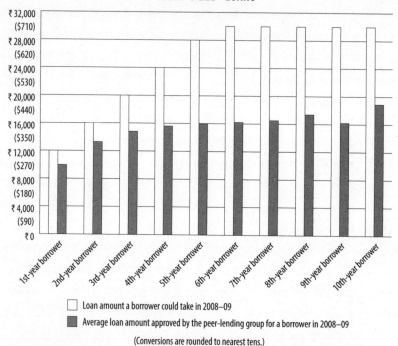

☐ Loan amount a borrower could take in 2008–09

■ Average loan amount approved by the peer-lending group for a borrower in 2008–09

(Conversions are rounded to nearest tens.)

The peer-group lending approach led to an SKS borrower receiving a loan that she could manage without becoming over-indebted. Data represents ₹43,988,000,000 ($978 million) disbursed to 3,950,000 borrowers in fiscal year 2008–09.

Source: SKS data from www.bfil.co.in/wp-content/uploads/2016/08/sks_annual_ report_2008_09.pdf. March 2010 exchange rate of ₹45 = 1 USD from: www. exchangerates.org.uk/USD-INR-31_03_2010-exchange-rate-history.html.

on behalf of a defaulter any given week. Moreover, if the four members could not manage this, the responsibility would escalate to the center, meaning fifty members who each needed to chip in about ₹5 (about 10 cents) a week.[6] A center could easily manage to cover for a borrower who had a cash flow problem with her business.

In fact, when I happened to come to village center meetings a few minutes early, I would see the cash-flow smoothing firsthand. Women would be handing each other notes of ten or a hundred rupees as "hand loans" so that everyone had their full repayment.

Then they would pay each other back during the week. So, it was not as if everyone was repaying 100 percent each week. Rather, there was a lot of internal cash-flow smoothing that allowed the center to have a near perfect repayment each week.

This is not to say that SKS insisted on a borrower repaying or a center taking responsibility even if the borrower was facing dire hardship. I've mentioned examples of having to enforce the lending rules in those early years despite having conflicted emotions about particular cases. Nonetheless, if there was a dire hardship, such as a fire or if a member had to migrate to the city for work, we would write off the loan. Such cases made up the 2 percent of our defaults. But otherwise, we insisted on the center covering the individual and sorting it out afterwards. Basically, we were sending the message that while being a member gave a person the benefit of receiving loans, one of the duties of being a member was to help others out in times of difficulty; that was the price of being in the center and having access to finance.

The group trainings were intensive; typically, a loan officer could train one to two groups a week (sitting, over the course of five days, with members in the evening, after women had finished their work and household chores and were free). I often used to say we were not a microfinance institution—we were a group training institution. The SKS logo itself was a silhouette of a five-member group:

Indeed, the group lending system worked well in Bangladesh, which had a much higher density of MFIs, for over three decades and it worked in India at SKS just as smoothly for over a decade, even in states like Andhra Pradesh, which had the three largest MFIs in India.

It's perhaps unsurprising that many of the new breed of MFI leaders did not understand, or perhaps deliberately ignored, some of these core processes, including group formation and group training. Rigorous group training—to the degree necessary to make sure that loans were the right size, that loans generated income, and that kept repayment rates high—was costly. This new breed of MFI leaders wanted to cut costs. The trend became to shorten group training— they would reduce it to four days, and then three, even two days. They would allow loans for consumption and not insist on income generation, so they could avoid costly loan utilization visits. They would not stagger disbursement and instead would give loans in one shot, which was more cost-effective (but which eliminated a critical component of staggered disbursement in the group lending system). While on the surface such measures may have seemed more efficient, the essence of Grameen-style group lending was lost, elements of the strong repayment culture diluted.

In a press interview in July 2010, before our IPO, I spoke in some detail to this problem, explaining that since many MFIs were not following proper group formation, that the Microfinance Institutions Network (MFIN), the MFI association of which I was a founding member, had capped the loan amount as well as the number of MFIs that could lend to a borrower.

> Though increased competition is good for the poor, we know that many of the newer MFIs don't necessarily follow the rigorous group formation process and as a result [don't follow] the loan approval process that the traditional MFIs do. Instead, they treat it more as a bank might lend to someone. In the absence of a credit bureau, we felt that it was prudent to limit the numbers of MFIs that can lend to a poor household and limit the amount to ₹50,000 so that inadvertently some borrowers don't get into a situation where they are over-leveraged. It is a good proactive move to protect the health of the industry.

Now, if the MFIs use the rigorous group process, you don't need the cap because in some ways the group itself would prevent that happening.

The way the system works is if any single person defaults, none of them get future loans nor does anybody in the village. The other reason the system works so well is it is a staggered disbursement. So, first two people get a loan, a few weeks later, the next two, a few weeks later, the last one.

We stagger groups (formation). It means in any 50-week period, someone is waiting for a loan. If the repayment doesn't come in on that day, the loan doesn't get disbursed. That person is going to pressure (the) one who is defaulting, or if there is genuine [hardship], help her out. If you have this strong group system, you don't need a code of conduct.[7]

New-breed practices contributed to group support morphing into group pressure. The critical message delivered to borrowers was ineptly reduced to: *If my fellow group member does not pay her loan, I will not get my loan.* Naturally, customers put pressure on each other. Statistical interpretations aside, did this type of pressure on individual borrowers lead to, tragically, some instances of suicide? According to the most reliable reports, I believe yes. Let me be clear that there is a role for group pressure in the Grameen lending system, as I have described earlier—for example, in a case of willful default. But that sort of group pressure made sense in a context of an overall approach that had *all* the elements of a Grameen lending system, especially the requirement to use loans to undertake income-generating activities. In the absence of that comprehensive system, group pressure can and did tragically lead to suicide.

Let me also clarify that, from the reports and evidence I saw, suicides among the borrower groups of major MFIs were typically not the result of loan officers putting pressure but often the result of group members putting pressure on each other. As mentioned, there may well have been rogue MFIs—the fly-by-night lenders set up by loan sharks—where loan officers directly pressured borrowers. It is difficult to precisely know what may have been their role in the suicides. As for the major lenders, those licensed and regulated by the Reserve Bank of India (RBI), it was more of a situation in which group members put pressure on each other—though there may have been exceptions. Of course, the tragedy of a suicide is a still a tragedy, regardless of the cause. My point is that the solution—at least for the major MFIs— was, in my view, to go back to basics, go back to the rigorous training that had characterized the microfinance industry in its early phases.

Some may wonder how group pressure could be so severe as to result in suicide. The answer lay in the idea of losing izzath, or "respect." As was explained earlier, losing izzath colloquially meant losing face. Losing face is a fairly devastating thing in a village con-text, and people will do anything to avoid it. Knowing the impor-tance of izzath, group members would sometimes inflict inordinate shame on a fellow member. They would sit in front of her house and hurl abuse at her and her children. In some cases, she might even be terrorized with the threat of sexual violence by the husbands of other members. For a family that was already economically vulnerable and for a borrower who may have been depressed or in a fragile emo-tional state, such shaming was and is quite devastating.

It is hard to explain something comparable in a Western context. Consider the front-page of your hometown newspaper carrying a headline that you defaulted on your car loan and, as a result, no one in your town can get any more loans. It would be tough to endure the resulting animosity and downright bullying that might result. That is the nature of the pressure that some of the Indian borrowers faced.

Let me offer one other example to illustrate what it means to lose izzath in an Indian village context. It is akin to cyber bullying in the United States, such as when a high school teen is tormented, threatened, harassed, humiliated, and embarrassed by other teens using social media. In today's American high school environment, where social media is omnipresent in the lives of teenagers, such cyber bullying is known to lead to suicide.[8] Part of the reason that teens have taken such drastic measures is that social media tends to dominate their social world, and that can be overwhelming. In the same way, if you live in an Indian village without the ability to escape into anonymity from other village residents, and you are from a poor family—and perhaps also face the marginalization that comes with being from a lower caste or minority community—and a group of angry women, maybe as many as fifty, come to your house and hurl abuses, well, then suicide might very well seem like the only option.

Mind you, there was an appropriate role for peer pressure in group lending. As discussed in earlier chapters, in a properly trained group, peer pressure would ensure that a borrower would not take more loans than she could handle; peer pressure would deter a borrower from using a loan for wedding expenses or consumer goods such as a TV instead of an income-generating activity; and peer pressure would prevent multiple lending because fellow borrowers would know when other customers had loans from other MFIs. But when rigorous group training was stripped from microlending, the system broke down. In a case of genuine hardship, when the group was supposed to support a member, there was peer pressure instead. It was as if an automaker eliminated the brake system from the car assembly process to save costs. There would invariably be crashes.

The worse part of this is that when new players cut short rigorous group training, existing players did so as well. Why did that happen? Well, imagine you're a loan officer at a large incumbent MFI and you painstakingly train a group for five days, and then a new MFI swoops in and lends to that group before you do. You are angry and frustrated. You articulate that to your branch manager. Branch managers percolate these issues up to the head office, resulting in a policy decision to mimic the new MFIs. Before they swoop in, give the loan, you are told, even if it means you cut short group training. All the major MFIs faced this problem, and virtually all of them succumbed.

To summarize the chain of events discussed thus far: Sequoia's landmark investment in SKS in March 2007 brought in a new breed of MFIs—those led by former bankers from mainstream commercial banks as well as those led by fly-by-night rogue operators. These new MFIs cut short the rigorous group training that had made microfinance successful in India for more than a decade. Incumbent MFIs mimicked these shortcuts. As a result, over-indebtedness started to emerge. Borrowers used their loan funds on items like TVs and weddings instead of income-generating activities. And group support morphed into group pressure, leading—regrettably—to instances of suicide of borrowers. In short, the industry made mistakes that led to tragedies.

Now, in just about any other industry, the situation would get corrected. Either the industry would self-regulate, as we had attempted to start to do through MFIN. Or the government would step in. When there are fatalities from FDA-approved drugs, the company will recall the drugs or the FDA will step in. When there are deaths from faulty airbags, the auto industry will recall vehicles and the regulator takes action. When there is a food poisoning issue, the Food Safety and Inspection Service of the U.S. Department of Agriculture (USDA) steps in.

The microfinance industry, however, was not a typical industry.

For starters, there were no regulations, per se. The major MFIs were under the purview of the Reserve Bank of India but were lumped together with mainstream lending companies. There were no regulations specifically developed for lending to the poor, who are a very different type of borrower than a middle-class consumer or a business. The RBI was working on regulations piecemeal, but at the time there was nothing comprehensive in place, which is simply the fact of nearly any social enterprise. By definition, social enterprise involves going to new frontiers. Those new frontiers are usually unregulated.

Accordingly, the microfinance industry was taking steps to self-regulate. In October 2009, the industry set up the previously mentioned Microfinance Institutions Network. In early 2010, MFIN had established a cap of only three MFI lenders to a borrower and not more than ₹50,000 ($1,100). We were working on sharing borrower data, a precursor to a credit bureau. We were, however, well aware that it would take time to establish a genuine credit bureau because first there needed to be a unique identification system. Indeed, a prodigious initiative from the Indian government set out to issue *Aadhaar* cards (the equivalent of social security cards) to all Indians. But it wasn't until 2014 when the Unique Identification Authority of India (UIDAI) was robust enough to start enrolling large numbers for Aadhaar cards. Until then, the microfinance industry continued to take steps to self-regulate. In essence, we were going through the maturation process of other emerging industries. However, there was another important difference between the emerging microfinance industry and mainstream industries: namely, that microfinance faced powerful vested interests that emerged as the industry gained traction and hence visibility.

CHAPTER 15

CULPRIT NUMBER TWO: VESTED INTERESTS

There were myriad vested interests aligned against microfinance. The biggest were "malicious, monopolistic" village moneylenders, loan sharks who were the main source of credit in rural India.[1] Known in local languages as the *mahajan* or *sahukar*, they often lent against security of some sort—whether that be gold, land, or bonded labor. The traditional village moneylender had a firm hold on credit in rural India. In the most exploitative predatory lending relations, "families have lost land, farmers have been asked to prostitute their wives to pay off debts, and, when all else has failed, they have tied the noose to end their misery," as described by the journalist and banker Moin Qazi.[2] Unsurprisingly, the most exploitative lending relations primarily occurred in underdeveloped regions, one of which happened to be the epicenter of the microfinance backlash, the Telangana region, which was part of the state of Andhra Pradesh at that time.[3]

In the 1970s, the Indian government tried to provide an alternative to village moneylenders through government-owned regional rural banks. But these were not successful. Microfinance, however,

Top: With my parents and brother in the early 1970s. *Left to right:* Akula Krishna, Padma Krishna, Gautham, and me.

Above left: With my mother, Padma Krishna, in Hyderabad on my first birthday.

Right: My grandfather, Akula Venkatramiah. Although a member of a "backward" caste, he used credit to work his way up from laborer to shop owner.

After college, I worked as a social worker for the Deccan Development Society (DDS) in Telangana, the region my family is from and where I first began working in rural development. Here, I am helping Narsamma, one of the local staff at DDS, with weeding on a farm.

Above, left: Participatory rural appraisal involves using highly visual group exercises to get villagers to talk about social and economic matters. Here, I am facilitating a participatory mapping exercise with a group of villagers. Since this is done in the open, it makes the exercise transparent, so villagers can understand the data being gathered as well as confirm its accuracy.

Above, right: Instead of using clipboard-based written surveys, which often intimidate semi-literate poor people, participatory appraisal uses tactile materials with which villagers are familiar. Using *rangoli* (chalk) powder, seeds, coins, and kernels of sorghum, a group of villagers creates a seasonal cash-flow diagram. We used this data to set our initial loan and installment amounts as well as frequency of payments.

Above, left: Sathamma, SKS's first member, in front of her thatched-mud hut. Her first loan was for ₹1,000 (about $25 at exchange rates at the time) to start a vegetable vending business. Over the years, she took more loans and eventually earned enough money to build a new house.

Above, right: SKS's first employee, the unflappable Rama Laxmi. (Photo by G. Bharat Bhushan)

Inset: Shenkar Rao, a landlord in Anthwar village.

In underdeveloped regions like Telangana, landlords owned vast tracts of land and were the traditional moneylenders. They charged high interest rates and often required collateral such as gold jewelry. Here, I have just visited the house of one of these landlords, along with Syed Hashemi of CGAP, a multilateral institution based in Washington, D.C. I am wearing one of the shirts I bought during my initial visit to the Grameen Bank. (Photos by G. Bharat Bhushan)

Staff meetings on the roof were a commonplace occurrence after we relocated SKS's Narayankhed branch office to the nearby village of Anthwar. I lived in this small bungalow. This was also where a group of men carrying crowbars tried to attack Shyam Mohan, our newly hired chief operating officer.

Above, left: The first step in starting a peer group lending center in a new village was to conduct a transect walk through the village. That provided initial information on the number of poor households and economic activities. Informal conversations with villagers along the way also served as a means of getting potential lenders curious about our program, as well as gauging the level of interest. Here, I am conducting this survey with Sandhya Rani, the third SKS employee.

Above, right: After surveying a village to determine that there would be sufficient interest, the next step was to have informal discussions with groups of borrowers. Here, I am engaged in such a discussion in our first village, Thumnoor. This was then followed by a formal public meeting in a village to present the procedures of SKS's lending program. (Photo by G. Bharat Bhushan)

Above, left: At a village center meeting, I give an SKS member a loan to purchase a milk-producing water buffalo. She will milk the buffalo, keep some milk for her family, and sell the rest, using the proceeds to pay off the loan in one year. (Photo by D. Ravinder Reddy)

Above, right: An SKS staff member uses cash and coins to explain the concepts of weekly repayments and interest rates to members in Islampur, one of the first villages in which SKS practiced microlending. The compulsory group training meetings incorporated visual group exercises to teach financial literacy and present our products and procedures to potential borrowers. (Photo by G. Bharat Bhushan)

A center meeting in Kondapur village. (Photo by G. Bharat Bhushan)

Above, left: Looking at goats with Nirmala Kambalimatam, who was SKS's second employee, and Rama Laxmi in the village of Islampur. They could tell when villagers tried to pass off one goat as another, even if I couldn't. (Photo by G. Bharat Bhushan)

Above, right: With the SKS staff from the first branch. Most of these staff went on to become managers in other areas as SKS expanded in various parts of the country. (Photo by G. Bharat Bhushan)

Though SKS was only in its second year of operation in 2000, the multilateral institution the Consultative Group to Assist the Poor (CGAP) awarded SKS its Pro-Poor Innovation Award that year. Here, Syed Hashemi, Microfinance Specialist at CGAP, presents the award to me and to Yadamma, one of SKS's early borrowers in the first SKS village, Thumnoor. (Photo by G. Bharat Bhushan)

ahul Gandhi, prominent Indian politician and the grandson of Indira Gandhi, attending a center meeting at Banda ?omaram village in the Nalgonda district of what was then the state of Andhra Pradesh. Here, I'm sitting to Gandhi's left nd SKS chief operating officer at the time, Praseeda Kunam, in red dress, is on his right. (Photo by D. Ravinder Reddy)

Above, left: Saailibai is a Banjara tribal woman who used her first SKS loan to purchase a buffalo. Over the years I knew her, Saailibai took larger loans to farm her land and invest in more buffaloes. She used some of her profits to build a new home with stone walls and to send her son to a private high school. (Photo by G. Bharat Bhushan)

Above, right: With the pioneer of microfinance, Nobel Prize winner Professor Muhammad Yunus, at the Reserve Bank of India.

SKS members used their loans to start or expand all kinds of businesses. Here a woman shows off her cobbler enterprise.

Above, left: Each SKS village center—308,000 in all as of January 2018—elected a leader. These leaders met annually in regional meetings to give feedback and suggestions to the SKS team and learn about new pilot products. Here they're voting on whether they like a new loan product we were designing.

On the red carpet at the TIME 100 Gala. Dubbed by the magazine in 2006 as one of the "world's most influential people," had the opportunity to raise U.S. awareness of SKS's endeavors in India. (Photo by D. Ravinder Reddy)

I met with thought leaders at the 2006 TIME 100 Gala. *Top left, clockwise:* With actress Jennifer Lopez; with then U.S. Secretary of State, Condoleezza Rice; with U.S. Senator John McCain; with then Mayor of New York City Michael Bloomberg. (Photos by D. Ravinder Reddy)

Inset: SKS logo on the six-story SKS corporate headquarters in Hyderabad. (Photo by Adeel Halim/Bloomberg via Getty Images)

The six-story SKS corporate headquarters in Hyderabad. (Photo by Krishnendu Halder)

Above, left: Receiving the 2009 Ernst & Young "Business Transformation" Entrepreneur of the Year Award, along with M. Damodaran, former Chairperson of the Securities and Exchange Board of India and Digvijaya Singh, former Chief Minister of Madhya Pradesh, with my son in attendance.

Above, right: With U.K. former Prime Minister Tony Blair in China in 2008.

Above, left: With L. K. Advani, Indian politician and a senior leader of the Bharatiya Janata Party (BJP), at a 2010 event for the release of BJP leader M. Venkaiah Naidu's book, *Tireless Voice: Relentless Journey.*

Above, right: On stage with then President of the Indian National Congress Party Sonia Gandhi and World Economic Forum founder Klaus Schwab, when I was selected for the Social Entrepreneur of the Year Award in 2006. (Photo by Manpreet Romana/AFP/Getty Images)

Timothy Geithner, then United States Secretary of the Treasury, met with me and Vijay Mahajan, founder of Basix, when he came to India. (Photo by Kunal Patil/Hindustan Times via Getty Images)

Above, left: SKS Microfinance's IPO ceremony at the BSE, formerly known as the Bombay Stock Exchange, in August 2010. (Photo by STR/AFP/Getty Images)

Above, right: Speaking on the plenary stage at the World Economic Forum Annual Meeting in Davos, Switzerland. I was on a panel with Bill Gates, the Prime Minister of Zimbabwe, and the head of the United Nations Development Programme. (Photo by Chris Ratcliffe/Bloomberg via Getty Images)

Speaking to a group of borrowers during a field visit with Pierre Omidyar, founder of eBay. (Photo by Pierre Omidyar)

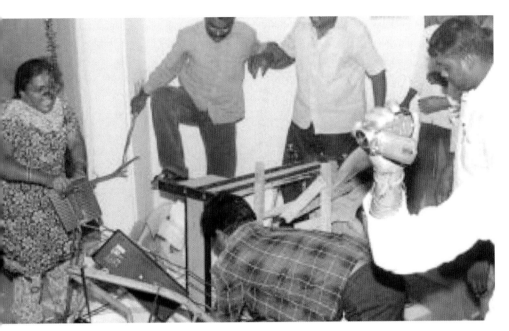

In the wake of incendiary comments against microfinance by the then Rural Development Minister of Andhra Pradesh, SKS branch offices were vandalized by local political thugs during late 2010. (Photo by Murali)

S. Dilli Raj (*left*), former chief financial officer of SKS Microfinance, and M. R. Rao, chief operating officer and later chief executive officer of SKS. Raj was arrested in 2016 for his involvement in a ₹665 crore ($115 million) fraud in his previous company and is awaiting trial. I gave evidence to the forensic auditor that, under Rao and Raj, bribes were paid to police to get reports that exonerated SKS from the charge of abetting suicide. The SKS Board never disclosed the results of that forensic audit. (Photo by Hemant Misra for Mint and HT Media Ltd.)

Above, left: Sumir Chadha led Sequoia Capital India from 2006 to 2011, when he left to found WestBridge. Sequoia became the largest shareholder in SKS by the end of 2007. Sequoia, WestBridge, and related entities earned proceeds of $121 million from the 2010 IPO and later sales. When I raised concerns about over-indebtedness of poor women borrowers, he emailed me: "You are not cut out for running a large company that SKS has become . . . I hope that you can hear this feedback in the right spirit and change yourself, otherwise you will suffer the most from this." (Photo by Pradeep Gaur/Mint via Getty Images)

Above, right: Translation: They Are Not "Micro" Deaths

Rangareddy Rural: NewsLine 2010

—Report concluded by district police department

—Report submitted to Collector

The district police have concluded that the recent suicides are not to be attributed to microfinance pressures. After thorough investigations, the department has concluded that these suicides are the result of personal financial problems. The final report was submitted to the district collector on Tuesday. In this month, news made rounds that the following people have committed suicide due to pressures by microfinance companies: Abdul Hameed (Annepally, Vikarabad); Narsimulu (Mominpet); Gopal (Nawabpet); Lalitha (Godumaguda, Darur); Arkala Narsimha (Malkapur, Chevella). Based on these reports, the police department has investigated the reasons for these deaths and established that these are not to be attributed to microfinance.

The district Superintendent of Police, Munu Swamy, briefed *NewsLine* that—post the local police authorities registering these cases—the regional police have specifically investigated from the angle of microfinance pressures. He clarified that these deaths are the result of personal financial problems and not MFI pressures. In addition, he mentioned that the small loans taken from MFIs are being repaid on time. He also reported that these borrowers have informal loans (to the tune of lakhs) and were burdened by these higher-size loans, which may have drawn them to this extreme step. In the majority of cases, he clarified that MFI staff do not visit borrowers' homes for recoveries, but they collect through the group members. (Photo courtesy of Jagati Publications Limited)

Above, left: My son, Tejas, as a ninth-grader at a school soccer game.

Above, right: My son, Tejas, now an eleventh-grader at a school tennis match. (Photo by David Lee)

Giving the keynote speech at a conference on good governance at the University of Oxford's Rhodes House in 2015. (Photo by Michael Brock, courtesy Linklaters LLP)

Above, left: Kavita is a borrower in my new microfinance company, Vaya FinServ. She and her husband have a flower business. They harvest marigolds from their one-and-a-half acres of land and make garlands and floral decorations for wedding ceremonies and other functions. In 2015, Kavita took a loan from Vaya for ₹24,000 (~$400) to lease more land and increase the size of their crop. Now that she has repaid the loan and earned greater profits, next, she wants a loan of ₹50,000 (~$800), so that she can expand her business further. (Photo by Omar Adam Khan)

Above, right: A Vaya center meeting. Established in 2014, Vaya is the capstone of my twenty-five year journey in financial inclusion. Vaya represents microfinance 2.0, blending the agility of a start-up with decades of experience. The *Wall Street Journal* profiled Vaya for pioneering the deployment of tablet banking in rural India in 2015. (Photo by Omar Adam Khan)

Speaking on a panel discussion in 2015 about the future of financial inclusion, with Romesh Sobti looking on. Sobti is CEO of IndusInd Bank Ltd., which announced in 2017 that it will acquire SKS Microfinance for $2.4 billion, making SKS the most valuable microlender in the world. (Photo by Abhijit Bhatlekar/Mint via Getty Images)

was. Beginning in the 1990s, nonprofit microfinance institutions emerged that provided a low-cost alternative to village moneylenders, and, by the late 1990s, commercial microfinance institutions emerged, including SKS. Where moneylenders asked for collateral, SKS and others did not. Where moneylenders charged high interest rates that did not allow borrowers to accumulate any profits for themselves, SKS and other MFIs charged—relatively—lower interest rates, allowing borrowers to gradually improve their economic well-being. As microfinance spread across the country, the village moneylender lost his dominant hold on rural credit and his hold over the village economy.

Naturally, moneylenders were upset. Their efforts to sabotage microfinance endeavors included, as described earlier, spreading false rumors and even the occasional violent attack. Our loan officers were frequently harassed or threatened. One of our loan officers was beaten so badly by a village moneylender that he permanently lost his hearing in one ear.

However, because village moneylenders were a disparate group, they could not and did not coordinate amongst themselves. So other than the occasional one-off resistance in a village here or there, they could not do much against microfinance. They simply watched as their control waned. If given the opportunity, however, they were ready to pounce.

The second vested interest was the government bureaucracy. In the 1990s, the government's National Bank for Agriculture and Rural Development, or NABARD, launched the Self-Help Group (SHG) Bank Linkage Program. State governments would fund and administer initiatives to form self-help groups in villages that they would "link" to government regional rural banks that had been set up but that were not lending to the poor. Though successful Grameen-style peer-lending groups were proliferating in neighboring Bangladesh, the Indian bureaucrats often looked down on Bangladesh. The prevailing attitude could be paraphrased as: "India is a great civilization.

Do you expect us to learn from an unstable, small country like Bangladesh!?" Bureaucrats certainly did not feel they should use Grameen-style peer lending. So the self-help groups in India were different in many ways, one being that the groups were less structured and less standardized. And generally speaking, bureaucratic government staff—whether those administering the SHG Bank Linkage Program or those working in regional rural bank branches—were less committed to their work than field staff at mission-driven organizations such as Grameen Bank, BRAC, and ASA in Bangladesh.

In India, sometimes nonprofits would assist government banks with the SHG Bank Linkage Program. I knew this program well because when I first came back to India in 1990 and worked with the nonprofit DDS, I did exactly that—facilitated these self-help groups.

I would spend days forming a self-help group, training the group members in numeracy, collecting small savings, recording accounts, and then taking the group of women to a local regional rural bank branch to try to get a loan. The women had to save up front for six months. They would lose wages and spend bus fares on days when they had to visit a branch. Then there was no guarantee the branch loan officer would be there, let alone approve a loan. In short, it was a nightmare to facilitate a "linkage."

The attraction, however, was that the loans were highly subsidized. In Andhra Pradesh, for example, under a program called *Velugu*, meaning "light," launched in 2000, loans were given at an interest rate of 12 percent because the AP government created the Society for Elimination of Rural Poverty (SERP) to manage this program, with the government underwriting all the costs of SERP staff. That certainly improved the "linkage."

In the 2004 elections, the then opposition Congress Party in Andhra Pradesh promised those SHG loans at 3 percent interest. The Congress Party won and delivered on the promise. Soon after, it appropriated the SERP Self-Help Group program and gave Velugu a new name—Indira Kranthi Patham (IKP). The name was a reference to Indira Gandhi, the slain former prime minister. Literally, it meant the "Indira Revolution," referencing the fact that the SHG program was for women. Many observers credited the campaign promise as a key to the election victory. As such, the SERP-administered IKP program was important. And the bureaucrat who administered the initial program, Koppula Raju, was heralded. Raju, in fact, went on to become a key policy maker in the federal government and later left the bureaucracy to enter politics, joining the Congress Party at the national level.[4]

At the time of our IPO, the senior bureaucrat in charge of the rural development department (and the SERP program) in Andhra Pradesh was Reddy Subrahmanyam. He had been a protégé of Raju, and he knew the importance of the SHG program for his career. He also believed, as did Raju, that microfinance should be the purview of the state, not the private sector. In a *New York Times* article, he described MFIs as worse than the village moneylender. "The money-lender lives in the community," he was quoted as saying. "At least you can burn down his house. With these companies, it is loot and scoot."[5]

In addition, there was a second category of bureaucrats who had a stake in the SHG program. These were lower-level officials, from the district to the village level. For these individuals, the subsidized loans provided an opportunity for getting bribes (as was true in virtually all government programs in the country). In India, bribery is a fact of everyday life, and poorly paid government workers view bribes as a necessary component of their income. In the Andhra Pradesh SHG Bank Linkage Program, it was well known that borrowers would pay bribes of as much as 20 percent to lower-level officials to access these loans.[6] Moreover, much of the funding for the SHG Bank Linkage Program in AP emanated, directly or indirectly, from the World Bank and other international development agencies. With the rise of private sector microfinance, there were questions being raised within these institutions about whether there should be continued funding for such programs.

Naturally, such sentiments worried both sets of bureaucrats. The ones who had a statist ideology, like Reddy Subrahmanyam, were worried about private sector microfinance occupying a space that they felt should be the purview of the state. Meanwhile, the petty bureaucrats were worried about losing their opportunities for bribes. Both groups had a strong vested interest in stopping microfinance. They just needed an opportunity.

Politicians comprised the final group with a vested interest against microfinance. They got involved in microfinance for several reasons. First, moneylenders (who were growing increasingly disgruntled because of the rise of microfinance) were also often the large landowners in villages and the ones who delivered votes in elections. In short, the politicians had a patron–client relationship with village moneylenders. Since the moneylenders were disgruntled, they articulated that to politicians. In the same vein, much of the local-level staff in the rural development department—including village SERP officials who took bribes—were recommended by local politicians. With the rise of microfinance and the possible discontinuation of international funding for SERP, this was also a group that had some anxiety about microfinance, and they made their views known to politicians. The disgruntled groups were not organized enough or large enough to get politicians to act. But they did draw the attention of politicians to microfinance, and this was augmented by senior bureaucrats—statist motivated people such as Reddy Subrahmanyam—lobbying senior political leaders with their concerns about private sector microfinance.

The real trigger of the backlash was the increasing awareness that there were high profits in microfinance. This is something I had talked about explicitly for years. It was, after all, my philosophy to use market forces to scale microfinance to deliver profits to investors, thereby enabling us to tap capital markets and provide more loans to more borrowers. This was my life's work.

In retrospect, I realized that politicians had not taken me seriously. How could a *chappal*-wearing, kurta-clad kid create a multibillion dollar company? Then I exercised stock options pre-IPO and sold shares in February 2010 for a gross amount of $13 million, which was widely reported in the press. I exercised stock options before the IPO because I had agreed to voluntarily lock-in my options for three years so that new public investors would have confidence in the company. In the parlance of the venture capitalist world, I had "skin in the game." In fact, because of a mistake I made in structuring my stock options—after all, who could have imagined when I first started SKS that they would be worth anything—I ended up having to pay very high 33 percent ordinary income tax rates, because I was a U.S. citizen in India, and not the lower 15 percent short-term capital gains rates typical with stock options. And because this was paid in one go at the time of the sale, I landed on the list of the ten highest advance taxpayers in India. I was by no means among the top ten wealthiest people in India, but I ended up having to pay an inordinate amount of tax at one time. Landing on that list gave people a sense that I had made hundreds of millions. In reality, post tax and post the cost of shares, I netted $7.8 million. Of course, even that was a huge sum—that too, for a chappal-wearing, kurta-clad kid who came to India after college with virtually nothing. It was certainly more than I had ever dreamed of making in my lifetime. I had been an accidental entrepreneur, and I had become an accidental multimillionaire.

Alongside these news reports of my multimillion-dollar share sale, politicians started to notice conspicuous consumption of other MFI leaders. In particular, then Rural Development Minister Vatti Vasant Kumar reportedly was shocked to learn that the founder of one leading MFI bet large sums at a pool hall. The MFI founder was apparently betting ₹100,000 ($2,200) on each pool game. Kumar was further surprised upon learning that the individual had a luxury imported German sports car (a costly purchase since there was an import tax of more than 100 percent on luxury vehicles) and apparently hosted lavish parties. Politicians like Vatti Vasant Kumar started to wonder about the level of profits in microfinance.

It was one thing for politicians to speculate about the level of profits. But after our IPO, SKS's $2.2 billion market capitalization was in the public domain. So were profits earned by SKS institutional investors. Sumir Chadha's entity Sequoia Capital and its affiliated entities cashed out $79 million at the IPO and had eventual realized proceeds from the IPO and later sales of $124 million. Ashish Lakhanpal's entity Kismet earned $47 million and had eventual realized proceeds from the IPO and later sales of $80 million. Paresh Patel's Sandstone did not sell at the IPO, but had eventual realized proceeds from later sales of $53 million. Sumir, Ashish, and Paresh earned significant personal profits through their profit share on those gains, known as "carry." They did not reveal the amount, but typically owners of venture firms take 20 percent of the gains, though Sequoia was known to take 30 percent.[7]

Andhra Pradesh politicians were observing all this, and at a time when there were no more than a handful of billion-dollar companies in Hyderabad. What's more is that founders of those billion-dollar companies frequently had to pay bribes to politicians. It was just the way things were done in Andhra Pradesh. That last sentence will get me in trouble, I know. But someone has to say it.

I also know that, having written that previous sentence, it is incumbent on me to at least give one documented example. But I can't. No one speaks about this openly, let alone on record. Take, for example, the most infamous case of corruption in Andhra Pradesh and possibly in India, Satyam Computer Services. The founder of Satyam, B. Ramalinga Raju, built Satyam into a $2 billion company. In 2009, Raju confessed to a ₹7,136-crore fraud, which was $1.5 billion at 2009 exchange rates. In 2008, Satyam reported it had $1.1 billion in cash when the real number was $78 million. Raju had been allegedly withdrawing $3 million (₹200 million) every month. In the accounts, the money was recorded as salaries for 13,000 nonexistent employees.[8] The fraud eventually unraveled. Raju went to jail for seven years.

For what purpose did Raju siphon those funds? Here are two opinions.

Gurcharan Das wrote about Satyam in his book, *The Difficulty of Being Good: On the Subtle Art of Dharma*. As mentioned, I had asked Das to serve as the first chairperson of the for-profit SKS Microfinance Pvt. Ltd in 2005, which he did. Das remained on the board until January 2010 (just before the SKS IPO). In his book, Das wrote the following about Satyam:

> Even as the story was unfolding, it seemed clear to me that the moral failing was not greed as everyone thought . . . Was it, perhaps, that Raju's stake in Satyam had dwindled to 8.6 percent, and the company was in danger of slipping out of the family's control? Raju has two sons and a sense of filial duty drove him, perhaps, to create companies in real estate and infrastructure, two sectors of the Indian economy that had not been reformed, and where politicians insisted on bribes to [be] paid upfront for favours delivered. Since revenues from the new companies were far away, Raju dipped into Satyam to pay politicians.[9]

Likewise, a *New York Times* article reported that "cash was siphoned for other uses, possibly land deals the family is involved in through Mr. Raju's sons' companies." In that article, Arundhati Roy, the novelist and activist, had the courage to go on record. She said, "No Indian believes that the Satyam scandal has to do just with those three executives . . . It has to do with huge land deals, with infrastructure projects and it all dovetails into the political system."[10]

In short, the suggestion is that Satyam funds were siphoned to pay bribes to Andhra Pradesh politicians. Raju described his situation as follows, perhaps referring to the widening gap between the real and artificial numbers in the accounts or perhaps to something else: "It was like riding a tiger, not knowing how to get off without being eaten."[11]

The Satyam case was extreme, both in the quantity of the fraud and in the fact that it came out publicly. That such payments were made by Indian companies, however, was common knowledge. They were just done in a way that sidestepped detection. Consider the fact that India ranked number 87 on Transparency International's 2010 "corruption perceptions index," meaning at least 86 countries were seen as less corrupt. That ranking has improved a bit, to 79 in 2014, the latest report available.[12]

Politicians had never asked me for bribes. I had naively thought that they did not do so because they believed we were doing good work. What I belatedly realized is that they did not do so because they did not realize how profitable the company was—until the SKS IPO. Then they came calling with a vengeance: "How dare you work in Hyderabad and create this kind of wealth and never come see us!"

That statement is concocted—no politician ever said that to me. Their approach was far more subtle and far more sophisticated. Here's how it worked.

Politicians in Andhra Pradesh had close ties with local local-language newspaper and television companies. The historical roots of this connection go back to the 1980s and 1990s, during which time India saw a great proliferation in media outlets. The classic example is the Telugu-language daily newspaper *Eenadu* (the term means both "this day" and "this region"). The paper was founded by businessman and media entrepreneur Ramoji Rao in 1974, and during the 1980s, new technology (offset printing, photocomposing software, and computers) enabled *Eenadu* to spread into smaller towns across Andhra Pradesh. Then, in 1982, N. T. Rama Rao (or NTR as he is known), a film-star with Reagan-esque appeal and political abilities, linked up with Ramoji Rao, who was from the same caste, the Kamma caste.[13] *Eenadu* featured NTR's handsome visage all over the front page, and for the first time in decades, the Congress Party lost power in Andhra Pradesh. NTR became chief minister in 1983.

In the 1990s, access to the television spectrum increased, and anyone could set up a channel with little barrier to entry. *Eenadu* launched ETV in 1995; many other channels, often affiliated with political parties, emerged. Though NTR died in 1996, the nexus between media and politics continued and thrived. The media promoted favored politicians via televised speeches and favorable coverage, likewise publishing slanderous exposés of the opposition— negative political ads in the United States are tame by comparison.

According to a 2012 article in *Business Standard*, more than a third of news channels in India are owned by politicians or political affiliates and 60 percent of cable distribution systems are owned by local politicians. The article said politicians use their channels as "political vehicles" to influence the course of local elections. "There are dozens of small and big newspapers owned by politicians or their family members that influence the course of several local elections. Many newspaper chains with political affiliations also own broadcast networks. Most now have Internet portals."[14]

In Andhra Pradesh, perhaps the most notorious example came from the media company ABN, led by Vemuri Radhakrishna. ABN seemed to be associated with N. Chandrababu Naidu of the Telugu Desam Party, though I cannot find any evidence of a direct link. Both men were of the same politically dominant Kamma caste. In October 2009, a few months after the ABN channel was launched, it aired a video exposé of Narayan Datt Tiwari in a sexual encounter with three women.[15] Tiwari was the governor of Andhra Pradesh and former chief minister of Uttar Pradesh. A governor is a largely ceremonial yet significant political post, but one important fact was that the governor in this case was from the ruling Congress Party, rival of the Telugu Desam Party to which Naidu belonged.

Media such as ABN and politicians such as Naidu did not pay much attention to SKS, until around the time of our IPO. Then they homed in, beginning with the suicide stories. One of the first

stories was in *Andhra Jyothi*, the newspaper that was part of the
ABN media company.

As the stories became longer and moved to the front pages, I asked
our CEO, Rao, to give me information about the allegations. After a
few days, Rao gave me a report listing all the suicides involving SKS
borrowers. There were seventeen names on the list. Rao's list indicated
the publicized cause of death and an actual cause of death for each
case. For example, an entry in the allegation column read, "died of a
heart attack because of pressure to pay a loan" while the actual cause
read, "had a history of heart problems and died of a heart attack." I
believed Rao. I had no reason not to. He subsequently even showed
me a newspaper clipping of a statement by a district superintendent
of police, in which the official exonerated MFIs of any responsibility
for abetting suicide in his district. (A copy of this newspaper clipping,
with translation, is in the photo insert of this book.)

Meanwhile, I was already being threatened by the local-language
media. Executives at media companies reached out to me directly
or through intermediaries, seeking payments in exchange for not
running stories of the alleged suicides, in which SKS was accused.
The most memorable exchange with an executive of a media company took place in late September. The executive reached out to a
lawyer who had represented me in the custody case about my son.
The lawyer passed on the message to me. Though at the time, I was
generally aware of pressure tactics driven by the media, I had faith
that I could convince the executive to treat us differently than other
targeted businesses. I felt I could persuade him or, in the worse case,
just refuse until he realized I would never pay—my same tactic
throughout my years at SKS, holding firm against petty bureaucrats
or village strongmen who threatened to impede our work as a means
of extorting bribes.

I first met him on a late September afternoon. I had just returned
from New York, where I had a famous debate with Muhammad
Yunus at a plenary session of the Clinton Global Summit. There was

a huge buzz about SKS's IPO and the success we were having. My lawyer accompanied me to the studio headquarters. We proceeded through a security check and were escorted to a second-floor waiting room, just outside of the executive's office.

After a few minutes, he opened the door and in a deep voice welcomed my lawyer first and then me. He was short and spoke choppy, broken English. A gold chain hung loosely around his neck.

We engaged in a bit of small talk while tea was brought in. Then the executive got to the point. I don't recollect the exact words he said, but it was something along the lines of, "You need to give me ₹5 crore and we will stop." That was the equivalent of $1.2 million. The executive wasn't asking. He wasn't bargaining. He matter-of-factly stated the figure, as if it was an everyday business transaction.

I had no intention of paying but needed to buy time. I did not want to appear to insult a media mogul and risk further negative coverage. I had to tread carefully. Hesitatingly, I went into my persuasion mode.

"We can't make a payment like this, sir," I started, deferentially. "It is against our principles . . ." I used all my go-to arguments. In the past, when we were a nonprofit, I used to pepper in the fact that our funds were from donors and that it would be unethical for me to make such payments with their donations. It wasn't my money to give. Now that we were for-profit, I amended my commentary to say that the money belonged to our shareholders. I could not do anything, I told the executive. We had a Big Four audit firm, Ernst & Young.

In the past, I'd had a lot more leverage. If a village strongman asked for a bribe, we could simply refuse and threaten to leave the village. Borrowers would then put pressure on the strongman so that they did not lose access to finance. Meanwhile, with higher-level officials, we could wait it out, as I'd done when refusing to pay a bribe for receiving permission to bring in the foreign donations I had raised from friends and family. Things were different now—in many ways. The pressure was not perpetrated by some village strongman; the executive held a powerful position in the media, with politicians at his beck and call. Also, we could no longer just walk away. We worked in nearly every village of Andhra Pradesh, and walking away would have meant walking away from millions of members, thousands of staff, and hundreds of millions of dollars in loans that were outstanding. And, of course, we were no longer a small nonprofit paying nonprofit salaries. We paid our staff, myself included, top dollar.

The other difference was that in the past, for the first several years, we did not make any profits. Indeed, we had losses. Then after our first break-even year, fiscal year 2004–05, when we converted to a for-profit, no one really knew how profitable we were. Now that we were a public company, our financials were in plain view: Our quarter ending June 2010 profits were $14.4 million (₹67 crore); our 2009–10 fiscal year profits were $38.6 million (₹174 crore). And with our market cap rising as of mid-September to $2.2 billion, this executive and his ilk were out for blood. They wanted to get paid.

After he made his demand, there was a lot of back and forth. I played dumb for a while. "Sir, I don't understand. What exactly are you asking me?"

He got irked. When he was perturbed, he spoke in very fast Telugu in his native Andhra dialect, the dialect used by those of the eastern part of the state, the Andhra region. I could barely understand this dialect given that I spoke the more rustic Telangana Telugu, which I had picked up from my family and refined during my decades in rural Telangana villages. I therefore legitimately said, "Sir, I don't understand your accent," which irritated the executive even further.

At one point, I said to him, exasperated, "I don't even know how I could possibly create that much cash."

At that, he raised his voice in turn and told me to "send Dilli Raj" to meet with him so he could "explain."

At another point, I pushed him on the issue of politicians who were making incendiary statements. He deadpanned something akin to, "I will take care of that once you make the payment." When I responded quizzically and suggested that maybe I could speak with the politicians myself, he bared his fangs. How had I survived in this city? Didn't I know how business worked? I should make the payment or we would both be "in a soup."

At the end of that first meeting, I left the frustrated executive without a promise to pay. "Let me talk with my board," I said, still with no intention of paying. I just needed to buy time to figure out what to do. Meanwhile, I was dealing with the ultimatum from Rao and Raj that we fire our CEO, Suresh Gurumani, as well as the shadow of the negative media attention about my child custody fight.

I spent my days shuttling between Hyderabad—where I was meeting with executives of local language media companies and keeping an eye on what was going on in the field—and Mumbai, where I was engaged in heated conversations with the board and a slew of lawyers about Gurumani's impending ouster.

Immediately after Gurumani was fired, I headed straight to the Reserve Bank of India to explain to two deputy governors the context, so that they did not have to read it in the papers first. But I did not have time to properly deal with or pin down the real source of the press fallout—much of it specifically directed at me—from having fired our CEO less than fifty days after our IPO. I had to race back to Hyderabad to turn my attention back to the media company executives, who were ramping up their stories about the suicides of borrowers. Alongside these stories, local politicians—each of whom was connected to one or the other media company—started to up the ante.

Kankanala Narayana, the leader of the AP chapter of the Communist Party of India, an opposition political party, held a press conference in which he told borrowers not to repay their microfinance loans and demanded that the state government ban microfinance. Naidu, leader of the main opposition party in AP, the Telugu Desam Party, called for borrowers to not only stop repaying their loans but to beat up loan officers: "If MFI agents harass you for repayment, tie them up in a room and call the TDP workers for support," Naidu exhorted in a mass rally.[16]

Naidu also tried to link the alleged transgressions of SKS with the ruling Congress Party in Andhra Pradesh. Because Rahul Gandhi had visited SKS in 2005, Naidu made false claims that Gandhi and I had been college friends at Harvard. In fact, we both happened to attend Harvard the same year: me as a graduate student; he, an undergraduate. But I never met him on campus. (Incidentally, both of us dropped out of Harvard to finish our degrees elsewhere.) Naidu's team located the famous picture of Gandhi sitting in on one of SKS's group meetings in rural Andhra Pradesh. *Look!* Naidu claimed. *The Congress Party is doing nothing about these practices because they are close to these scoundrel MFIs!*

Then, in early October 2010, the attack came to our corporate headquarters. A local leader of an opposition party rallied a mob of 150 people who surrounded SKS's Hyderabad headquarters. They brought the corpse of a man who had allegedly committed suicide because of a microfinance loan. He was the husband of one of our members. In reality, the man had died of a heart attack. But that did not matter to the mob. The local leader stood on a jeep and whipped the crowd into a frenzy. Through back channels, the same leader demanded the rupee equivalent of about $20,000—which he said he would give to the family.

At the time, Rao and Raj were on a two-day religious pilgrimage to the temple town of Tirupathi. Admittedly, when Rao told me he was leaving for two days in the midst of the political backlash, I was shocked. We needed all hands on deck to deal with the series of attacks that made up the onslaught—in this case, the angry mob that was now threatening to drag the corpse inside. Rao was pious and had been adamant about turning to prayer. While away, he was barely reachable by phone since he was walking up the 3,555 steps of the six-mile trail to the top of the seven hills, an act that he deemed a greater expression of piety.

Atop the hill was the temple of Lord Venkateswara, "destroyer of sins." It was said that Venkateswara took a large loan from Kubera, the Hindu god who is the treasurer of wealth. To help Venkateswara repay his debt, devotees offer him wealth and in return Venkateswara fulfills their prayers. Perhaps the trip Rao and Raj were taking was to thank the lord for the firing of Gurumani; perhaps it was to offer wealth in exchange for getting SKS out from the destructive political juggernaut; perhaps it was to thank Lord Venkateswara for a successful IPO. After all, Raj had named our IPO prospectus after Kubera. I don't know. All I know is that, during our toughest challenges, Rao and Raj abandoned ship to pray.

I was eventually able to defuse the mob situation by calling a former member of Parliament of the same party who spoke with the local leader and got him to back down.

Meanwhile, out in the field, our members, fearful of the heated political climate, hesitated to repay loans. Even if they came to the weekly microfinance meetings with their payments, these meetings were disrupted by the mobs, who often scared away loan officers with the threat of violence.

Around this time, a person I will call "Harish" reached out to me. I use the name "Harish" for fear of using his real name publicly. He contacted me through a mutual acquaintance, who said Harish could help. Desperate at this stage, I agreed to meet with Harish.

I called him and set up a meeting at his office in Jubilee Hills, a posh area of Hyderabad. When I entered the office, which was in a brand-new building, I saw a large empty space filled with office furniture but just a handful of people: two armed security guards in familiar gray Indian "safari" suits, a young female receptionist, and a male office assistant, dressed in white pants and shirt.

Harish was perhaps in his early thirties. He spoke softly but in the same fast-paced Telugu of the Andhra region as did the above-mentioned media executive. When I first met him, he made the effort to speak in English. I appreciated this, but his English was halting, so I asked him to speak in Telugu. His message was simple. He could organize payments to the rural development minister. He could also coordinate with other representatives for other politicians—from both the ruling and the opposition parties—and their media companies. He was offering a turn-key, one-stop brokerage services for paying bribes to everyone involved—at a cost of ₹50 crore, about $11 million. He offered specific suggestions on how to channel the money from SKS to him.

He was not threatening. He was not intimidating. His tone was matter-of-fact, as if this was just an everyday transaction. He was patient, even gentle. So why do I not want to use his name? This was the Indian underworld, its players as ruthless and powerful as what the term "mafia" conjures up. I had a very real sense of the great power that Harish wielded behind the scenes. During my various meetings with him, I always saw one or two other meetings going on in the office space. Once, I saw an elected Member of the Legislative Assembly (MLA) whom I recognized. He was meeting with two others—my guess was to arrange a kickback for some infrastructure contract. Another time I saw a uniformed policeman in the waiting room; maybe he was there to take a payment to make sure a murder case went away. I frequently saw people meeting with the brother of a minister in the central government. The minister was one of the most powerful politicians in the country, and lucrative contracts under his purview were one area notorious for large-scale kickbacks. In short, over time, I understood that this was the hub for fixers and brokers, and Harish had created a clearinghouse of sorts. If I wanted to get SKS out of the backlash through paying bribes, I was in the right place.

I still never intended to pay anybody anything. I was just buying time, trying to figure out my next move. Meanwhile, I had more meetings with other media heads. I even met the above-mentioned media executive again, twice—once at a hotel, which I had requested, because I was wary of being caught on camera in his studio office and how he might splice together video of our meetings. The final meeting was at his home around the second week of October 2010. It was the meeting where I told him, finally, that I would not pay. He got the message and abruptly ended the meeting.

In the midst of these myriad meetings with media, bureaucrats, and politicians, the SKS team also had daily "war room" meets with other MFI leaders. At these meetings, I pleaded with the industry to organize a mass rally of our customers. While there was no doubt the industry had made mistakes, at this stage, the issue was one of politics. Since we were signaling to politicians and local language media that we were not going to pay bribes, we had to show that there would be political fallout if they went through with their attack on microfinance. A march of hundreds of thousands of borrowers would be significant. With a combined membership of six million customers in the state, with at least a half million close enough to Hyderabad that we could mobilize them for a march, we could realistically draw at least 100,000 to 200,000 people. That would be a show of strength.

While there was support from some of the more grassroots-oriented MFI leaders, many of the new breed—especially the former bankers—were aghast at the thought of a rally of customers. They said, "We are businessmen, not activists!" I knew that unless politicians were able to see our strength and our ability to influence our customers—their voters—we would lose this battle. I also knew that we had a lot of goodwill from our members. They were coming to center meetings, money in hand—ready to repay. But they also were being told not to repay. They needed to see some sign from us that we were with them. Unfortunately, the idea of a march on the capital was shot down by the majority of MFI leaders.

My board was also no help. I spoke with several board members, and their replies ranged from shoulder shrugs to, perhaps unwittingly, supporting payments. Pramod Bhasin offered to make an introduction to Nira Radia. Though it was not known publicly at the time, Radia helped broker deals between businesses and politicians. In November 2010, *Open Magazine* did an expose on Radia, printing transcripts of government tape recordings of her phone calls from 2008 to 2009, in which Radia was speaking with (then) Indian telecom minister Andimuthu Raja and other politicians of the ruling Congress Party as well as with senior journalists and corporate houses. The tapes led to Raja's resignation and indictment for his role in the 2G spectrum scandal, in which politicians and government officials allegedly took kickbacks in exchange for undercharging mobile telephone companies for frequency allocation licenses, which they used to create 2G spectrum subscriptions for cell phones. The alleged loss to the government was estimated at ₹3,098 crore ($4.8 billion).[17]

Other SKS board members gave similar advice, perhaps unwittingly. Sumir Chadha of Sequoia introduced me to a Hyderabad-based businessman who was part of a large conglomerate. Sumir said something akin to, "He will be able to guide you." I met the businessman, expecting him to give me strategic advice. Instead, the businessman proceeded to explain various ways of creating and channeling large cash payments to politicians. Needless to say, I abruptly ended that meeting.

I made one final attempt to solve the problem. I, along with Vijay Mahajan of BASIX, and a few other MFI leaders, tried go over the head of Reddy Subrahmanyam, even over the head of the rural development minister, to meet the ruling Congress Party Chief Minister of Andhra Pradesh, Konijeti Rosaiah. The problem was that the backlash—led by the opposition parties—was so severe that the chief minister refused to even meet with us publicly. He did not want us to come to his office, where we would be seen by the press and others. We had to go to the Taj Krishna hotel, and from there we were taken in a different car—with tinted windows—directly to the CM's house. Upon meeting the CM, we tried to explain our policy views. But it was in vain. Rosaiah was not ready to buck the populist tide.

In parallel, I was meeting—often along with other MFI heads—with bureaucrats. We tried in vain to have some reasonable dialogue about how market-based financial inclusion had a role in complementing government efforts. But the bureaucrats had ideological blinders. There was the "loot and scoot" Reddy Subrahmanyam with his statist views. He was patient, polished, and subtle in his replies. But intractable. Others were less polished, though no less dogmatic. Budithi Rajasekhar, the head of SERP, for example, was a firebrand. In one particularly heated discussion, Rajasekhar—visibly enraged—said he would not rest until I was in jail. He looked right into my eyes. I held his gaze, hand on my chin, but I stayed silent and expressionless, refraining from taking the bait.

One thing I will say about these senior bureaucrats is—while I did not agree with their statist dogmatism—they were not personally corrupt. There were never any intermediaries who approached me on their behalf asking for a bribe. No fixers in the middle. In fact, in some moments, I even admired their ideological passion. It is an odd statement, I know. But the reality is there was a common commitment to trying to do what was best for the poor. It's just that our prescriptions were radically different.

I think Reddy Subrahmanyam felt this odd kinship as well. In one of our one-on-one meetings, he even said something along the lines of, "I know your reputation, Vikram. Why don't you go back to who you once were?" In fact, Reddy Subrahmanyam was right about my reputation. I had sat in that same chair in front of his predecessor, Vijay Kumar, and in front of Kumar's predecessor, K. Raju, and twenty years earlier in front of their predecessor, the late Smarajit Ray. I even knew their ideological mentor, the late S. R. Sankaran, the bureaucrat known as the "People's IAS Officer." In my early days, I was in fact in sync with the ideologies of Sankaran and Ray. The wife of the late Smarajit Ray, Nandita, was even part of the founding board of SKS when we began as a nonprofit. I used to have dinner at their home and had regular meetings with Smarajit Ray, both at his office and in the field. I became friends with Ray's son and daughter-in-law.

But, of course, over my twenty years of working in India, I saw the merits of and need for a market approach, whereas Reddy Subrahmanyam represented the now outdated straightjacket ideology of his predecessors. The world had changed, but the officers sitting in those powerful bureaucrat chairs had not. Yes, we were perhaps kindred spirits in our concern about poverty. But we were on different paths. And when my path—the market-based approach—was showing promise and threatening their turf, Reddy Subrahmanyam and his colleagues had to assert themselves. And they did.

Politicians and the bureaucrats struck their final blow on live television. Vatti Vasant Kumar of the ruling Congress Party made an official statement—widely televised on a live broadcast—telling borrowers not to repay loans and instead "beat up MFI loan officers with brooms." Key bureaucrats stood alongside the Rural Development Minister when he made the statement.

After the incendiary statement made by Kumar on live TV, the situation in the field became untenable. Loan officers were brutally beaten; our branch offices were viciously attacked. The day after the broadcast, on October 14, 2010, the AP cabinet hurriedly passed the Microfinance Ordinance (which later became an Act).[18] The ordinance required MFIs to obtain government permission for each new loan, which effectively ended the estimated 500,000 loans per month given by MFIs in Andhra Pradesh. As explained earlier, the government's refusal to give permission for MFI loans under this ordinance further weakened borrowers' already shaky confidence.

At SKS, we actually tried to test the new governmental loan approval process and submitted 100,000 loan applications the first week the Ordinance was in place. Several months later, with extensive lobbying by borrowers (that SKS helped organize), about seventy loans were approved. Whereas before the ordinance a borrower would say she needed $200 to buy a cow for her family and, within seven days, she would have that money to buy her cow, now it would take a borrower months of hands-on lobbying to get a loan reviewed, and even then only a miniscule .0007 percent—less than one hundredth of 1 percent—of loans submitted finally were approved.

Adding to their blossoming concerns about the state of MFIs, borrowers witnessed loan officers being brutally beaten and sometimes jailed because the ordinance allowed any government official to issue an arrest warrant. In fact, more than a hundred loan officers from a wide range of MFIs were thrown in rural jails without the possibility of bail after the ordinance was implemented. Rural Indian jails are horrible places. Reeking with the stench of urine, they are filthy and crowded. With no chairs, prisoners typically sit on cold cement floors, and the rural Indian police were notorious for beating prisoners. One SKS loan officer was in jail for more than three weeks before being arraigned. While the eighteen-year-old was waiting in jail, his father suffered a heart attack, and the young man was not allowed to attend his father's funeral.

In light of this assault by the state on microfinance, borrowers soon stopped repaying en masse. It was the reverse of a run on a bank. If people think a bank is going to close, they race to pull their money out of savings accounts. In this case, borrowers saw the signs that MFIs were going to be shut down. The natural impulse was to stop paying loans. Any of us would do the same. In a matter of weeks, SKS repayment rates plunged from 98 percent to 11 percent in Andhra Pradesh. For the industry, it meant ₹7,200 crore (or $1.5 billion based on exchange rates in 2011)[19] in loans held by six million borrowers in Andhra Pradesh were at risk. SKS's share was $280 million in loans held by about two million borrowers.[20]

The irony of the actions of the AP government is that they did not actually have the right to regulate MFIs, at least not finance companies that were licensed by the Reserve Bank of India, which included the large players, such as SKS, Spandana, Share, and BASIX. The only MFIs the state could legally regulate were non-RBI-licensed entities, or the rogue MFIs.

The MFIs asked the High Court for a stay order. The court agreed to look into the case but asked the MFIs to comply with the ordinance in the interim. Effectively, it left the ordinance in force. The government—and more crucially, political thugs who were beating up loan officers in the field—were emboldened. Eventually, the case went to the Supreme Court, but it was a moot question after the several months it took to get on the docket. By that time, repayment rates in Andhra Pradesh had plummeted and MFIs were already writing off unpaid loans.

Soon after the Act, the RBI established a subcommittee of its board to recommend regulations for MFIs. It was chaired by a member of the board, Yezdi Hirji Malegam, who was the former president of the Institute of Chartered Accountants of India. But it would take the committee more than a year to make its recommendation and the RBI another year to issue official circulars, too late to avert the backlash as it was emerging in 2010.

In one last-ditch effort, I decided to travel to New Delhi to try to meet with Rahul Gandhi, who had risen to the position of General Secretary of the Congress Party of India, which was in power in the central government. Of course, practically all of India had been following the AP microfinance backlash. The optics were not good. The stories were out about the rash of suicides and over-indebtedness. The political capital it would take to fight against this backlash was great. But I was hoping that one of India's young and open-minded politicians would have the courage to act. After all, Gandhi had spent a day visiting an SKS field site with me in 2005. He had seen SKS operate in its early days and had been interested in microfinance because it could accelerate financial inclusion. He had even disbursed a loan with his own hands.

I flew to New Delhi and, first thing in the morning, went to Gandhi's home office on Tughlak Lane. I went through the outer security gate, into the waiting room, and gave my business card to the receptionist. Then I sat down, and I sat, and I sat, and I sat.

Periodically, I would check in with the receptionist, and she confirmed that my card had been given to his assistant. They knew I was there. I would simply have to wait until they called. As I sat, I saw others going in through the second, inside, security scanner and coming back out again after they had finished their meetings. It was reminiscent of my early days at SKS where I would sit—sometimes for hours—waiting to meet with a district collector.

After a few hours, I finally asked if I could speak with Gandhi's chief of staff or anyone of the people who had accompanied Gandhi when he'd spent the day with me. I was told that none of them were available. By mid-afternoon, the receptionist asked me to come to her desk, and she handed me the phone. A junior member of Gandhi's team spoke with me and apologized that it would not be possible to meet Gandhi or anyone from his staff. At this point, I was exasperated and hungry, and blurted out, "What the hell is this? You can't even offer me a cup of tea?" The staff member apologized. I gave the phone back to the receptionist and sat down, trying to decide if I should finally give up and leave.

Soon after, one of the housekeeping staff—dressed in a crisp all-white uniform—brought me a cup of tea. I drank it and left.

As I left Rahul Gandhi's house, I reflected on the events of the last few weeks. I had landed back in Hyderabad from New York City on September 23, following my debate with Muhammad Yunus at the Clinton Global Summit plenary session. SKS's market capitalization had hovered around $2.2 billion at that time. I was about to do a tour for my first book, *A Fistful of Rice: My Unexpected Quest to End Poverty Through Profitability*, with scheduled appearances at places at which I had always dreamed of speaking, such as the CNBC Power Lunch, the Commonwealth Club, and the World Bank. And then everything had turned upside down.

The political backlash had grown from a muffled ticking in the background to a full-blown explosion. Soon after the October MFI Act, SKS repayment rates in Andhra Pradesh plunged from

98 percent to 11 percent. Field staff were beaten and jailed; branch offices were ransacked, with doors broken and computers smashed. SKS lost more than a billion dollars in the value of its market capitalization in two months, with its share price plunging from its mid-September peak of ₹1,491.50 ($33) to ₹673 ($15) by mid-November. What took me thirteen years to build was about to collapse in an onslaught that took about two months.

Eventually, the microfinance industry received only 10 percent of loans that were due and wrote off the remaining ₹6,500 crore of loans in Andhra Pradesh, which was $1.2 billion based on exchange rates in March 2013 when the final write-offs took place. Many MFIs went bankrupt and closed shop. Six large MFIs had to go into corporate debt restructuring, a precursor to bankruptcy. SKS's share price ultimately dropped to an all-time low of ₹54.40 ($1), virtually wiping out its entire value. SKS went from a peak market capitalization of $2.2 billion in September 2010 to an eventual low of $80 million by June 2012. SKS survived because it was sitting on the cash it had just raised in the IPO; SKS used that to repay banks for loans that borrowers were not repaying. If not for those IPO funds, we also may well have been on the fast path to bankruptcy.[21]

Industry-wide, upwards of 35,000 field staff jobs were lost, most in Andhra Pradesh, but there were also jobs lost in other states because the sector had to scale back throughout the country.[22] SKS had the biggest layoffs, eventually letting go of 15,000 field staff.[23] Naturally, shareholders lost a lot of money.

But the biggest losers were our members. After the MFI Act, there were no more loans in AP. Economists who examined consumption data a year before and a year after the ban found that the average household expenditure dropped by 19 percent in AP compared to those who continued to have access to microfinance in the rest of the country. Notably, the largest decrease was in expenditure on food. As of this writing, the region—which has split into two states—has had virtually no private sector microfinance loans. The state government has tried to substitute government lending, but the government's own studies show that poor borrowers have gone back to predatory moneylenders.[24] In addition, the nearly six million borrowers who did not pay back their loans because of the backlash have been declared defaulters on the now more robust credit bureaus that have emerged. Those six million can no longer access formal finance, unless the lender ignores the negative credit bureau reports that are now attached to their names.

The one saving grace was that the microfinance crisis did not spread to other states in India. MFIs, including SKS, were able to continue operating in other states in India, albeit at a slower pace because banks radically slowed down lending across the country until they were confident there would be no contagion.

Eventually, the industry hobbled back. Oddly, relative to others, SKS ended up benefiting from the crisis. While SKS no doubt was hurt and wrote off $280 million in loans, because it had just completed the IPO, SKS had cash to repay banks.[25] Therefore, it did not have to turn to corporate debt restructuring. Most of the other large players did, which made them less competitive because banks who owned their debt forced them to recover more than they lent in new loans; it was, in effect, a winding-down operation. Meanwhile, the rogue operators were wiped out, which was actually the main positive outcome of the backlash. From an SKS perspective, we were among the last ones standing and eventually could come back. Others who benefited were those MFIs that did not have a presence in AP. This ranged from Bandhan—which was in the northeast of India, and which soon became the largest MFI in India—to a handful of players in other states, such as Ujjivan, Equitas, and Janalakshmi, all of which had some presence in AP, but not significant enough to lead to corporate debt restructuring.

Despite the eventual recovery of the industry, great damage had been done not only in terms of borrowers losing access to finance, loans written off, dollars lost, and jobs eliminated, but also in terms of the reputation of the industry. In the immediate analysis, the cause and effect was simple. Because of the IPO, politicians understood, for the first time, how profitable SKS was, and they asked for bribes—indirectly through brokers and media companies. I refused to pay those bribes, and they responded by destroying the microfinance industry in AP. But complicating that simple calculus was the recognition that something had, indeed, gone wrong with the microfinance industry. Mistakes that we had made—in terms of process dilution that led to over-indebtedness—gave a foothold to corrupt politicians, their political thugs, strong-arming moneylenders, extortionist local-language media, and bureaucrats entrenched in statist ideology. Yes, those vested interests brought the industry to virtual collapse—but it was the industry's mistakes that gave them a foothold.

CHAPTER 16

CULPRIT NUMBER THREE?

Was SKS also a culprit? Was I?

So far, I have talked about the issues in the industry: a slew of fly-by-night MFIs jumped into the sector and ran amok, and a new breed of banker-led MFIs cut short group training. These things led to tragic, unintended consequences.

But I have conveniently sidestepped any mention of SKS being at fault. In my mind, that just was not possible. SKS was above the rest. I had carefully cultivated the company for more than a decade before handing it over to new leadership. During that time, SKS had set the standard for best practices. We could not be at fault.

I was wrong. I came to realize how wrong I was almost by accident. In November 2010 MFIN, the industry association, hired an independent researcher, Davuluri Venkateswarlu, to determine whether the series of suicides had been the result of over-indebtedness of borrowers. We needed hard evidence to counter the Andhra Pradesh government. Davuluri's report would come after the October Microfinance Ordinance had jolted the industry, of course, but the hope was that the central government, the Reserve Bank of India, or even the Supreme Court of India would step in. I had known Davuluri for years, ever since I had moved to India in 1990. An anthropologist trained at the University of Hyderabad, Davuluri had been conducting research in those years that exposed the abusive practices of using child labor to pick cotton. He was a solid academic with an impeccable reputation. We had an easy familiarity and respect for one another.

On a Thursday afternoon in January 2011, I received a phone call from Davuluri. "I need to meet with you privately, before I present my report to MFIN," he told me. "You need to hear the audiotapes we have of these borrowers."

Why did he want to meet with me privately, in advance? I thought to myself. Did he want to ask me for a bribe to alter his findings, in the same way that the local-language media had been trying to get payments from me in exchange for not running trumped-up stories of suicides? It was a paranoid thought, I know. But at that time, I felt like I could not trust anyone outside of my colleagues at SKS. Nonetheless, I gave Davuluri the benefit of the doubt and agreed to meet with him.

We met a few days later, at the SKS office in Hyderabad. He came with two researchers. January is the cool season in Hyderabad, its weather like a perfect New England summer day, and I had spent that Sunday morning as I often did, enjoying time with my son. After we had lunch, I walked into our six-floor office building. My back-corner office was next to our stately boardroom, and it was in the boardroom where I sat with Davuluri. Our CEO, Rao, and my key aide, Sivani Shankar, joined us.

Davuluri is a lean, weathered academic with a slightly sunken face whose upper lip is brushed with a thin mustache, a common trait among Indian men. He is gentle and soft-spoken. He ran a small research group, GLOCAL, and he and his staff had traveled from Hyderabad to the rural parts of Andhra Pradesh to interview family members of individuals who had committed suicide.

He started to play the recordings of SKS borrowers, prefacing each recording with a brief description of the family background.

Then he played an excerpt of the tape. Davuluri's researchers had simply asked people to speak about what had happened and why. These family members spoke of over-indebtedness, pressure from their group members to pay, public shaming, verbal abuse, and even threats of physical attacks and sexual violence. Davuluri had brought with him tapes of seventeen cases of borrowers who had received loans from SKS; they had also taken loans from multiple other MFIs.

When he first started playing the recordings, the defensiveness I had felt since the initial newspaper stories kicked in. Despite that defensiveness, I listened. There was the single mother, whose husband had passed away, leaving her to raise four children on her own. She had taken loans from SKS and other MFIs as well as from a local moneylender. With little income to manage her household expenditures and loan repayments and facing pressure from group members as well as the local moneylender, she jumped into a local pond in the village. Unable to swim, she drowned.

Davuluri stopped the tape. The other two researchers looked at me, and one of them asked, "Can't you even give her one extra day to make the payment!?" I started to explain that wasn't how it was supposed to happen in the model SKS adopted from the Grameen Bank. "We train borrowers that they have to help each other out in times of hardship," I said. "The group pressure is only to be used when someone has the money and refuses to pay—a willful default."

Davuluri played another tape.

An SKS borrower described how fellow group members had stopped her from bringing her young son, weak with diarrhea, to the hospital, demanding that she first make her loan payment. She said the other borrowers, who could not get any new loans until she paid, told her that if she wanted to die, they would bring her pesticide. She drank the pesticide but survived.

After listening to that recording and the anguish in the voice of that woman, I did not try to defend. The fact that she was an actual borrower, speaking firsthand about harassment from other members, made it even more real for me. I needed to hear more.

Davuluri played an excerpt of another tape. I listened. He played more: tape 3, tape 4, tape 5, 6, 7, . . . 17. I listened and tried to absorb what I had heard.

There was no denying the authenticity of the voices.

"If this is true, I have to resign." There was silence among the half-dozen people in the boardroom. As I looked around, I could hear my own breath. The three researchers looked at me. Sivani looked at me, and then looked away. Rao—his lips pursed—looked down.

In the lengthy silence after I spoke those words, what was running through my mind was, *How could this have happened?* How could a company that I had painstakingly curated over a decade to be focused on the member, focused on the poor women to whom we lent, how could my company have done this? What went wrong?

Until that meeting with Davuluri, I interpreted every piece of information as confirmation of a conspiracy against us. I had no reason not to. I knew the system that we adopted from the Grameen Bank had a series of mechanisms to ensure against over-indebtedness. Then there were the statistics, mentioned earlier, that the number of suicides among microfinance borrowers was in line with statistical averages of other regions. Then Rao gave me a report from the field that exonerated us. Even if there were suicides linked to MFIs, I'd felt that those cases could be attributed to rogue MFIs using their traditional strong-arm tactics or—worst case—new-breed MFIs led by former bankers.

The meeting with Davuluri was really the first time that someone credible gave me an alternative view. Before that, everyone had an ulterior motive. Local-language media and politicians that were trying to extort us. Bureaucrats who wanted to get rid of us. So, I'd defended SKS, and defended, and defended. I gave newspaper interviews, wrote op-eds, and spoke on television. I was the most vocal and the fiercest defender of the industry. That is, until that Sunday in January with Davuluri.

―――――――

I had a restless sleep that Sunday night. First thing Monday morning, I asked our internal audit team to give me a report about the seventeen cases in which SKS was implicated. I explained to Rao that I was unsatisfied with the reports I had received from him and that I wanted our internal audit team to determine if we had responsibility for these tragedies.

Meanwhile, that week, I went to Davuluri's office, taking along Sivani, and listened to the full recordings. Davuluri had played excerpts during our Sunday meeting. This next meeting was long. For the whole day, Sivani and I listened to the full tapes of the tragic accounts of how people took their lives after falling into deep mounds of debt. By the end of the meeting, I was convinced that SKS had done something wrong in at least several of the cases.

By the end of that week, I received the internal audit report. It exonerated SKS and echoed the explanations earlier provided by Rao and the management team—that the seventeen deaths of SKS borrowers were not suicides, but were, in fact, caused by other issues, such as a heart attack or domestic violence. I began to wonder how independent our internal audit team really was. Technically, internal audit reported to the board, but in reality the team was housed in the same headquarters as Rao and was under his administrative purview.

I began to doubt whether I was getting accurate information. I would have to find out the truth myself. Given the political climate, I could not go the field myself. And, to ensure independence, I did not want to use any of the SKS field team. I turned to an independent nonprofit, Guardians Human and Civil Rights Forum, led by Rajender Khanna, who has the same last name—but was not related to—our board member Tarun Khanna. I know this sounds absurd, asking a third party to investigate the practices of the very company I had founded and of which I was chairperson of the board. But I needed to learn the truth. I needed to know what was happening. Was information being purposely withheld? Or was Rao also not fully aware of what was going on in the field?

I met with Khanna in mid-January, about ten days after Davuluri initially played the audio tapes for me. I asked Khanna to investigate the seventeen cases of suicides that involved SKS members, including traveling to these rural, remote places in Andhra Pradesh to video-tape interviews with the surviving family members. I wanted to hear them tell their stories, unfiltered.

There were four people aware of what I was doing: myself, Sivani Shankar, our Executive VP for Facilities and Administration Ramesh Vautrey, and Rao. Though Rao was aware, I told Khanna to give the reports directly to me first, so I could ensure they were authentic. I received the reports one at a time, as they were completed. Khanna would bring them personally and hand them over to me in my office. After viewing them, I gave them to Ramesh, who kept them in a safe. Typically, Khanna sent out teams of three people, one person to ask questions and two others to record videos.

By late February, I had the full findings of the seventeen cases. Each individual case had a detailed file composed of two parts. First, there were the videos, recordings lasting anywhere from one to as long as thirty minutes. Second, there were the written reports Khanna and his team compiled.

The videos were heartbreaking to watch. I first viewed them in early 2011, and I watched them again in 2017 as I wrote this book. Each time, I was saddened by the anguish of the victims' family members. I was also outraged when I realized how the microfinance lending system had utterly and completely broken down. Each victim had multiple loans. None of the victims had used loans for income-generating activities—whether loans from SKS or other MFIs. In some instances, there seemed to have been no group training at all.

And in all cases, what was supposed to have been group support had morphed into group pressure. The pressure by fellow group members was downright abusive and struck at the core of losing izzath, the devastating loss of respect that I described earlier.

I closely examined the seventeen cases that involved SKS borrowers. SKS seemed to have played a role in seven suicides. I will describe one of those cases here without revealing names. In the aftermath of the suicides, families of victims had to deal with dozens of visitors—from politicians to the police to the media—which compounded their ordeal. The family I will describe has moved on as best as they can. I won't use their names out of respect for their privacy.

One caveat is that this particular story involves the suicide of a teenage girl, the daughter of an SKS borrower. That was not typical. Most often, the borrower took her own life. Other family members typically did not commit suicide.

Everything that could have gone wrong in this lending situation did.

The family was Madiga, the lowest subcaste within the scheduled castes of the Telangana region. They had two acres of dry land, which was of poor quality—as is typical in drought-prone Telangana. The couple mainly earned their livelihood as day laborers, working in the fields of large landowners. The family had three children and had taken loans of ₹52,000 (about $1,155) to pay for wedding expenses and dowry for their eldest daughter. The loans were from four MFIs, including SKS. (I won't single out the other companies by name. All the major MFIs working in Andhra Pradesh were lenders to several of the various borrowers who took their own lives.) In addition to MFI loans, the family took an additional ₹60,000 (about $1,335) in loans from friends and family and from a local landlord. To pay off the loan from the landlord, the husband of the borrower had to work for the landlord as bonded labor for one year.

It appears that the borrower did not undergo any group training. It is not clear whether the other MFIs involved had mandated group training for potential borrowers. SKS did, but it appears that either the SKS group training had been diluted so that the borrower had not understood the requirement to use loans for income-generating activities, or maybe the borrower did not even participate in group training.

Since the husband was not earning any wages during the period of his bond, the loan repayments had to be made from the earnings of the borrower. Both of her other two children—the second child (the daughter who committed suicide) and a younger son—were in school and not yet earning income. Her weekly repayments probably totaled ₹800 or ₹900 ($17 or $20) for three of the loans, spread over three days of the week. In addition, one MFI loan required a monthly repayment of about ₹1,500 ($35). So her monthly repayments totaled ₹4,000 to ₹5,000 ($90 to $110). As a daily laborer, earning perhaps ₹50 ($1.10) a day, maybe ₹100 ($2.20) a day in peak season, she would have been able to earn ₹1,500 ($35) or at best ₹3,000 ($65) a month. It would have been impossible for her to service the loans. To make repayments, the couple started selling their assets—gold jewelry and household items—as well as borrowing from friends and family.

The peer-lending group and village center, in a properly executed MFI operation, would not have allowed her to use the loan for a wedding or to take such large loans from multiple MFIs. If the group failed to do this, the loan officer should have noticed the breakdown in process and halted the loan. Regardless, if the loan had somehow slipped through the controls in place, the fellow members should have been helping her out with repayments in a shortfall situation.

Rather than providing support, the group pressured the borrower to make repayments because approval of the future loans of other group members was contingent on her repayment. The borrower described a large number of fellow group members coming to her home and verbally abusing her. She wanted to avoid losing izzath. So on one particular day, when SKS's weekly installment happened to fall on the same day as the monthly installment of another MFI, she and her husband went to another village to borrow money from a relative. Since the borrower was absent from the weekly lending meeting and the payment was missing, the SKS loan officer sent group members to her house to collect, an egregious violation of SKS policy. Of course, what should have happened and didn't is that the other members of her group should have jointly come up with her repayment and then collected from her afterward. If the borrower had a genuine hardship (as clearly she did), the group, as guarantors of the loan, had the responsibility to continue to make her repayments.

When group members arrived at her home, the borrower, of course, was not there, but her daughter was. The SKS group members brought this teenage girl to the meeting, another egregious violation of SKS policy. At the meeting, SKS group members began scolding and cursing her, not an uncommon occurrence among adults in villages, but not something to direct toward a teenage girl. She gave them the money she had in hand. But the group members kept pressuring her to get the rest of the repayment. She frantically called her parents from a pay phone in the village. They would take more time to return with the payment. In the meantime, the girl could not bear the abuse. No doubt, the economic stress that the family was under along with the taunts and jeers on that day were more than she could withstand. The girl returned home and wrote a note to her parents: *Work hard and earn money. Do not take loans.* She then drank pesticide and died.

I cannot convey with words the depth of my sorrow.

———————————

The other cases are also heartbreaking. Through the trust set up with SKS sweat equity, I have provided financial support to these seven families. I did this anonymously—through trusted colleagues—in the initial years. Now that enough time has passed since those tragic events, I have started meeting with the families personally, beginning in 2017.

Whatever support is provided to them, it will never be enough. Every time I meet with a family, my heart breaks again. I cannot imagine the loss. Nonetheless, when we meet, we do not dwell on the past. The focus is on the future. When I met in 2017 with the parents and brother of the teenage girl described above, we talked about what was going on right then. I asked them: How was the harvest that year? How was their eldest daughter getting along at her in-laws' home? I asked the brother: How was school going? What subjects did he like the best?

Likewise, back in 2011, in the immediate aftermath of watching the videos, I focused on the future. What corrective steps could we take to ensure this would never happen again? As a starting point, I wanted to understand how the process lapses that led to the tragedies could have happened. It seemed that all the safety measures we'd put in place to prevent over-indebtedness had been ignored. The question for me was, were these cases unique in terms of how SKS staff operated in the field? Was there simply a small number of staff who had flouted our standard operating procedures? Or were such problems more widespread?

To find out, I demanded meetings with the field staff and managers responsible for the regions where these suicides had taken place. Unfortunately, in the wake of the crisis, many of the staff responsible for managing the groups and centers that threatened and harassed borrowers to take these drastic actions had fled. They were nowhere to be found, and we could not track them down. The tendency to flee had partly to do with the fact that, throughout the AP microfinance backlash, aggressive police officers and the politicians behind them were arresting field staff and throwing them in jail. More than one hundred microfinance field staff had been jailed in the latter half of October, including SKS staff.

In many instances, our loan officers—often the sons and daughters of our borrowers—had done nothing wrong. So perhaps the field staff involved in these seven cases had fled for fear of imprisonment. Or perhaps they fled with guilty consciences.

In late February 2011, I—along with Rao, Sivani, and a couple of other executive managers—met with those staff that we were able to find. Some were district managers, a skip level away from the field staff; others were field staff working in the same branch but in neighboring villages. During the day-long meeting, I probed about the events leading to the deaths. In many cases, the staff did not have firsthand knowledge of what had occurred. But I also probed deeply about training. Where did the staff get their training? When? From whom? Did they understand how group responsibility worked? Did they understand how to train the borrowers in group responsibility? How did they conduct members' training? What was the day one curriculum? Why was it important to use the cooperation game? And so on.

I wanted to find out not only what had happened in each specific case but also if these incidents were indicative of a larger systemic problem. That is, was this a situation of a handful of rogue field staff ignoring procedure, or was there a fundamental process failure?

In the end, there was evidence to support my initial assessment. SKS seemed to have played a role in the seven cases. I did not find evidence to suggest that the staff put strong-arm pressure on borrowers, but they nonetheless sat by and perhaps even encouraged borrowers to put pressure on a defaulting member.

Moreover, I was shocked to learn how little the field staff understood about group training. They did not know the curriculum, let alone understand the logic behind each carefully curated aspect of the group training modules. The system of training borrowers, which was a foundation of everything we did at SKS, seemed to have broken down. That heightened my worry. I was also troubled by Rao's seemingly indifferent attitude during the meeting. He attended because I insisted, but he showed little interest—constantly shuffling in and out of the room.

I dug into the question of why field staff had a limited understanding of how to train borrowers. I spent the first half of March poring through documents to decipher the last couple years of SKS operation. From the time I'd transitioned out of the CEO role, SKS management had gradually reduced their attention to products, pro-cesses, and systems that were the core of SKS—especially during a period of unbridled growth in late 2009 to 2010. For example, in 2008 to 2009, the core group training was reduced from five days to four. In 2009, management decided to allow a loan officer to train three groups at a time (fifteen women instead of five), further water-ing down the training delivered.

This reduction in training actually occurred during the time an independent study by EDA Rural Systems, which we had commis-sioned at my insistence, said we should increase, *not reduce*, our train-ing days because of new products, particularly insurance products.

In addition, I reviewed the incentive structure, which revealed that nearly all field incentives related to quality of groups had been eliminated. Only growth targets were being incentivized. Moreover, even the parameter related to branch grading (which had a small component on group training) was eliminated by 2010. The param-eter of Loan Utilization Checks—which are visits to ensure loans are used for income-generating activities—did not even figure in the incentive structure.

The pinnacle of this dilution of processes occurred during the "Incentive Galore" drive of December 2009 to March 2010 (just prior to the SKS IPO), which, according to Rao, was initiated to exceed the growth targets of the company. During this drive, field staff were encouraged to form more than sixty-seven groups a month in order to receive a package of consumer goods, including a "TV+Fridge+WM+Mixer+DVD+10Gms gold." The value of these items was five to ten times the average monthly salary of field staff, giving them a tremendous push toward unbridled growth. Moreover, even branch managers, who were supposed to test the quality of group formation, were also incentivized along these lines, leaving no check for quality of training and group formation. There was no maker–checker dichotomy.

Everyone was a maker, and everyone's incentives were pegged to giving loans, not checking whether the proper processes were followed. The result was that SKS gave a staggering number of prizes to loan officers and branch managers. Such rewards were given to 5,211 loan officers; some received multiple items. The total was 8,800 televisions, refrigerators, gold coins, mixers, washing machines, and DVDs as rewards in more than 300 districts nationwide.

During the three-month contest period, 2,910 loan officers formed sixty or more groups (translating to about twenty groups a month). One loan officer formed 273 groups in three months. In normal course, with an undiluted training, a loan officer would typically be able to form a maximum of two (perhaps three) groups a week or eight (at best, twelve) a month, for a maximum of thirty-six in three months. The contest numbers were a sure indication that groups had been formed without due consideration for the poor communities in which we were introducing microfinance. These village women were intelligent and motivated but also semiliterate and completely unfamiliar with lending concepts. It was clear that without sufficient training, many of these group members would not have fully grasped the idea and intention of the peer support foundational to our lending processes. Instead, group support morphed into undue group pressure—that is, coercive recovery tactics, likely involving shaming and threatening—that had tragic outcomes.

The more stories I heard about how borrowers were being trained and how SKS employees were being compensated, the more I understood that the problems with SKS Microfinance were not just those of a few rotten eggs. We needed to fix the foundation. We needed to get back to basics. And the microfinance industry needed to do that as well.

In retrospect, I feel like I should have figured all of this out sooner. I was the founder and chairperson of the largest MFI in India. I was a founding member of MFIN. Before our IPO, I had publicly voiced my concerns about overlending. I had enough firsthand knowledge of microfinance to understand the problems of cutting short the group formation process; no one in India was better equipped than I was to recognize and address the issue. I had ample opportunities to gain field-level insight; no one had more access to grassroots field staff in Andhra Pradesh than I did. But I did not see the scope of the crisis threatening the industry.

Was it that I could not see it? Or that I did not see it? Or that I did not want to see it?

Was I a culprit too?

In a postcrisis discussion with our investor Vinod Khosla, he explained that entrepreneurs who have had huge success in their first endeavors often suffer from confirmation bias. Such entrepreneurs have struggled to succeed against all odds, and when they do, they receive adulation and accolades. That happened to me. Everyone told me over and over again how remarkable I was and SKS was, so I ended up believing that nothing could go wrong. Such entrepreneurs interpret data in a way that confirms preconceived views. When things go terribly wrong, we are blindsided. I know I was.

I had a blind spot. I suffered from confirmation bias. Throughout the first eleven years of SKS, we always hit numbers that were too good to be true. In fact, they were true. We had great processes and a talented team, and we worked incredibly hard. My blind spot was in thinking that the same mode of operation and philosophy toward our endeavor had continued, which allowed me to accept without question another period of "too good to be true" numbers. I assumed that the same quality of process remained in place. I never imagined that those processes had changed. I also failed to take into account the broader, hyper-competitive environment, which had not existed when I was running SKS.

Was I responsible? Was I the real culprit? Professor Yunus feels I was. He made this statement about me:

> The key is that the whole thing was triggered by SKS. They were the ones who kind of overdid things in a big way. The aggressiveness that it brought into the picture created all the problems.[1]

Professor Yunus may be right. After all, I brought in the venture capitalists. I handed SKS over to commercial bankers. Then I left, thinking everything would go smoothly.

On the other hand, there's no way I could have anticipated fly-by-night loan sharks jumping into the sector and donning the garb of microfinance. I had no way of knowing that a new breed of banker-led MFIs would start diluting group training or that SKS would blindly mimic them. Moreover, I had left the CEO role at SKS in December 2008, and it was during the two years since my departure that SKS management diluted group training without my knowledge. I was literally 8,000 miles away, in Chicago, for a year. And when I came back to India, I focused on the IPO preparations and not day-to-day management. Besides, I was busy, finally, being a dad—trying to make up for lost time with my son.

Seven of our borrowers' families suffered the tragic loss of a family member, and who knows how many borrowers were struggling under the weight of over-indebtednesss. Was SKS the third culprit? Was I the third culprit? Sometimes I feel like I was. Sometimes I feel like I wasn't. What I do know is that things went horribly, horribly wrong.

CHAPTER 17

SANGAM MITRA

In the wake of what I learned from Davuluri's and Rajender Khanna's investigations, and after my meetings with SKS managers and other local staff, I knew something had to be done—and fast. In my mind, this meant a return to the principles that had made us great, a return to the basics of microfinance that characterized SKS in its first decade.

In March 2011, I recruited a two-person team to help formulate a plan. They had to come from outside of existing operations. Considering the inaccuracies now apparent in the reports on suicides that had been prepared by insiders, I recognized the possibility that people within SKS were giving me false information. I was able to find two very talented rising stars. One was a recent graduate of the Tata Institute of Social Sciences. The other was a recent SKS recruit from the Institute of Rural Management, Anand; she was working in our business development group at the time and thus not directly involved in field operations. Working intensively and on a tight time line, we came up with a plan.

The first part of the plan involved a complete cessation of lending for two months so we could pause and get back on track. The analogy I used was the cyanide murders involving Tylenol that happened in

1982 in the United States. I was in high school at the time. Someone had laced Tylenol capsules with cyanide, resulting in seven deaths, including that of a twelve-year-old girl. Johnson & Johnson, the maker of Tylenol, swiftly addressed the key issues surrounding the crisis and changed not only their company but the pharmaceutical industry for the better. Johnson & Johnson recalled the existing bottles of Tylenol—that had a retail value of $100 million—and placed ads in the national media advising individuals not to consume any of its pain relief products. Next, Johnson & Johnson invented the triple-sealed tamper-proof bottle, which is now ubiquitous. Though at the time of the scare the company's market share collapsed, dropping from 35 percent to 8 percent, it rebounded in less than a year, a move credited to the company's prompt and aggressive reaction.[1] Within several years of introducing the tamper-proof package, Tylenol had the highest market share for over-the-counter pain medicine in the United States. Today, no one thinks twice about taking Tylenol or giving it to their children. I recognize that the Tylenol example is not parallel. Whereas it was a malicious act to lace Tylenol with cyanide, that was clearly not the case in microfinance. I use the example nonetheless because it represents the type of major overhaul I thought we needed at SKS Microfinance. We had the potential to change not just our company, but also the industry.

What was the tamper-proof bottle for microfinance? In the absence of a credit score or even a sufficiently robust credit bureau for microfinance (which would take India several more years to develop), I proposed a plan to spend $10 million to create *sangam mitras*, which means "friend" (*mitra*) of the "lending group" (*sangam*). These would be financial counselors who would make sure members weren't getting into too much debt and were using their loans for income-generating activities. The idea was that the sangam mitras would work alongside our loan officers, called sangam managers. The sangam mitras would ensure that sangam managers were delivering the level of rigorous, methodical group training needed. In fact, my original idea was to transform all sangam managers to sangam mitras, but at the time we had about 20,000 field staff, and I knew that would be a daunting task. The model of a single field person who would have the responsibility for both managing loans and ensuring responsible lending—something that we had in our first decade—would be hard to revive. So, I proposed we create a parallel cadre of 4,000 sangam mitras to work alongside sangam managers, at a ratio of 1:4.

The idea was to cull the 4,000 staff who were the best at quality group formation and have them lead the remaining 16,000 staff through a retraining in the first month and then, in the second month, lead all staff in retraining every single member in each and every group—more than seven million members across the country. My two recruits and I planned out each step, using detailed pivot table Excel spreadsheets.

No doubt, my plan was drastic. But I felt we needed to reclaim our original ethos and standards. We needed to re-educate all our members about what our responsibilities were as lenders and what their responsibilities were as borrowers, responsibilities not only to SKS Microfinance but to their peers in their village lending circles.

Of course, this back-to-basics plan—along with the cessation of lending for two months—was going to cost us. The retraining plan would cost $10 million and with lost revenue for two months, we could expect a loss of $15 to $20 million. These were steep numbers, to be sure, but, just as Tylenol took losses in the short term to launch safety reforms and ultimately win back public confidence, I felt we needed to address head-on the stresses imposed on our borrowers and likewise assure the public that we were taking action.

In the process of researching this plan, my two-person team and I discovered major issues with our insurance products. I'd had ongoing concerns about insurance, and some of the comments on Davuluri's tapes had confirmed those concerns, but the insurance problem ran even deeper than I thought.

I had been a huge advocate of insurance for the poor. Historically, poor Indians have been almost entirely uninsured—a real impediment to moving up the economic ladder. As mentioned, an illness or a death in the family could be catastrophic. Early on, SKS had offered a term life insurance product alongside each loan. With the product built into the loan repayments, administering a claim was straightforward. When the borrower or her husband died, the claim was paid.

While term life insurance was important, we also knew that there were numerous risks besetting the poor and we wanted to develop insurance for all of them. In 2007 we started with a health insurance product. The health insurance product was especially challenging; this type of insurance brings into high relief all of the classic challenges of providing insurance. There are "moral hazards," meaning that people may change their behavior if they know they are insured; "adverse selection," where people who think they may have a problem in the future are the only ones who get insured; and fraud, people submitting bogus claims about medical conditions or medical bills.

One of the ways we initially tried to alleviate these concerns was to simply provide catastrophic health insurance, that being coverage for when someone falls life-threateningly ill or has an accident. Yet even then we ran into problems with discerning just what "life-threatening" meant. Imagine trying to explain the outlines and contours of a health insurance policy to one of our illiterate, rural members. Let's say you get past the idea of not covering pre-existing conditions. How do you then go on to explain the difference between illnesses that were pre-existing and those that are new? The problems were so difficult that when I'd raised these issues in front of the board back in 2009, the board agreed to discontinue health insurance after the pilot stage.

We also offered whole-life insurance, life insurance that pays a benefit on the death of the insured and also accumulates a cash value. Whole-life insurance premiums are typically higher than term life insurance, and they also carry a surrender value if the buyer decides to discontinue paying premiums.

For the whole-life product, as described earlier, we worked closely with Bajaj Allianz to develop a product that suited the needs of the poor: It was inexpensive (only 20 rupees, about 50 cents, per week); and it would never lapse—even if members missed payments. Normally, such a small premium to be collected from millions of members would make such a product unviable. But since our micro-finance channel already had a built-in marketing—after all, our members trusted us—and distribution mechanism, the micro-insurance product could work. Initially, it did. It worked very well—at the pilot stage and at the early roll-out stage. At the time we were ready to scale it enterprise-wide, I was transitioning out as CEO. Gurumani came on board. Rao, who had joined as COO in late 2006, had an insurance background, so I left SKS thinking the product roll-out was in good hands. It ended up being a disaster.

From the outset, there was a problem with the way whole-life insurance was presented to borrowers. Staff were explaining the product as a kind of savings account. This makes sense on its surface—you are paying money into an account for a greater reward later on. For the poor, this was attractive because banking regulations did not allow us to collect savings deposits; only full-fledged banks could do that and MFIs were not given such banking licenses.

But whole-life insurance is not a savings account; it's an insurance policy. And we had members who paid their weekly premiums and then, months later, thinking this was their savings account, wanted to take out the money they had deposited. They were, understandably, irate when they learned there would be a surrender charge, typically 30 percent—*after* a lock-in period of one year. Slowly, we were losing the goodwill and trust that we had developed over more than a decade.

In addition, the software to manage the back end was repeatedly delayed, and a team was entering data manually on Excel spreadsheets. As a result, there were significant data reconciliation issues, where there was uncertainty about claims payouts. Rao's Excel-based system was not able to provide real-time data on turnaround time (TAT), the time it takes to process claims; it was unable to even state how many claims were paid on time and how many were outstanding.

Both in individual meetings and in board meetings, I raised these issues. We had very heated board meetings over these issues. In one particularly explosive board meeting in July 2009, just after I'd returned to India to help lead the IPO, I took Rao to task for what I saw as the failure of ensuring quality of insurance products. Insurance was critically important in the lives of our members. We had a responsibility to get it right. Subsequently, the board designated fellow board member and Harvard Business School professor Tarun Khanna to write a detailed policy memo on the criteria for taking new products, such as whole-life insurance, to enterprise-wide roll-out. The hope was that such a memo would bridge the divide and we would have a way forward. Despite elegant policy memos such as this one, and despite my protestations, there continued to be problems in the field with the whole-life product. Even MFIN raised concerns, which I shared with the SKS board.

The board, however, continued to support Rao. You see, whole-life insurance was extremely profitable. We had already built the marketing and distribution channel, so costs were minimal. Moreover, with whole-life insurance policies, the distributor gets a large upfront commission (around 15 percent of the premium collected for each policy in the initial year of the policy). So rapid enterprise-wide scaling significantly boosted profits.

I was so frustrated that at our board meeting in October 2009, I blurted out, "You know, why go through all this hassle of whole-life insurance as a means of improving profitability? You can always just steal from the poor. That would be a lot easier."

I insisted that we stop the whole-life insurance initiative until we fixed the problems, while Rao continued to assure the board that everything was fine. The board conceded to allowing me to get an independent assessment done. I reached out to EDA Rural Systems, the go-to organization for microfinance assessments. EDA conducted its research and presented its findings in December 2009. The report recommended that "an additional day should be added to the compulsory group training of new members and an annual refresher training [should] be administered for old members for the purposes of providing comprehensive education on what insurance is and the terms and conditions of the product offered by SKS."

As I discovered through the research with my two-person team in 2011, it appeared that SKS had not made any corrections after the EDA report. To the contrary, SKS not only reduced training days but also discontinued other reinforcement initiatives such as Center Leader meetings, which had been discontinued in mid-2009. My hope and expectation had been that changes would be made. I was wrong.

In December 2010, the Insurance Regulatory and Development Authority (IRDA) sent us inspection reports of our practices and cited numerous violations. The IRDA report highlighted several of the problems that I had cautioned about and that EDA had documented a year earlier. The IRDA inquiries confirmed the fears I had been articulating in past board meetings. When I confronted Rao about these reports, he wrote me an email, dated December 25, 2010, that said: "Every insurance company is fined by IRDA . . . Typically it is a token fine."

In April 2011, as part of my broader inquiry into issues that had led to the problems with group training, I took a poll at our national area managers meeting. Ninety-two percent of areas reported major issues with whole-life insurance.

At that same meeting, I also uncovered a host of revelations about having cut short group training. When I expressed shock that no one had ever expressed their concerns about training, a few area managers came up to me afterward and explained that Rao would warn them before meetings that if anyone said anything negative or revealed any problems when I was present, they would be disciplined or even fired. Having seen Rao bully staff, I could imagine how a twenty-something, recent graduate area manager would be hesitant to go against Rao—especially in a public forum like a national area managers' meeting.

By mid-April, what I saw as Rao's mismanagement of insurance came back to haunt him—and SKS. On April 21, 2011, the *Hindu Business Line* carried an article with the headline "MFIs Now 'Default' on Payment of Life Insurance Claims of Poor."[2] The article reported that SKS Microfinance was "defaulting on payment of life insurance claims to some of their members." Rao's reply as paraphrased in the article: "There were 6,537 deaths among its clientele in AP during October 2010 to February 2011." The reporter went on to quote Rao: "Of this 5,455 claims were approved and 3,102 have been paid. We don't have exact data from our field staff on whether the remaining 2,253 claims are paid."[3]

In fact, it was even worse than that. While the journalists focused on the insurance inspection, I found out that our whole-life insurance software had data reconciliation issues for 2,198,373 clients out of 2,864,284 if one looked at the entire country.

The day after the news article came out, Friday, April 22, I was at the airport in Hyderabad, boarding pass in hand, waiting to board a flight to New York. I was going for half a day to be at the wedding of a close cousin of mine. I was intent on going—if only for a few hours—because over all the years I had spent in India, one of the drawbacks was that I often missed important family functions in the United States—weddings, birthdays, reunions, holidays. The wedding was on Saturday, and I was determined to be there.

As I was waiting in line to board, I received an email from Rao saying he was going to resign. I immediately called him.

When I asked him if he genuinely wanted to resign, he said, his voice softer than normal, "Yes, I am going to resign."

Because of the issues with insurance, Rao wanted to resign as CEO, a position he had held for a mere seven months.

My shoulders sank. I would not be getting on the flight.

We had pushed out Gurumani just after our initial public offering, and now, months later, his replacement was poised to resign during one of the worst crises our company had ever faced. If his intention got out, I knew there would be chaos. I needed to be present to ensure the company didn't collapse. Reluctantly, I informed the gate agent I would not be flying and went to meet with Rao at his home.

I had to turn around so immediately because SKS was now a public company. If Rao were to send a formal letter, I would have to inform the board and we would have to disclose it immediately as price-sensitive information. I could not be out of the country if that were to happen. So, I made a beeline to his house.

I asked Rao to hold off on letting the board know about his decision to resign. I told him to give me some time to get a new CEO in place and that then we would take it to the board. Rao promised to keep his intention to resign between the two of us.

I immediately started to work on a leadership transition plan. From among the executive management team, I felt that a relatively new recruit, A. V. Sateesh Kumar, was the strongest candidate. He was brought in as executive vice president to head the entire field operations. I found him to have the right blend of being both data-driven and having good instincts. He also had excellent strategic insights. What's more, he had joined SKS just before our IPO, so he had been at SKS only about two months before the series of crises hit. As such, I felt he had a fresh perspective on SKS. If there had been bad habits that had crept into SKS after I left the CEO role, Sateesh would be less likely to have picked up those bad habits. I took him into confidence about Rao's intent to resign and asked him if he would be open to taking on the role. He was.

Along with Sateesh, I put together an executive committee that included the CFO Raj and his deputy CFO, the head of human resources, and the head of administration. My plan was to work closely with this five-member team on implementation of the back-to-basics plan. As the executive committee started to take on more responsibilities, with me steering the committee, Rao started to come to the office less frequently.

My next step was to start letting the board members know about my proposed sangam mitra plan. I did not tell them about Rao's intent to resign. I wanted to make sure the executive committee was fully in charge and the sangam mitra plan fully vetted before bringing up the issue of Rao's resignation.

CHAPTER 18

BATTLE IN THE BOARDROOM

D ay by day, the executive committee was stabilizing and running day-to-day operations as Rao started to let go of all responsibilities. Meanwhile, the external environment had calmed. Since there was no microfinance activity in Andhra Pradesh, the region's politicians, bureaucrats, and the media left us alone. In January 2011, the RBI Malegam committee submitted its report. It would take time—it wasn't until June 2012 that the RBI finally accepted and implemented all the recommendations—but the fact the report was submitted was significant because everyone could see that regulations were on the horizon. It was enough to calm the heated environment. The Malegam committee recommendations included some of the 2010 guidelines from MFIN, such as restricting the number of lenders to three MFIs per borrower. The committee also recommended new provisions, such as capping interest rates.

The recommendations were not market-oriented regulations in that they stifled competition and created a barrier to entry. But in light of the Wild West microfinance environment of the previous year, replete with rogue MFIs, it was a needed step. It created some structure where there had been none. In addition, banks—which bore the brunt of the financial hit because of the need to write off about $1 billion of loans in AP, slowed lending outside of AP as well. So, the industry was in slow gear. There was finally some stability.

Internally, I focused on implementing the sangam mitra program. My first step was to publicly take responsibility. After having defended SKS for months, on Tuesday, May 11, 2012, I held a press conference and admitted to lapses in the company's operations. "There may well have been some process lapses even at SKS. So as a result of the AP Act, we have examined these systems and have taken steps to strengthen them," I said. These steps, of course, were the plans behind the sangam mitra program.

My statements were widely carried in the television and print media. *Times of India* ran a big headline, "Akula Admits to Lapses at SKS." The first line of the article read, "For the first time since the AP crisis erupted eight months ago, SKS Microfinance founder chairman Vikram Akula finally admitted that there may have been procedural lapses at India's largest microfinance player and that [the] AP MFI Act had forced it to set its house in order."[1]

Now that I had uncovered information about mistakes SKS had made, I felt I had to stand up and take accountability. It was the right thing to do—not only because I was the leader of SKS but also because I was widely seen as a leader of the microfinance movement in India.

I think many people in the industry and among the broader population appreciated my stance—many people, but not the SKS board. I did not realize how they felt at the time, but my board saw that press conference and appeared to panic. Throughout the microfinance backlash, board members seemed wary because the AP Microfinance Act specifically said that directors of an MFI could be held accountable for any violations, which meant board members could be arrested and face criminal charges. In fact, SKS board members refused to come to our corporate headquarters in Hyderabad. Since the backlash erupted, our meetings were held in Mumbai, where the board was safe from the tentacles of the AP government.

The fear was not unwarranted. In all the suicide cases involving an SKS member, Rao, as the CEO of SKS, was the one who appeared as the prime accused on the police charge sheet. As discussed earlier, the majority of these cases were falsely attributed to SKS; in the cases in which SKS genuinely had a role, it was the village member groups that had put pressure on borrowers, though perhaps with the knowledge of staff. My point is that it would not have been difficult for any AP government official to bring charges against the entire board of directors.

This was why my admission of mistakes was so troubling for them. After the press conference, I received a flurry of calls from my board members. I am sure Rao received calls as well, as the board of course had no idea that Rao had intended to resign. While the board was panicking about my press conference, I had also finalized and started circulating the sangam mitra plan, first within the management team and also within the board. Because the sangam mitra plan involved such a large expenditure and disruption to our current business, I needed board approval, so I had to wait until the next board meeting in July.

In that context, I went ahead with a long-planned three-week vacation in June. I was taking my son to the United States, his first visit back to the States in two years. Now that all the legal appeals to my custody victory in court had been completed and the Interpol notice had been removed, my son and I could finally travel without fear. Since we are both avid tennis fans, we planned to see the French Open en route to the States in the first week of June and then see Wimbledon the third week of June on our way back. More than the tennis, I wanted to give my son (and myself) a break. I had been working at breakneck speed for almost two years—first with the IPO prep and road shows and then dealing with the microfinance backlash. Meanwhile, my son had to deal with a very public custody battle and swirl of media around him. Now that the dust was settling on both fronts, we needed a respite.

Before leaving for the States, I started to sense distance between Rao and Raj and me. It was understandable in Rao's case. The rift had been created when I started digging into SKS's field operations. I assumed any tension with Raj had to do with the stress of the last eight months. In an effort to make an overture of peace, I went to some trouble to find thoughtful gifts for Rao and Raj before I left. Rao loved expensive pens, so I went to the one Montblanc store in Hyderabad—in the luxurious Taj Krishna five-star hotel—and bought him a beautiful platinum-coated pen. Raj loved single-malt scotch, so I got him a bottle of eighteen-year-old Glenlivet, which I procured from an uncle of mine—since Glenlivet is not sold in India but can only be brought in by foreign travelers. With both gifts, I included handwritten, personalized notes. Despite being upset with Rao's blunders at SKS, I did not wish him ill. I was fine with him resigning, but I wanted him to land on his feet—and would do every-thing I could to make sure he would. As for Raj, I knew we would be working together again—even more closely than before—so I wanted to be sure to bridge any distance that had crept in during the tumultuous IPO backlash.

At the French Open, my son and I watched Rafael Nadal at the Stade Roland Garros venue, and then continued on to the States to spend time with family. On the way back, as planned, we stopped in London to see the opening day of Wimbledon. We were having a wonderful trip, sharing our love of tennis. I played tennis in college, and my son was developing a passion for the game as well. For the first time in a long time, I was able to forget about microfinance and forget about India and just enjoy being a father.

Unfortunately, the respite did not last long. A few days before the Wimbledon Championships, I received an email from Sumir, requesting that I join a conference call with the board. I assumed that the board had found out about Rao's intention to resign. I drafted talking points about the sequence of events and the creation of the executive committee. I asked Sateesh Kumar, my CEO candidate, to be available for the call. I circulated his résumé in advance of the call and waited.

The call took place on a Sunday afternoon. I focused on assuring the board that there was a transition plan in place. They asked about the executive committee, and I explained how it was in place to serve as a bridge for the new CEO. I asked if they wanted me to conference in Sateesh, and Sumir said no. The call ended soon after. I hung up and did not think much more about it that day.

The following morning, en route to opening day at Wimbledon, I received another call from India, this time from Pramod Bhasin, a board member who was then CEO of a General Electric spin-off company called Genpact. He'd been the one to perhaps unwittingly suggest that we engage Nira Radia—later revealed to be a high-priced corruption "bagman"—to help with the MFI backlash. He said something along the lines of, "I speak on behalf of the board. You are to stop interfering with Rao's management of SKS."

What!?

I asked questions, and Pramod mentioned how the executive committee I had set up undermined Rao. I tried to explain that Rao had told me back in April that he intended to resign. I also explained that as executive chairperson of SKS, a position to which the Board had appointed me effective April 1, I had the authority to establish the executive committee. But Pramod did not stay on the call long. He was merely delivering a message.

Shocked, I hung up the phone. I had the sudden realization that Rao had told the board something different than what he'd told me.

My son and I went to the matches that day, but my thoughts raced back to India. Was Rao having second thoughts about resigning? Did he have a change of heart? Maybe he never intended to resign and was just setting me up. I did not know the answer, and it did not matter. Whatever the reason, while I was away, he must have woven a false narrative about my undermining him.

I canceled the remainder of our trip, and my son and I flew back to India the next day.

When I returned to the SKS office, I could immediately feel that things were different. My floor at SKS was largely composed of senior management, and when I walked around that floor, my colleagues kept their distance. No one would make eye contact. My greetings of "hello" received curt replies.

A few staff who were close to me explained what had happened. Rao had told the senior management team that the board was upset with me about the May press conference and the sangam mitra plan. He told them the board was going to ask me to resign—essentially fire me. The indirect message was that Rao would be solely in charge and that any staff that appeared to support me would eventually get fired. Of course, I am not sure exactly what Rao said or whether the message was subtle or more direct, but the staff seemed to clearly understand the message.

To help explain this to those less familiar with business in India, employees in Indian companies always make sure they manage up. That is, they curry favor with the boss, especially since the predominant model of Indian business is (or was at that time) family-run business, which means that bosses don't come and go. They tend to be family members, and they are there to stay. Staff—who are mostly middle class and for whom the loss of a job is devastating, especially in a highly competitive labor market—would not dare risk crossing the boss. Though SKS was not family-run, the culture of obsequiousness was likely still at play among the senior management.

Besides, many of the managers had been recruited by Rao during the time that he served as COO under me and then under Gurumani. They were loyal to Rao, having been brought in primarily from other companies where he had worked with them.

When I returned to the office from my London trip, I tried to engage some of the staff in the office, including walking into the staff cafeteria to have lunch, as opposed to my usual practice of eating at my desk. But the reactions were ice-cold.

To give you a feel for how much fear there was of Rao finding out that someone was talking to me, consider an incident with Sateesh, the executive I had proposed as the new CEO. Since Sateesh—and other executives—were hesitant to come to my office lest they be seen by Rao, we started speaking by phone. But Sateesh was so fearful that Rao was tracking my calls and calls of senior executives that, when Sateesh wanted to speak with me, he borrowed the phone of my key aide, Sivani Shankar.

For one of these calls, Sateesh happened to be in the bathroom out of sight of Rao. Unfortunately for Sateesh, Rao walked in when Sateesh was talking to me. Sateesh hung up immediately but was worried that Rao had overheard my distinctive, raspy voice on the other line. He was in a panic.

Later, Sateesh bought a burner phone so that he could speak to me undetected. Out of abundant caution, he and I started speaking only after office hours. He also pleaded with me to get a burner phone as well, as my calls would also be in the company call logs.

I did not think that Rao would have the audacity to look at my call records. It just seemed too brazen for someone to track the calls of the executive chairperson of the company. I never imagined that Rao would monitor my calls. But since Sateesh was insistent, I asked the executive in charge of administration, Ramesh Vautrey, about it.

I felt comfortable confiding in Ramesh, both because Sateesh had trust in him, and because I'd had a chance to closely interact with Ramesh during the private investigation of the suicide cases. He was the one coordinating with the private investigator, and I'd also entrusted him to safeguard the case reports, so he had a chance to read them.

He did. One night he came to my office visibly upset. The suicides were "bad karma," he said, shaking his head. He did not want to be a part of SKS anymore. He felt we should just close down. I listened to him, empathetically. I was also disturbed by the investi-gator's reports. Eventually that led me to creating the sangam mitra plan, but at the time that Ramesh came to me, I had no words for him—except to commiserate with him.

After those heartfelt interactions in January, I trusted Ramesh enough to ask if Rao had asked for my call logs. I was shocked when he told me yes, Rao was tracking my calls, and also reading my texts on the company server. He'd accessed all my emails. Moreover, he even had the driver of my company car report to him where I went and with whom I met. Ramesh shared with me that Rao had done the same thing to Gurumani in the months leading up to the former CEO's exit.

I immediately got a burner phone and recruited a new driver from outside of the company.

I thought back to the ultimatum by Rao and Raj against Gurumani, just a few months earlier. Could something like that happen to me? The situation looked ominous—especially since Raj's behavior toward me was puzzling. Rather than avoiding me, as most of the staff had been doing, the CFO Raj took a more aggressive stance. On one of my first days back to the office, he said, "I'm not going to be part of your executive committee." I had never heard him raise his voice before. He was always soft-spoken, even deferential. Up until that moment, I had counted on him to support the leader-ship transition to Sateesh and the new executive committee. If Rao was going to resign, naturally Raj would have a more prominent role in the new SKS leadership. But his ardent refusal to join the commit-tee made it clear to me that Raj would not be supportive.

When I realized how bad the situation was, I knew that there was one person who could probably give me advice: Gurumani. I called him. We had not spoken since he left SKS, but he was gracious and agreed to meet. I met him in Mumbai and shared what was happening in the office. He listened with a knowing expression and then shared with me a shocking revelation. Soon after Gurumani had joined as CEO of SKS, Rao had invited Gurumani to his home and proposed a plan to oust me. Gurumani had not taken the bait. He made it clear that he did not want any part of such a plot, and he encouraged Rao to forget any such notions. He told Rao that there was an opportunity for them to lead SKS to great heights and urged him not to jeopardize that.

At the meeting, Rao told Gurumani he would forgo his plot to oust me, but in retrospect Gurumani felt Rao instead set his sights on getting rid of Gurumani—and then me. Rao did this by masterfully planting seeds of doubt about Gurumani among various members of the board, including me. This included allegations of financial impropriety, which the board eventually investigated and deemed false. Finally, Rao organized the ultimatum of the management team to quit if Gurumani was not removed. Gurumani felt, in retrospect, that Rao had been holding a grudge that Gurumani had been selected as CEO over him, and so had a deep desire to get rid of both Gurumani and me.

When I realized what Rao had been planning, I knew I would have to explain the full sequence of events to the board. In any event, that was my main reason for returning to India ahead of schedule. I also never had any doubt about my ability to explain the facts to the board. I had faith in the board members. I felt they were reasonable and simply did not have a full picture of the scenario. Upon being fully briefed, they would make better decisions. They just needed to hear the facts and circumstances directly from me. I started by emailing the board and asked to have an emergency board meeting; we could do it by conference call since it was too short notice to convene in person. Paresh Patel, one of our board members—nominated by his investment firm, Sandstone Capital—replied that I did not have the authority to call a board meeting at short notice. There was a meeting scheduled for a few weeks later in July; I could meet the board then, said Paresh.

I was disappointed but undeterred by his response. I set out to meet each board member individually, which they made difficult to do. Each one had a range of excuses: *Sorry, no time . . . Away on a business trip . . . Too busy . . . Aren't we having a meeting in a few weeks?* When I pushed harder, offering to meet them wherever and whenever they could free up even fifteen minutes, some board members acquiesced. I started crisscrossing the country to meet board members wherever they were at whatever time they would give me—late night, early morning, when they were traveling between other meetings. From Hyderabad to Chennai to Delhi to Mumbai—back and forth I went.

Some of the board members were polite, listening silently, poker-faced—perhaps trying to placate me. Other conversations were downright absurd. For example, I met with Tarun Khanna, the professor at Harvard Business School and an independent director. He was based in Boston but happened to be in India on one of his regular trips. At first, he refused to meet, saying he already had back-to-back meetings scheduled for the entire week in India. I offered to fly to Mumbai and stay the night at the same hotel he was in, so that I could drive with him to the airport and have thirty minutes during the car ride. I made it such that he really could not say no.

I flew to Mumbai and stayed at the Taj Mahal Palace Hotel, where Tarun was staying. The next morning we drove to the airport in a hotel car, a black sedan. During the drive, I shared what I learned from the private investigator about microfinance and microinsurance process lapses, and I outlined the logic of the sangam mitra plan as a means to address those issues. I explained that Rao had intended to resign, which was why I'd set up the executive committee. I said that I had identified a proposed CEO and was ensuring a smooth transition.

As Tarun's car pulled up to the Mumbai airport and my time was up, he turned and looked at me for what seemed like the first time. "Vikram," he said. "You may be absolutely right, but you should resign." I stared at him, incredulous. The two ideas didn't seem to hold the same space. How could I be absolutely right but still be wrong? Something was amiss.

My conversation with Tarun was particularly troubling because I had full faith in his ability to be reasonable. He had a stellar academic reputation, and there had always been mutual respect between us. We were both academics. He taught at Harvard, and I had a PhD from the University of Chicago. I felt we were kindred spirits—interested in SKS not merely as just another company but as the manifestation of a new form of capitalism, a model of a transformative social impact–creating business. He and I had coauthored a *Wall Street Journal* op-ed comparing microfinance in China and India. So when he confronted me with the absurd statement that I was right but I should resign, it was a jolt.

I tried to explain away his reply. Maybe Tarun was particularly concerned because a colleague of his at Harvard, Krishna G. Palepu, had been an independent director on the board of Satyam, the Hyderabad company that was mired in a fraud scandal. Palepu had resigned as a director of Satyam in 2008 and in 2014 was found guilty in the government's prosecution of Satyam and fined $430,000 for conflict of interest. Surely, the Satyam scandal must have been on Tarun's mind as he was not only a colleague of Palepu's, but they'd also coauthored a book (the 2010 *Winning in Emerging Markets*, published by Harvard Business School Press) that came out around the time the Satyam fraud scandal made news.

All my conversations with board members reinforced my feeling that something was strange. Another thing that puzzled me was that they kept asking my opinion about lending against gold. We had discussed the idea in past board meetings and had rejected it. I was surprised to hear board members raise the topic again.

Loans against gold involve taking people's jewelry as collateral and giving loans against this security. Rao was a big fan of gold lending and had advocated for it for more than a year—well before our IPO—but I was dead against it. In the past, I had always been able to persuade the board that gold-backed loans were not a good idea for SKS. I made the same arguments as I had in the past. I had no intention of turning the company that I had built into a pawnbroker.

First, microfinance was about making sure our members did well. Our success was tied to their long-term success. If they did well, we did well. And as such, through the group appraisal method, we were careful to make sure loans were the right size and were used for generating income, so that a borrower could repay loans and have a surplus left over or at least the windfall of an income-generating asset at the end of the loan period. The entire thrust of my sangam mitra plan was to get back to that ethos, to regain what we had done in our first decade and what had made us such a great company.

Lending against gold was different from microfinance. Gold lenders did not care about the purposes for which loans were used; they had gold collateral in case of a default. For a traditional lender against gold, it did not matter whether the loan was used to generate income, host a lavish wedding, or buy a color TV. Lending against gold was no doubt more profitable than microfinance—at least in the short term. There was no need for an elaborate group training method, no need to check what the loan was used for.

What was likely especially attractive to our board members, particularly the directors nominated by investors, was that, in the backlash against microfinance since our IPO, gold lenders were thriving. Our members who had lost access to microfinance loans were turning to borrowing against gold, either from the traditional village pawnbrokers they had gone to before microfinance or from gold-loan companies such as Muthoot and Manappuram. In fact, our investor with the largest ownership, Sequoia—whose nominee on the board was Sumir Chadha—was an investor in Manappuram. Meanwhile, Muthoot had just completed a successful IPO. The board was also probably intrigued by the fact that at the same time as politicians were viciously attacking us, they were saying nothing about groups like Muthoot and Manappuram.

I could certainly understand the attraction of short-term profits, especially in light of the defaults that resulted from the political backlash and certainly in contrast to my sangam mitra strategy—which would have resulted in short-term losses (though, I was convinced, it was a strategy that would protect our members from over-indebtedness and win back public confidence and, in so doing, result in increased shareholder value in the long term).

Perhaps one could even make an argument that the cavalier attitude of gold lenders may be okay when lending to the middle class or even the lower middle class. After all, Indians had often bought gold as a way of storing surplus—a practice rooted in tradition and bolstered by people's historical unfamiliarity with and lack of faith in banks. In fact, at that time, India had the highest per capita consumption of gold in the world. Many Indians kept gold, whether it be jewelry, gold coins, or even gold bars. An argument can be made that gold lenders like Muthoot and Manappuram provided the middle class—who were financially literate enough to understand the risks—an important service because it allowed them to monetize surplus gold.

But for me, lending against gold to the poor was different from lending against gold to the middle class. While gold lending for the middle class may be a means of monetizing surplus, the poor borrowed against gold only in hopeless situations. For poor women, this often meant pawning *streedhan*, a form of heirloom jewelry gifted to a woman by her family at the time of her wedding. It is the last resort, pawned only in the most desperate of times. I have witnessed this firsthand, when a poor woman removes a few strands of gold from her string necklace, perhaps even her bridal *mangalsutra*, a special necklace symbolizing the sacral bond of matrimony, and her hand quivers as she turns over the jewelry to the pawnbroker.

Typically, at the end of the loan period, such poor borrowers end up not being able to repay their loan and have to continue to pay the interest so as not to lose heirloom jewelry that has deep sentimental value. As a consequence, poor borrowers are put into a debt trap. I pointed out that, with the way Rao was proposing to structure loans against gold, interests and fees could easily skyrocket to 50 percent. And if those rates were not paid, the jewelry would get auctioned.

Gold loan companies have no qualms about this. As stated on gold lender Manappuram's website: "As for a borrower facing temporary difficulties, the only compulsion is to keep on servicing the interest component, till his situation permits repayment . . . Defaults are settled by sale of the pledged gold."[2] In our board discussions, Rao and Raj used to say that our loans against gold would be secure because of the fallback of "asset stripping," a crass euphemism for auctioning off people's heirloom gold jewelry.

Even the Reserve Bank of India, in a new microfinance framework that had come out just a few weeks prior, was averse to loans against gold to microfinance customers. The new RBI rules stated that at least 90 percent of microfinance loans were to be "qualifying assets," which included loans being given without collateral. Otherwise, loans given by banks to the microfinance entity would not be considered as satisfying the government-mandated "priority sector" lending. Moreover, the 90 percent figure was not intended to create a space for 10 percent lending against gold. The industry understanding was that it was a buffer in case MFIs did not meet the now strict qualifying assets criteria that included everything from restrictions on the number of lenders to a borrower to the income level of borrower. The 10 percent buffer was simply intended to allow some leeway for inadvertent errors in complying with the qualifying assets criteria.

But Rao did not see it that way. There was 10 percent leeway, so we could do 10 percent of lending against gold. Rao's proposed plan was to then gradually hive off all our members into a new separate gold lending company that was not a microfinance institution—and that did not have such restrictions. Lending against gold would be done in that company but to the same borrowers, essentially using MFI staff to cannibalize MFI lending.

Rao wanted to implement a program whereby microfinance loan officers would receive an additional 100 percent of their standard microfinance incentive: ₹100 ($2.20) each for each client who visited the gold loan branches and then ₹3,000 ($66) if eighty members took gold loans in two months. This idea meant that loan officers would informally start insisting that visiting and taking a loan against gold be a prerequisite for processing unsecured microfinance loan applications of poor women, driving them into gold loans whether clients need it or not. Once again, a skewed field incentive system was being proposed by Rao. We had seen the result of "incentives galore" in microfinance. In fact, even prior to microfinance incentives becoming an issue, I had fiercely argued against a similar incentive system for the SKS whole-life insurance product—which I had been able to stop.

Rao had no plans for advertising in the way traditional gold lenders do, which further supported my concern about cannibalizing our existing member base. Just as I had done in past board meetings, I pleaded with board members during my one-on-one meetings to realize that as a result of such incentive policies to promote lending against gold, gradually we would end up with heirloom jewelry from a high percentage of our women members. This would pretty well ensure that many borrowers would fall into the debt trap of just servicing interest or having their heirloom jewelry auctioned. In addition, though interest rates on gold loans that were paid on time were proposed to be 25 percent, Rao's proposal also involved charging interests and late fees that amounted to 38 percent if the repayment was a mere *four days* late. Aside from what I saw as the unethical cannibalization of a group-lending business that had taken more than a decade to create, I felt we would face a public backlash far worse than the post-IPO backlash against microfinance.

This time, my arguments fell on deaf ears. I remember coming back to the office in between my whirlwind travels for my one-on-one meetings with board members and walking down the hall past

Raj's office. Rao and a few senior managers were sitting listening, in rapt delight, to Raj as he demonstrated, replete with hand gestures, how to use a few drops of acid to test whether gold was real. The image made a strong impression: It was so far removed from the way in which I'd started SKS, sitting on a patch of dirt with grassroots field staff and poor women borrowers in small groups. Now I was in the midst of middle-aged mainstream bankers talking about how to test whether the heirloom gold of poor people was real or not.

Realizing that the moral argument or the argument about long-term shareholder value might not hold sway with board members, I also pointed out strategic flaws in SKS taking up gold lending. For example, there was the issue of core competence. Groups such as Muthoot had been in the gold lending business for eighty years, while we would be new to the business. Rao talked about creating software in three months. I pointed out that his track record suggested we would miss that deadline. I reminded board members that our whole-life insurance software had data reconciliation issues for 2,198,373 clients out of 2,864,284, three years after launch. Imagine if our software did not properly track heirloom jewelry.

Then there was the concern about starting a gold lending initiative at a time when gold prices were at their peak, which was the case at that time. If there was a correction of 20 percent or even 10 percent, we would have a problem, whereas gold lenders who had been in the business for decades would have a lower average loan to value of the gold collateral. I further pointed out that the proposed ad hoc approach to gold lending did not adhere with our internal guidelines for new businesses, based on the 2009 memo written by Tarun Khanna, which had been drafted after I'd pointed out the myriad problems with whole-life insurance and persuaded the board to mandate Rao to take corrective measures.

Tarun wrote:

Key elements for each business should be a well-vetted business plan, a pilot phase to test the business plan and a separate set of highly qualified management to operate the business. Within the business plan, important issues will include capital outlay, unit sustainability, core business compatibility, market prospects and a set of well-defined management qualifications and descriptions. Businesses with a high coefficient to the SKS core business will likely become subsidiaries of SKS Microfinance. Businesses based upon our customer niche but less aligned with the core business could be joint ventures or SKS could be a minority shareholder . . . Key to all businesses is separate, highly qualified management teams.

The memo continued, advising further company guidelines for piloting any "new initiative," including recruiting both internally and externally to position a team possessing core expertise and experience in scaling. It indicated that in the interest of further refining the relevant business strategy, Rao and Raj might be called upon to provide "guidance and mentorship as needed" to initiatives that met or exceeded milestones during their pilot phase. "The board would be pleased to consider MR Rao and/or Dilli Raj being part of the leadership team for one of these new initiatives at some point in the future," it noted, "however it would be crucial that prior to that the following important conditions are met." Such conditions included that SKS achieve key operational milestones and be on track to meet specific financial goals; that a "deep and talented pool of managers" was recruited and mentored in key functional areas of the proposed business; that the performance of such key hires indicated their ability to function effectively and independently; and that the SKS board would continue to assess the managerial performance of key hires and determine whether additional support was needed in a given area.

The memo was beautifully written, as you would expect from a Harvard Business School professor, but none of these measures were in place when it came to lending against gold. Yet Tarun, who wrote these words on behalf of the board, appeared ready to launch headlong into lending against gold—and to ask me to resign.

The whole thing was surreal.

Needless to say, my whirlwind of one-on-one meetings with board members had failed. I had one more chance at the upcoming July 26 board meeting. I had to persuade the board to fully hear me out, and this time I decided that rather than informal discussions about the suicides and our role, I would have to put things on record. It seemed that would be the only way to jolt the board into coming to terms with our moral responsibility for the process lapses that led to over-indebtedness and suicide as well as to explain, in concrete detail, what I saw as the best way forward.

By this time, I was working from home to avoid any surveillance from Rao and his cronies. In the weeks leading up to the meeting, I worked solely with Sivani Shankar and one other trusted colleague—a graphics specialist—to help me put together a PowerPoint presentation that would go on record.

The July board meeting took place in Mumbai, in the offices of Paresh Patel's Sandstone building in Nariman Point. At this time, board members were still reluctant to come to Hyderabad for fear of arrest. We'd been holding our board meetings in Mumbai since the the adoption of the October 2010 AP Microfinance Act.

I got to the meeting early so I could put together presentation packets for board members. I had so many documents, I had to bring a small suitcase to carry them all. I was offered tea, and I sat in the conference room collating each packet. When Rao and Raj arrived, they did not come to the conference room but went into Paresh's main office. Other directors strolled in, but rather than sit with me in the conference room, they proceeded inside to Paresh's office as well. The only exceptions were the nominee of SIDBI, V. Chandrasekaran, and the company secretary, who was collating his own packets for the board.

When the meeting time came, the directors who had gone inside now walked into the conference room together, along with Rao and Raj. I sat down amidst my stacks of PowerPoint printouts. Behind me was my suitcase and stacks of backup documents—the field reports from the Guardians Human & Civil Rights Forum, the EDA report on insurance, and so on.

The company secretary, under Rao's direction, had circulated an agenda where my presentation was to come last, under other business. As chairperson, I called the meeting to order, and then told everyone that we would have my presentation first. No one said anything, but some glances passed around the room.

My presentation was supposed to be about an hour long—a detailed explanation composed of five major topics: (1) Rao's stated intent to resign, the context for me setting up the executive committee, and Rao's furtive surveillance of me; (2) the policy changes that led to improper borrower group formation and thus over-indebtedness; (3) the investigator's findings about the seven cases of suicide for which I felt SKS had to take some level of responsibility; (4) the legal and regulatory compliance issues that SKS Microfinance had faced due to Rao's mismanagement of our insurance division; (5) the problems with changing SKS into a company that loaned against gold.

I asked Rao, Raj, and the company secretary to step out of the room so that we could have an open discussion—especially since much of the content was very critical of Rao. It was unusual to send the CEO out, but it was not unprecedented. In the past, our board had held executive sessions without the management team and the CEO in attendance, even though the CEO was also a member of the board. Once the three of them left the room, I gave each board member a stapled copy of the presentation. Packets in hand, board members began to flip ahead as I gave introductory remarks.

Because I knew board members might be surprised that I'd asked Rao to step out, I started with his stated intent to resign and his surveillance of me. I did not get very far. Several of the board members had flipped ahead to the section on the seven suicides. They were visibly shaken. I had entitled the final part of the presentation "Appendix," and this section was a detailed explanation of all seven suicides—who the people were; what village, branch, and district they were a member of; how long they had been a member of SKS; and what had driven them to take their own lives. Every man sitting around the table was already aware of the information he was reading. Ever since returning from London, I'd been telling people informally about what I had learned from the investigator and about the sangam mitra plan. No one had listened, so here it was, on record. Now, I thought, the board would have to reckon with all I had learned.

Soon after my presentation was underway, Pramod tossed his handout toward me. We all watched the thick packet of papers slide across the table. Pramod was the one who had called me in London to deliver the board's message to quit interfering with Rao's operations. "I don't want this," Pramod said now. Other board members followed suit, and soon most of the packets I had handed out came sliding across the table. Except one. Geoff Woolley, who had been nominated to the board by Unitus, kept his.

I continued speaking and explaining things, to the obvious discomfort of my audience. I pressed on. The board members were literally squirming in their chairs, looking at each other, looking down, pursing their lips. Realizing that they would not let this go on for much longer, I announced that I would pause the presentation and discuss the appendix—which outlined the suicides. I spoke for about ten minutes more before Pramod finally protested, saying something along the lines of: "Why are you telling us all this?"

No one had wanted to listen even when I'd chased them around the country to meet one on one, so I needed the facts to be on the record, I explained.

Pramod looked at Sumir and then at Paresh.

Sumir told me to stop, that we had other business to deal with. I did not want to stop, but I had little choice. Sumir effectively controlled the company and the board, since the two other major investors, Sandstone led by Paresh and Kismet led by Ashish, were allied with him, not to mention Pramod and Tarun, the two independent board members he'd brought in.

Sumir said that I should share the information presented with Rao and Raj when we were back at headquarters. He also said my comments were better suited for discussion with the strategic initiatives subcommittee of the board. The subcommittee could then assess the information in-depth and report back to the full board. It was a delay tactic, I knew. But at that moment, I did not know what else I could do. The board was not ready to continue the discussion.

Sumir then asked Rao, Raj, and the company secretary to come back in. We finished the other agenda items, and the meeting was adjourned. Most of the board members quickly walked out of the conference room. The SIDBI nominee, Chandrasekaran, lingered with me for a few moments, looking as if he had something to say. Whatever he might have wanted to say to me went unsaid. He just bid me farewell and went out the door.

I should have realized the extent of the board's opposition to me. I was still a naive optimist. Perhaps it was my doctoral training. I had always thought a logical argument, backed by hard data, would make people listen. I now realized that the SKS boardroom was not like a University of Chicago seminar room. The board was not even ready to hear the facts. Maybe their collective reaction was one of self-protection, a desire for plausible deniability, in light of the AP Microfinance Act. Maybe they felt I was exaggerating. Whatever the reasons, their actions had conveyed that they were not going to accept the validity of what I was saying, regardless of the merits of my argument, regardless of how much evidence I presented.

Rao, Raj, and the company secretary were the last to leave the room. I stayed because I had to gather together all the paper—the copies of the presentation and the reams of backup documents that I had brought. As the three of them were leaving, Rao walked behind my chair on his way out. Thinking back on how he had outmaneuvered me over the last couple of months, I turned to him and said,

"Wow, you really got me." He gave me a jovial slap on my back, smiled, softly chuckled, and walked out.

It was one of the only times we'd spoken in about two months.

I sat there for a few minutes alone, amidst the piles of paper. I stared out the window.

CHAPTER 19

ROUND TWO: BACK IN HYDERABAD

As Sumir had suggested, when I was back in Hyderabad I scheduled a meeting to share my board presentation with Rao and Raj. I met with them on Thursday, July 28, 2011, in my office at our Hyderabad headquarters. At the scheduled time, the two of them came into my office and sat down. Tea had been brought in for them—a standard courtesy for any such meeting.

I had again printed copies of my board presentation, which I started to share with them. They both became very defensive, very quickly—and understandably so. After all, I was essentially pointing out that Rao's field staff incentive system and dilution of borrower training had led to over-indebtedness.

Rao started to raise his voice. I do not remember the exact words he said, just that he got angrier and angrier, louder and louder. Raj did as well. I tried to calm them down, but Rao stood and leaned his body across the desk, his right hand raised. Then Raj stood as well. I don't know if Rao was preparing to hit me or just wanted to intimidate me. I looked up at both of them—stunned. "Get out!" I yelled firmly. "Get out."

Rao sat back down and said, "I am not leaving until I finish my tea." He sat back and sipped his tea. He took his time. Raj sat and did as well. It was the height of defiance—full of insult and insolence. I could only sit and watch, red-faced. They took a few minutes to finish their tea and then left.

Sumir later called me and said not to go to the office. I tried to explain what happened, but he was not ready to listen.

"Okay," I finally said, "I will go to the field."

"No, you cannot go into the field either. It might confuse the workers."

"If you don't want me in the office and you don't want me in the field, what am I supposed to do?" I asked in exasperation. "Where am I supposed to go?"

Sumir was smooth. He was always the friendly voice, the good cop. "Give me some time, Vikram. I will speak with them. We will work it out." His words were kind; his tone, reassuring. I agreed to stay home until he had a chance to speak with Rao and Raj.

A few days later, the company secretary emailed the minutes of the July 26 board meeting. My presentation had been completely excised from the minutes. I called the company secretary—who, along with Rao and Raj, had been asked to step out during my presentation. I asked why my presentation had been left off the record.

He said something akin to, "This was not part of the board proceedings." (In a subsequent email he wrote, "As per my notes, this was not part of the board proceedings. It has therefore been deleted.")

"What do you mean? I gave a presentation in the meeting. It's not there. Even if you were not there, I can summarize the content for you for the minutes, just as I have done in the past."

He responded that the chairman is not the one who writes the minutes. He said the company secretary does, based on what the entire board says.

I was beyond astounded by what I was hearing. Events had been purposefully manipulated. Fact: I had made the presentation at the board meeting. Fact: Geoff Woolley had kept a physical copy of my presentation. Fact: Another board member, P. H. Ravikumar, who could not make the meeting, had asked me for a copy of the presentation. Ravikumar chaired the audit committee of the SKS board. I'd sent the presentation to him by email soon after the meeting, and we subsequently had a conversation about the report. He not only acknowledged receipt of the packet but also wrote the following in reply to the concerns I'd raised: "As mentioned when we spoke, as a board and as a part of the audit committee, we are committed to process controls and compliances including regulatory compliances."

I called Sumir to ask about the omission in the minutes. He replied that my presentation needed to be sent forty-eight hours prior to the meeting to be included in the minutes. It was an absurd statement, as we had never had such a rule in the past. But that is what he said.

The board's position started to become clear to me. It wasn't that they didn't understand the issues I had been presenting to them. They knew the issues, but they were willfully choosing to ignore them (including keeping them out of meeting records) for what appeared to be the same reason we were having board meetings in Mumbai and not Hyderabad—they seemed afraid of legal liability. Whereas to me, it was a moral issue. I was trying to do the right thing by both taking accountability and changing the company to ensure nothing like this ever happened again. Of course, I understood the fear of legal liability, which is why I'd flown around the country to have in-person conversations. What I had been trying to do was to have an honest off-the-record conversation, so we could figure out what to do and then do it—working, first and foremost, in what I believed was the best interest of our members and thereby in the best interest of the long-term health of the company as well as the long-term transformative potential of SKS. Board members, on the other hand, seemed to be focused on how to protect themselves.

In retrospect, I understand their desire for self-protection. But they had known about the nature of SKS before they joined the board. SKS was not a typical company. It was a social enterprise. We were different.

The latest turn of events made me realize that I would have to further escalate things. Stunned, hurt, and more concerned than ever about what would happen to our members and to the soul of the company that I had cultivated for so many years, I called Vinod Khosla, who had led our first round of investment and who continued to hold a 7 percent stake in the company.

I knew Vinod embraced my view of social enterprise: that a market-based approach was a channel for increasing social impact and that, in a social enterprise, profits were not an end in themselves, and certainly were not to be made at the expense of the mission. And I knew Vinod had the gravitas to get the attention of the board. He was not on the board, but he was one of the most important investors in venture capital. The board could dodge or ignore me, but they could not do that to Vinod.

He listened patiently over the phone as I laid out my concerns. "Okay, Vikram," he said from his office in Silicon Valley. "I'd like to set up a conference call with the rest of the board."

We set up a call for August 9 at 9 AM India time (7:30 PM in the San Francisco Bay Area). A day before the call, the board canceled. The email came from Paresh Patel, the head of Sandstone. He said that something urgent had come up and that the call needed to be canceled. We rescheduled for August 19.

Meanwhile, Rao and Raj had been taking control back at SKS headquarters in Hyderabad. When bankers came to the office, they were told that I was traveling, when in fact I was in town. Rao held a national area managers meeting (on August 7), something that I had consistently attended in the past. But I did not participate, heeding Sumir's request to stay away from the office until he had time to sort things out. In the same month, SKS hosted a meeting of the Microfinance Institutions Network (MFIN)—of which I was a founding and current member—at SKS's offices. I was not even told about the meeting.

It was sad to be sidelined by my own team, but my solace was that the rescheduled board call with Vinod would take place on August 19. Things would change then. I just knew they would. But I was also worried the board would cancel again. As such, I felt I had to put things on record, just in case. In light of what happened with the July board minutes, I opted for something more concrete—something that the board could not ignore. I summarized my presentation in a letter and emailed it to each board member. The context for the email was the meeting of the strategic initiatives subcommittee of the board, which was scheduled for August 17.

Before sending the letter, I consulted a personal lawyer. I was sensitive to the board's concern about legal liability, so I asked the lawyer how I should present the information. I wanted the board to take the matter seriously, but I understood their fears about legal trouble with the AP state government. Having closely examined the cases of the seven suicides, I knew that the circumstances did not rise to the level of legal culpability for SKS. On the other hand, I knew the board was afraid of exactly that. By this stage, however, cordial discussions had stopped. We did not meet in person. We did not speak on the phone. I communicated with other board members in formal meetings and through emails only, so those were the only media available to me.

I was not ready to back down on my position that we should take moral responsibility for the process lapses that led to over-indebtedness. And, at the very least, if the board was not ready to do that publicly (as I had, of course, already done), at least they should do so privately and take steps to fix faulty processes. But so far, all my attempts at getting the board to align with my thinking had totally and utterly failed. I needed to jolt them, and the way to do that would be to play on their fear of a criminal case, to bring them to the precipice without them falling over the edge. In short, I did not want to give the board yet another opportunity to sidestep the facts. If I sent the letter in advance and they still ignored it, I could at least insist that this time the contents not be omitted from the meeting minutes. I sent the email on August 11 from my personal email, as my lawyer had suggested, and using phrasing that he had crafted:

> I am writing to you in my individual capacity to request feedback on my proposed DRAFT comments to the Strategic Initiatives Committee (scheduled to meet on August 17, 2011).

So how did the board respond to my letter?

Pramod Bhasin resigned one day after I sent the letter. He went on to insist that his name immediately be taken off the website and any other communications material. I think he realized that I was not going to back down on the strategic and ethical arguments I was making. He wanted out. And fast.

Other board members, particularly those who had substantial investments, could not just run. Instead, they went on a rapid-fire attack. The first salvo was, in time-honored fashion, character assassination—using the dreaded *F* word: founder's syndrome. For any founder who is labeled as suffering from founder's syndrome, it is tough to counter because the term implies that the person may have shown brilliance in the initial stages of an enterprise but—in later stages—no longer has the requisite skills to grow a company. It is the perfect way to sideline a founder.

Sumir—perhaps the most savvy venture capitalist of the lot— knew this well, and he knew how to deploy the term. I suspected that he knew that he could whisper it in the ear of other board members and investors and undermine me. That is how I understood his email reply of August 14th, in which he wrote:

> I find your behavior erratic and unprofessional . . . You are not cut out for running a large company that SKS has become . . . You are having the problem that many founders face—giving up control when the time comes. Please face this reality . . . I hope that you can hear this

feedback in the right spirit and change yourself, otherwise you will suffer the most from this.

I knew I would have a tough task fighting this reputation smear.

For starters, the short-term financial interests of the major investors and their board nominees were not aligned with my approach. A sangam mitra plan would be costly; I believed that it would create long-term shareholder value, but they did not concur. Nominee directors like Sumir stood to lose tens of millions for their investors and millions for themselves in profit-sharing. Meanwhile the independent directors, to whom we had given stock options, had a similar financial interest—if not in degree, at least in kind. They presumably felt they would lose hundreds of thousands of dollars.[1] Aside from their financial interests, it probably did seem to them that I suffered from founder's syndrome. There I was, making a passionate argument against lending against gold. From a banker's perspective, which was the background of most of the board members, they were watching me pound the table and say that unsecured lending was better than secured lending. They were hearing me say this as they watched us write off $280 million of unpaid loans. Surely, I looked like a fool—from the perspective of a banker. I could understand why founder's syndrome was an appealing label.

The other problem was that the board was more inclined to believe Sumir than me. Over the years, Sumir had masterfully seen that the board was composed of his close friends and associates. After Sequoia had invested in March 2007, one of Sumir's early initiatives was to "strengthen" the board. I did not realize it at the time, but in retrospect this appeared designed to bring in people he knew and could influence and removing people he did not know and could not influence.

Before Sumir had invested, SKS had a seven-member board, including individuals who had a background in development or had corporate sector experience but were committed to using a market-based approach for development. For example, two key board members were Gurcharan Das and the late Sitaram Rao. Sitaram Rao was a seasoned banker who had made a career shift to development. While he had spent his career in the corporate sector, he had a deep commitment to principles of social entrepreneurship. Meanwhile, Gurcharan Das was the first chairperson of SKS after it became a for-profit finance company in 2005. Like Sitaram Rao, he had spent his career in the corporate sector, but he brought to SKS a desire to blend capitalism and philanthropy. Anyone who had the honor of knowing Sitaram Rao when he was alive or the pleasure of hearing the thoughts of Gurcharan Das knows that they would be part of a dream team for any social enterprise board. The three of us were kindred spirits, and we anchored a board that was united in a common cause.

Slowly and subtly, Sumir changed that. First, he suggested adding an independent director who had an academic background. I immediately thought of Orlanda Ruthven, a stellar academic who had coauthored the 2009 book *Portfolios of the Poor: How the World's Poor Live on $2 a Day*. She had extensive field experience with our customer segment, and she would have been a great addition. Instead, Sumir suggested Tarun Khanna of Harvard Business School. Though Tarun did write about India, I felt Ruthven would bring more relevant experience. Besides, she lived in India, unlike Tarun, who lived in Boston. Ruthven had even visited SKS in its early stages when she was working for the UK's Department for International Development. But I deferred to Sumir. After all, Sequoia had just made an $11.5 million investment in SKS, the largest venture investment in microfinance up that point. Besides, I thought that, as a venture capitalist, Sumir had a lot of experience with a wide range of company boards and knew better than I who would be a good board member. Of course, it was only later that I learned that Tarun and Sumir were very close; perhaps that closeness lent context to Tarun's bizarre statement that while I might be correct I should nonetheless resign.

As mentioned, two other HBS graduates had joined the board.

The first was Ashish Lakhanpal, with whom I had been interacting since 1998, from the time of the original $50,000 donation from Ravi Reddy and Sandeep Tungare. When I spoke with him (which I had to frequently because he was the one administering the grants), Ashish made me feel like he was doing me a favor by taking time away from "corporate" matters. Those were the early days, when SKS was a nonprofit, experiencing losses, and no one had any idea of how big it would become. We did not get a lot of respect, especially from the likes of Ashish, who was far more interested in Ravi and Sandeep's for-profit ventures, from which he would earn his carry, the percentage of profits that he could keep for himself.

At times, Ashish seemed just plain bored by our work at SKS. During his requisite annual field visits, he appeared more interested in making sure he filled out his expense reports for each cup of tea than in what was going on in the field. A telling—although later— example of his attitude was his comment, reported widely in press reports, about SKS's rapid growth leading to suicides of the company's borrowers: "The growth was very rapid. That growth led to some suboptimal outcomes."[2]

During the dot-com bust of 2001, Ashish's was the first and loudest voice to tell Ravi and Sandeep to stop giving funds to SKS. I remember his words well. "Maybe we need to let SKS fold if it can't sustain itself," he said to me.

Of course, SKS did become sustainable and then profitable. And when it did, Ashish jumped back into the picture. By the time we were raising money from Sequoia in 2006, Ashish had arranged with Ravi and Sandeep to set up his own fund, Kismet Capital, which would manage the money of Ravi and Sandeep as well as many of their friends. Then Ashish wanted Kismet to invest in SKS. Though I did not want Ashish to be a part of SKS, Ravi and Sandeep insisted on giving their investment rights to Kismet. Perhaps there was some behind-the-scenes coordination between Ashish and Sumir. But what is certain is that Ashish (through Kismet) and Sumir (through Sequoia) both invested in SKS in March 2007. The pair controlled 36 percent shareholding as of that time.

Then they'd teamed up to bring in another HBS alumnus, Paresh Patel of the hedge fund Sandstone. Ashish and Paresh were very close; Ashish was best man at Paresh's wedding. In October 2008, Sandstone invested $51 million in SKS. By then, the threesome controlled the majority percentage of the shares of SKS.

Throughout this fundraising process, I deferred to Sumir for each investment round. I did the presentations, explained microfinance, and told the SKS story. But—since I had no idea about the private equity world—I relied on Sumir to guide me. After all, he was the head of Sequoia's India operation, and Sequoia was among the world's premier venture capital firms (or least that's what everyone kept telling me). So—on Sumir's advice—we ended up rejecting other premier investors such as General Atlantic for Paresh Patel's Sandstone. Not taking equity from General Atlantic was particularly painful because the firm had been a major donor of Echoing Green, the social venture group that had given me a two-year start-up fellowship back in 1998, enabling me to launch SKS. Indeed, in recent years I have had the privilege of interacting with the General Atlantic team on other social enterprise initiatives. They are, undoubtedly, some of the finest people I know. Perhaps SKS might have averted the microfinance backlash had General Atlantic been selected as an investor.

But they weren't.

To summarize, Sumir joined the board after his investment in 2007; then Tarun joined in early 2008. Later that year, Sumir insisted that Sitaram Rao and another director (who had been nominated by Ravi Reddy as his family foundation's nominee) step down. Ashish and Paresh took their places in late 2008.

Once Sumir, Ashish, and Paresh were in place on the board, the three asserted more control. At his very first board meeting in November 2008, Paresh pulled me aside and said that the chairperson,

Gurcharan Das, had to go. I was troubled by his suggestion, but Paresh's firm had just invested $51 million, and had done so in the unsettling aftermath of the Lehman Brothers collapse. How could I say no? On a break, I gently relayed the news to Das and explained that the request had come from Paresh. That was hard to do. Das had been SKS's first chairperson. And he was always there for me— whether I needed to discuss strategy or products or whether it was to give a speech at an all-staff meeting. When I asked him to step down from the board, I am sure he was hurt. But Das is a seasoned, gracious, old-school gentleman, and he kept his feelings to himself.

I felt so bad that during the lunch break I spoke with Paresh and suggested a compromise. Das would step down as chair but not leave the board. He stayed on as an independent director but eventually resigned before our IPO about a year and a half later. So Sumir and his cohorts had four of the nine board seats. They could not replace any others because virtually all of the other directors were nominated by other investors, such as SIDBI, so the quartet had no say.

Sumir suggested to me that we add another independent director. In what was becoming a trend, I presented to an unenthusiastic Sumir a number of great candidates: How about Sandeep Parekh, a lawyer who formerly had a leadership role with the securities regulator in India and was known for high standards of corporate governance? How about Farzana Haque, a rising star as the Global Head for Strategic Group Accounts at Tata Consultancy Services? Sumir demurred. Okay, what about Ankur Sarin, a professor at the Indian Institute of Management in Ahmedabad who did research on policy related to the social and economic life of marginalized communities in India? Sumir said we already had an academic in Tarun.

Instead, Sumir suggested Pramod Bhasin of Genpact, India's largest business process outsourcing company. I really did not see how Pramod's background was more helpful for us than any of the aforementioned three. But again, I deferred to Sumir, presuming he would know better about what type of board members we needed. His efforts gave his group five of ten seats.

As I look back, the subtle change in the character of the board is clear. In March 2007, before Sumir and Ashish had invested, SKS had a board anchored by Gurcharan Das and Sitaram Rao. By early 2009, in less than two years, Das, Sitaram Rao, and others were out and Sumir, Paresh, Tarun, Pramod, and Ashish were in. After Gurumani was fired, Ashish had to leave the SKS board to ensure the requisite balance of independent directors required by the Securities Exchange Board of India, but Sumir's allies still dominated the board—and controlled the shareholding of the company.

When it came to the board battles in July and August 2011, the board had no particular history with me. They did not know the long arc of SKS—the early struggles, my philosophical approach, my instincts that had helped me make the right decisions at various crossroads. No, they only saw what appeared to them to be a raving founder, ranting about unsecured lending being better than secured lending. There was no way I could even begin to try to reason with them. That ship had sailed.

As noted above, on August 11, 2011, I sent my letter to the board. On August 12, Pramod submitted his letter of resignation. On August 12, SKS received an inquiry from the editor of the *Economic Times* about the board wanting me to resign. As I would find out later, on August 14, Ashish, along with three other key investors whom he had rallied, sent investor grievance letters to the board asking for my ouster. August 14 was the date Sumir had emailed me, advising that I change myself or I would be the one to suffer. On August 16, the *Economic Times* ran a front-page, lead-headline story about the board wanting me to resign. Then the strategic initiatives committee meeting, slated for August 17, was canceled last-minute.

Admittedly, the week was rather masterfully orchestrated behind the scenes. For example, the editor from the *Economic Times* emailed the inquiry to our communications head on August 12, asking for a reply to a series of questions by the end of day August 15, as the story would publish the following day. That email wasn't forwarded to me until around noon on August 15.

August 15 is India's Independence Day. As I usually did on that holiday, I left early that morning, taking my son with me to one of the rural schools that SKS Trust had set up as part of our philanthropic work. Children would hoist the Indian flag, sing the national anthem, and perform skits throughout the day about India's independence struggle. On return from the field in the afternoon, I saw the email from the *Economic Times* editor, asking a series of questions about the strategic debate going on within SKS's board. There was also a question about allegations that board members had asked me to resign. I thought we'd had a genuine leak. I called Sumir, and we quickly organized a call for whichever board members were available. I took the call while driving back from the Independence Day celebration at our rural school. The agreed-upon decision was for me to reply with "no comment." I did exactly that.

The next day's front-page article (excerpted below) had a series of quotations from unnamed SKS board members, suggesting that everyone wanted me to resign. "SKS Microfinance Wants Vikram Akula to Step Down" claimed the top right column headline, with the catchy subtitle, "Macro Troubles for Akula."

> Vikram Akula, the one-time poster boy of microfinance and founder-chairman of SKS, India's largest microfinance institution, is under threat of losing control over the company he launched in 1998. Some board members of SKS, the country's only listed MFI, have suggested that Akula step down as executive chairman. They feel since Akula has to travel frequently, it is difficult for him to devote time as a full-time executive.
>
> Instead, he should use his experience and understanding to guide the company as a non-executive or part-time chairman, said a person familiar with the developments in SKS.

While the board did not consider a formal proposal or move a resolution, the suggestion has not gone down well with Akula. He fears assuming a non-executive role may diminish his control and importance in the firm he founded. Akula, sources said, has recently approached AZB, a leading law firm in Mumbai, to explore possible legal options if the board eventually decides to turn against him.

When contacted, he said, "I can't comment." The SKS spokesperson did not respond to ET's email query. Said an industry source: "There may not be a revolt by the board. Most of the directors are known to him for years. But they may keep on nudging Akula for giving up his executive powers in SKS."

"Except ESOPs, Akula owns little or no shares in SKS. He is an employee and a director. It's not clear what kind of powers the law gives him," the person pointed out . . .[3]

No comment.

CHAPTER 20

SHOWDOWN AT THE ROSEWOOD HOTEL

I won't pretend that I wasn't blindsided and, frankly, hurt by the back-room politics that I believed coalesced in the *Economic Times* piece. But there was far more at stake than my wounded ego. I felt like SKS was losing its essence, abandoning the mission and culture that had made it a transformative company that was helping to positively impact millions of poor women. I still thought it morally impera-tive to follow the Tylenol example, to take corrective measures for the process lapses that led to over-indebtedness. And I believed that doing so would strengthen rather than harm SKS in the long run.

I had a last chance to appeal to Vinod Khosla during the upcom-ing August 19th conference call with the board. Unfortunately, but not surprisingly, the board cancelled that conference call as well. In desperation, I called him and explained just what was at stake and pleaded for the need to take action. Realizing the magnitude of the problem and perhaps miffed that he was being ducked, he asked the board members to come to San Francisco to meet with him, which we did on August 27, 2011. We met at the Rosewood Hotel, the famous Silicon Valley hotel on Sand Hill Road in Menlo Park. The

Rosewood was right across the street from Vinod's office—and, for that matter, the offices of Sequoia and Silicon Valley Bank, which were also investors in SKS. Four board members attended the meeting in person: Sumir Chadha of Sequoia; Geoff Woolley, the Unitus nominee; Rao; and me. Three members joined by phone: Audit Committee Chair Ravikumar, Paresh Patel of Sandstone, and HBS Professor Tarun Khanna. The SIDBI nominee, V. Chandrasekaran, could not attend.

Though it was planned as a meeting only for board members, most of the board wanted Raj to attend. He was SKS's CFO but not a board member. I vehemently protested Raj coming with us to Menlo Park. I wanted to be able to debate Rao one on one. I ended up succeeding in that effort. Raj was not allowed to attend. However, the one board member who was on my side also did not attend. V. Chandrasekaran represented the Small Industries Bank of India, a government bank with a development focus. SIDBI had a division—funded by international agencies—that promoted microfinance, and, as such, they were an early lender to SKS and an early investor.

Chandrasekaran was a retired career civil servant. I have voiced my preference for the characteristic mind-set of individuals from the private sector, where one sees the drive and dynamism needed in nimble businesses. At first glance, Chandrasekaran was not dynamic. He wore tired old suits and walked slowly. My interactions with him forced me to rethink my own bias against career civil servants. What was most striking is that Chandrasekaran was a stickler for governance. He always spoke up for doing the right thing, even when outnumbered. For example, when some members of the SKS board tried to take over leadership of the trust that I had set up with SKS sweat equity, he firmly and loudly spoke up that the SKS board had no business in the affairs of that trust. When it came to the concerns I'd been raising of late—our responsibility in the microfinance backlash; sales practices that led to over-indebtedness of borrowers; concerns about lending against gold; the future direction of SKS—he was the one board member who vocally agreed that we needed to address the issues.

Though he was keen to attend, taking an international flight to attend a meeting in California was beyond what SIDBI would permit. Even though SKS would pay for the flight, such travel was outside the scope of what a government institution—especially one devoted to development—could allow. At the last minute, Chandrasekaran had to pull out, although I was able to set up a call between Vinod and him directly before the morning meeting.

By the time the Menlo Park meeting had been finalized and travel plans set, I had very little time to prepare for the meeting. On the twenty-two-hour flight from Hyderabad to Frankfurt to San Francisco, when other passengers turned off their lights and drifted to sleep, I asked the flight attendant for more coffee and worked on what was perhaps the most important presentation I would ever give. The plane landed late afternoon, and I made my way to the Rosewood Hotel. The rooms were spacious and luxurious, but I kept working through the night—starting with a flurry of emails to get source data to back up the presentation. Then I put the final touches on the presentation, slept a couple of hours, got ready, grabbed a coffee to go, and left for a 7:30 AM pre-meeting with Vinod at his office.

It was just after sunrise when I arrived. Vinod was already there. We chatted for a few minutes. I thanked him for helping me. Though Vinod may not have realized it, when I said thank you, I really meant it. I was in a desperate situation. There was so much more at stake than a typical board battle over strategy. For Vinod, SKS was one of many portfolio companies and represented a minuscule part of his assets. Yet he cared enough about SKS and its mission to make time for calls with me from India and then to spend a whole day with us in Menlo Park. I know what it meant for him to carve out so much time. I was truly grateful, so much so that when I said thank you that morning, my voice cracked.

About 7:45 AM, Vinod called Chandrasekaran from a speaker phone. They spoke. I listened. Their conversation started with small talk, then they quickly covered the various events that led up to the meeting. Then Chandrasekaran got to the point. "Vikram has raised important concerns about what is happening to SKS borrowers, and the board has not taken these issues seriously," he said and went on to explain the various ways in which I'd been thwarted, despite the important issues I had raised. I had to blink back tears. Those words meant so much to me. It was the truth, of course. But Vinod got to hear it from someone other than me, especially in the face of near-united opposition from the rest of the board. Chandrasekaran was always supportive, but in the last several weeks he'd been less vocal. Now he finally said—out loud—what I wanted Vinod to hear. For the first time in months, I felt like I would get a fair hearing on a level playing field, refereed by someone with genuine authority. We could set aside the shadow boxing and ad hominem attacks in favor of a genuine debate about the best path for SKS.

Vinod and I hopped in his car and went across the street to the Rosewood. I felt confident as we walked down the stairs to one of the meeting rooms. Sumir and Geoff were already there. We greeted them. Rao walked in after a few moments. I am sure the jet lag was hitting him, as it was me. We set up the conference call on the Spider speakerphone. Ravikumar, Tarun, and Paresh dialed in.

I was to present first. I went to the head of the rectangular table and fired up my PowerPoint file. I gave some background on the crisis and the current crossroads and then outlined the two divergent paths for SKS. One path was what Rao called "cross-sell on war footing," which involved aggressively getting into lending against gold and doubling down on faulty insurance policies as well as pushing other (untested) products. I noted that I was in favor of using microfinance as a distribution channel; I had been one of the earliest to adopt this strategy, and I had summarized it in early SKS business plans and published articles. But the products had to be well designed in the way our core loan product had been; this was key. I then outlined the path I was recommending: SKS should reclaim our core principles and reinstate the careful processes that had made it possible to successfully and responsibly lend to the poor. I described the sangam mitra program that involved pausing lending and retraining staff and borrowers: "If you want to win back public trust, then get back to the core principles that made SKS great, get back to basics. After that, we can start methodically leveraging the distribution channel for other products, but we need to do so systematically and do so in a way that ensures quality."

Vinod was seated at the other end of the table, taking notes on a pad of lined white paper. He had put his phone on silent. Despite it being a weekday, he did not take any phone calls except one that came in the afternoon from his daughter—and he apologized to us before taking that call. I was appreciative of his time, attention, and care. I knew how busy he was.

I concluded by emphasizing what truly mattered: our members—and their dreams and their hopes. When we did right by them once again, SKS would come back stronger. "What happens here today," I told the board, "is about more than numbers on the page. It is nothing less than the beginning of the rejuvenation of SKS or the beginning of its end. And that decision will have wider implications for financial inclusion and social enterprise throughout the world."

I was speaking in terms of a broader vision, the vision I had for SKS from the onset. It was a vision, I knew, that Vinod believed in. His presence in the room made a difference. There were no packets tossed back at me across the table. Instead, I got to finish my presentation. Then there were some genuine questions from the group.

Next it was Rao's turn. His presentation was well organized and flashy, and it used many of the slides and templates that I had created over the years. I asked him tough questions that he stumbled on. Not for the first time, I picked apart his "cross-selling on a war footing" rationale. Many of my concerns came from my deep understanding of our members. For example, how did he intend to effectively communicate the concept of a "surrender value" for a whole-life insurance product to a semiliterate or illiterate customer? If there was an incentive to field staff for successful leads for "loans against gold," how would he ensure that loan officers didn't start, informally, to make a loan against gold a prerequisite for the unsecured loan that members really wanted—and needed? If that happened, wouldn't that be the epitome of mis-selling? What were members to do when the mobile phones he proposed to sell failed, as they had in the pilot; would SKS be responsible or would the device manufacturer be responsible, and, if the latter, how would SKS protect its reputation if phones failed?

Interestingly, Rao gave the example of the U.S. bank Wells Fargo, showing data that their customers had multiple products and therefore its profitability per customer was high. *If Wells Fargo could do it, then we can too* was the message. It is well known now that Wells Fargo tacitly encouraged staff to meet their aggressive sales goals by opening unwanted or unneeded accounts in customers' names—often without even telling customers. Wells Fargo did the same with car insurance, leading to customers having their cars repossessed. What Wells Fargo did was comparable to Rao's "incentives galore" scheme. As a result of that fiasco, in 2016 the Wells Fargo CEO was fired as was their head of community banking, and they were forced to give back $69 million and $67 million in compensation respectively.[1]

If someone judges these two strategic options on the merits, they will see that my proposed path makes sense, I thought to myself when Rao finished. We broke for lunch, a buffet outside in the Northern California sun. Vinod pulled Sumir aside for a one-on-one and he did the same with Geoff, and then with Rao. He had told me that he was going to do this, so I was unfazed.

When lunch was finished, we returned to the conference room. By then, it was just Vinod, Sumir, Geoff, Rao, and me as the board members who had called in during the morning did not rejoin. It was the middle of the night in India. Vinod started to ask questions. He had taken extensive notes on his writing pad, and he would glance at his pad, then direct a question to Rao or me.

"Vikram," he asked at one point, "is there a way to allay your concerns about forcing customers to take loans against gold? Can we ensure that heirloom jewelry does not get auctioned—perhaps by putting a condition that the entire group or even the entire center has to approve of such an event?"

We had discussed the option of lending against gold only in cases of income-generating loans and, as Vinod's question spoke to, including the stipulation that jewelry would not be auctioned without the approval of the village group. By now, you must realize how painful it is for me to even write that previous sentence. Nothing in my vision of SKS, and nothing we had done while I was CEO, remotely included lending against—let alone auctioning off—heirloom gold of poor women.

Nonetheless, Vinod's comments were perceptive and conciliatory, and clearly aimed at resolving our differences without taking sides. The upshot of his questioning was an attempt to blend the two positions. The discussions went on for the remainder of the afternoon, spliced with more individual meetings that Vinod held with me, with Rao, and with other board members.

Toward the end of the meeting, Vinod huddled with Sumir and Geoff, and then asked me to join them. He told me that everyone appreciated my ideas and vision. Sumir and Geoff nodded. But we could not have two people running the company, Vinod said. Rao was the CEO, and he should run the company. Vinod asked, though, whether there was some role I could play that would address the legitimate concerns I had about the dilution of group training and the problems of lending against gold as well as the quality of our insurance division and other products. He suggested that I stay on as chairperson for some time and then, when I felt that my concerns were addressed, I could move to chairing a Client Protection Committee, a new committee the board would create whose responsibility it would be to continue to address quality issues. Geoff and Sumir nodded affirmatively.

This was not what I wanted to hear. And Vinod could see that. He pulled me aside for yet another one-on-one discussion and spoke to me about power versus influence. He wanted me to give up the former and pursue the latter. I don't remember his exact words, but he said something to the effect of, "I have seen you grow over the years. You have earned my respect and the respect of the microfinance industry. I know what you are capable of. You can do this."

His words were hard to hear. Nevertheless, realizing that I did not have much choice and that Vinod had done all he could to find a middle ground, I tried to read the positive in this proposal. I was still distrustful of the board and Rao, but perhaps now that Vinod was involved the board would take my concerns seriously—and therefore Rao would have to as well. I agreed to the plan.

We broke for dinner on the outdoor patio of Madera restaurant, which was part of the Rosewood Hotel. Vinod ordered a bottle of pinot grigio, and we sipped the cold wine. The others made small talk. I stared at the glistening wine glasses as the evening sun slowly disappeared over the hilltops.

———

That night, jet lagged and weary from the events of the day, I quickly fell asleep. The next morning, I felt better. I am ever the optimist, and, as I readied to return to India, I thought maybe there was some possibility that this new arrangement might work. Indeed, I felt hopeful.

En route to the airport I sent Vinod a heartfelt email:

> Thank you so much for your guidance yesterday. On behalf of all of us at SKS, I am grateful for your care and concern. We will become a much better company because of your intervention yesterday.
>
> On a personal level, I am grateful for your advice. Though it was not the outcome I wanted, I will take to heart what you said about trying to exert influence and not exert power. This will not be easy.

But I will do my best and am sure the effort I make will result in my becoming a better person and better guide to all of the SKS Team.

Vinod replied immediately:

Thanks. I think influence is much more powerful than power. And it is much more rewarding to exercise. I thought we made a lot of progress towards the strategy you desired.

His words gave me even more hope. When I was back in the office, I caught up with Sateesh Kumar, my one-time CEO candidate. I had called him immediately after the meeting to give him a quick update, but now I had a chance to give him a full briefing. I told him about the meeting, the presentations, the discussions, the compromise that had been struck, and how I was to be the chairman of the Client Protection Committee.

Sateesh looked at me with a mixture of sympathy and acrimony. "You're a fool, Vikram," he said. "They've absolutely destroyed you. It's over. Why are you still talking as if there is hope?"

CHAPTER 21

IF YOU SCORCH THE EARTH, YOU MIGHT GET BURNED

Soon after I got back to Hyderabad, I received phone calls from board members asking me when I was going to resign. It was as if the elaborate discussion about blending the two strategies had never happened.

The board had some leverage over me. I had a set of stock options that would expire in mid-October. In normal course, extending stock options is a routine matter. But in this case, the board refused to extend my options. On my end, I could not simply forego the stock options. SKS shares had lost tremendous value since the political backlash, but those options were still valuable. As mentioned, I had sold some of my stock prior to the IPO but had not had a chance to do so afterward because of lock-in restrictions. I had a son to provide for, and it was not as if—as a social entrepreneur—I would move on to the next lucrative financial opportunity. The wealth that was created through SKS would be a once-in-a-lifetime windfall. I could not just leave it. The board had me in a tight spot, and they used that leverage.

I was at a crossroads. As the pressure mounted, I called Vinod. I felt ridiculous reaching out to Vinod again, after he had been so gracious with his time already. I felt like a child running to his father when he was getting bullied on the playground. But I did not have any other choice.

Vinod said he would find out what was going on.

While he was looking into the matter, I did not wait. I had one last Hail Mary. I turned to the two people who had made my vision for SKS possible in the first place: my relative, Ravi Reddy, and his partner, Sandeep Tungare. As mentioned, they'd made significant donations to SKS NGO, the nonprofit precursor to SKS Microfinance, and then became angel investors in SKS Microfinance, alongside Vinod. I knew they believed in my mission and the mission of SKS. Of course, as discussed, they now invested through Kismet Capital, which was headed by ex-SKS board member Ashish Lakhanpal. My hope was to appeal indirectly to Ashish via Ravi and Sandeep, who were the initial and largest investors in Ashish's fund. Even though Ashish was no longer on the board, he was still part of the close-knit quartet from HBS. My hope was that Ravi and Sandeep would prevail on Ashish to listen to my side of the argument and reconsider his support of Rao's handling of SKS. After all, Ashish owed his lucrative career to Ravi and Sandeep.

A complicating factor was that there had been a significant change in the relationship between Ravi and Sandeep. Though they had been close partners in their early days together, by 2011, they had split their business interests. I was still close to both of them, though naturally, being his relative, closer to Ravi. His advice was to meet with Sandeep, as he was now the main person interacting with Ashish. So, I flew to New York, and then drove to Sandeep's office in Parsippany, New Jersey, forty minutes west of Manhattan.

Though I was not related to Sandeep, I called him "Sandeep Uncle"—an honorific title that was a function of both familiarity and respect for elders within close-knit Indian-American circles as well as an acknowledgment of the fact that he had been an early supporter of and angel investor in SKS. Sandeep's investments in SKS actually ended up making him a huge amount of money. Kismet entities cashed out to the tune of $47 million from the SKS IPO, and Sandeep had the largest holding in Kismet.[1] I expected him to help me. Beyond his profits from SKS, I banked on the fact that he knew me well. He'd seen how I'd struggled to build the company.

We met on a Sunday. I arrived before him and sat outside in my rented car because his office was closed. He pulled up shortly after in a white Porsche, hopped out, and greeted me warmly. His familiar smile was bright below his thick mustache. We went into his office and chatted. I explained the problems facing SKS Microfinance over the past year—from our IPO, through the AP microfinance backlash, and into the power struggle for the direction and integrity of the company. He nodded and asked questions. Toward the end of the discussion, he suggested heading outside as he wanted a cigarette. He pulled on his buttery leather jacket, and we headed outside. He leaned on his Porsche and between puffs of smoke, he said he would do what he could. He was also quick to manage expectations, explaining that he had not really followed the SKS investment after delegating that responsibility to Ashish.

Despite his tapering expectations, I was hopeful. As a follow-up and a thank you, I wrote an email to him on September 5.

"Sandeep Uncle," it began, and I went on to reiterate what we had verbally discussed. I wrote about the two ways forward for SKS and my fear that taking Rao and Raj's road would cause the company to fail in the long run. I asked Sandeep for two specific outcomes: the first was to arrange a meeting with Ashish Lakhanpal in the hopes that I could change his mind about aligning Kismet's investment with those of Sandstone and Sequoia. The second was that, if Ashish was unwilling to listen—which I was pretty sure would be the case—I hoped Sandeep would facilitate, including attending, a meeting with other limited partners at Kismet with the goal of persuading them about the merits of the direction I was proposing for SKS Microfinance. Finally, I attached several background documents,

including the full July 26 presentation that had been omitted from the board meeting minutes as well as the presentation I had given in front of the board and Vinod in Menlo Park at the Rosewood Hotel.

A few days later, Sandeep wrote back. An excerpt is below:

> Today, I feel strongly that I really do not have the time to devote to helping resolve this issue. As you may know, in addition to running Vistaar, I am also running Think Capital, since Ravi Uncle is no longer involved in running Think Capital. I am also spending an inordinate amount of time helping Ashish with our Thailand investment.
>
> As you requested, I spoke to Ashish about your concerns and he had several counter points, and I could see that it would be a long, long call. In short, it is a complicated set of issues that you have raised, and I simply don't have the time to understand all the nuances, rationales, risks and other factors involved. You know that I have always been a strong supporter of you and SKS from its inception, but today it is a public company. I just don't feel that I can advise you like I did in the old days . . . To truly provide value, I would have to get at least as deeply involved as your Board Members are before I could opine on anything.

Naturally, Sandeep's reply was disappointing. Even if he was busy, couldn't he make the time in my hour of need? I thought back to the various instances when he had made the time. He'd come to an awards ceremony when I was named the Ernst & Young Entrepreneur of the Year in the start-up category. We shared a Scotch after I was profiled on the front page of the *Wall Street Journal*. Of course, I was pleased to have him share those moments, but I was let down that he was happy to celebrate the high points, happy to cash out, but now he did not have the time to help me avert SKS from veering off its mission.

———————

Meanwhile, Vinod had spoken with various board members and emailed me on September 8, just after I landed in Hyderabad and less than two weeks after our meeting at the Rosewood Hotel.

I think you will need to step down in the next 2–4 weeks or they will force it.

I do think if you make it cooperative and issue some joint supportive statements of the new strategy you can get them to extend your [stock] options though I have not been part of that discussion. If you step down voluntarily and issue some joint supportive statements on the new strategy you will retain more influence and get a chance to build it over time as you build trust that you won't fight them in the press or in the courts. I would highly recommend that strategy.

His words stung. I could go back and tell him that this is not what we had agreed to at the Rosewood. But I felt like I had already asked too much of Vinod. He had been generous with his time when we were in Menlo Park, but I wasn't sure how much he could continue to influence from afar. Worse yet, there was no one else I could turn to for advice because the deliberations of the board were confidential, and because, now that SKS was public, the details of the discussions involved were insider information. If I shared it with anyone and they traded SKS shares based on that information, it would be a securities violation. In fact, involving Vinod and Sandeep had probably already pushed the limits of what I could do. I knew Vinod and Sandeep would not trade SKS shares, but I could not trust anyone else. Anyway, I was not sure that running to Vinod again would have made any difference. I believe Vinod genuinely cared about the mission of SKS and had respect for me as an entrepreneur, but I also know that venture capitalists do not like to fight publicly. I think Vinod got worried because he saw rumblings that I was about to do that; I, of course, noticed that in his email and calls to me he often used the phrase "make it cooperative."

Indeed, he was right. I was moving in the direction of a public fight because the board was forcing my hand. Now, the board changed SKS's official legal counsel (without informing me, let alone getting my approval, which would be expected as I was still executive chairperson). The new law firm sent me an aggressive letter on

September 9, 2011, about not extending my options. This came the day after I received Vinod's email about the board being ready to "force" my resignation.

Naturally, in light of the board's letter, my lawyer matched the tone in his reply. The posturing got very heated. Vinod emailed me once again a few days later, on September 13. This time he wrote:

> I do suggest you take a super cooperative posture with the board. I think it will help everyone get less polarized, which will help your position in the long run. You should reach out to Geoff [Woolley] and talk to him and try and de-escalate things and start rebuilding relationships for the longer term. You will have a lot better influence if you build relationships and stop any legal action etc.

Notice Vinod's words change from asking me to be "cooperative" to "super cooperative." As I mentioned, I have great respect and admiration for Vinod. I know he cared deeply about the mission of SKS. But when I read these words, I knew he was not getting the full picture. Frankly, it wouldn't have mattered whether or not Vinod got more involved. The board went on a full attack: I received a flurry of emails and letters from board members, delivering a range of outlandish and false accusations. All the missives used the loaded word "conduct." It seemed the board members had held discussions with legal counsel and were seeking to build a case for termination for cause.

I'll describe three of the messages.

On September 16, two independent directors, Ravikumar and Tarun, sent an email accusing me of threatening physical violence against Rao and Raj. It was a reference to the meeting I'd had with Rao and Raj after the July 26 board meeting. It was the meeting in which Rao and Raj had at one point stood at my desk—Rao with his hand raised—and then they'd refused to leave until finishing their tea. Afterward, they'd told the board I had physically threatened them. And now, two months later, the board was writing to me about this. Though the email came from Ravikumar and Tarun, Ravikumar later admitted to me that Paresh Patel brought him the letter and sat in his office and said to sign it. Indeed, in the email thread of the message sent by Ravikumar, one can see an email from Paresh, prompting Ravi to send me the email.

The second missive came on September 21, this time from a new committee called the "Committee for Review of Senior Management." In this letter, Paresh alleged that I ". . . violated my obligations to the company under my employment contract and the Company's Code of Conduct." There were no specifics, just a vague statement.

On September 24, I received a third letter from Ravikumar mentioning "concerns about your conduct." Ravikumar was writing in his capacity as chairperson of the Shareholder and Investor Grievance Committee, another newly established committee. It was a short letter, with seven attached letters from major shareholders, which is where the substance was. Two of the letters were from Ashish Lakhanpal.

Ashish's letter was replete with a series of false allegations. He blamed me for the firing of Gurumani—an absurd allegation because, being a board member at the time, Ashish knew full well that the board had fired Gurumani because of the ultimatum from Rao and Raj to resign if Gurumani were to stay on as CEO. Ashish also discussed my opposition to the gold lending strategy, casting this as irresponsible while failing to note my social and business arguments against this strategy. He brought up my son, discussing the fact that I had been in a child custody battle and the public nature of it. The correspondence from Ashish included letters of concurrence from three other significant shareholders.

Though Ravikumar emailed me on September 24, Ashish's letter had been emailed on August 14, which was interesting relative to the timing of my August 11 letter to the board asking for a response to my proposed comments to the Strategic Initiatives Committee. Then had come the August 16 front-page article in the *Economic Times*, with statements that the board wanted me to resign. It seemed to me that the board had held onto the August 14 letter from Ashish and other investors until now, perhaps in the hope that the news article and coaxing from Vinod would get me to back down on the strategic and ethical arguments I was making.

I had not backed down.

Ravikumar's September 24 correspondence also included a second missive from Ashish, dated September 7—a few days after I'd met with Sandeep in Parsippany. Ashish's main new complaint was that I had shared information with one of his investors; he then went on to repeat the allegations from his earlier email. Sandeep had emailed me back on September 7. Ashish's email had been sent one minute prior to the SKS board (though not to me), suggesting that Sandeep had possibly coordinated with Ashish. The timing of their emails seemed too coincidental.

Ashish's email begins:

> This e-mail is a follow-up to my note dated August 14, 2011 . . . Vikram has written to one of my largest investors seeking his support for Vikram's position against the board and claiming that he has the support of Vinod Khosla, SIDBI, and the SKS Trusts. What is most damaging and concerning to me is that he has shared material, non-public, information with someone who has no fiduciary responsibility to the Company. Specifically, he apparently has shared confidential board information with an outsider who has no background, context, or information with respect to what is going on at the Company.

My September 5 email to Sandeep was attached at the bottom.

It was one thing for Sandeep to not want to help me but another to participate in an attack on me. I am not sure what may have been going on between him and Ravi Reddy, but I would be saddened if it were true that Sandeep directed his animosity about that conflict toward me. I don't know, as I have never since spoken with Sandeep.

As for Ashish's contention that I had spoken with *his* investors, there is no doubt that I had. But the reference to "his investors" is to Sandeep and Ravi, two individuals who had been involved with SKS from the beginning—and one of whom is my relative. In fact, I had spoken to many of our outside investors—often at the request of their nominee board members—over the years as I sought to build consensus on SKS's strategic direction. In any event, I did not view the discussion with these investors as involving insider information, but rather as necessary steps to ensure that the board was acting in the manner that was aligned with the core shareholders.

Calling on Sandeep was the final move I had left. This attempt had not only failed but, even worse, backfired. I was cornered.

Now I had to decide what to do. I oscillated between flight or fight. Some moments, I felt outraged by the greed, the destruction of the soul of SKS. I vowed to fight. The next moment, I wanted to just curl up in bed. The argument for fighting was, first and foremost, that I cared deeply about the loss of lives, as well as SKS and its mission. If I gave up, everything that SKS had once stood for would be diminished. In short, pressing on was the principled thing to do.

I wanted to reach out to a journalist for an off-the-record conversation. If I were to go public with what was happening at SKS, it had to be off the record. All said and done, I was still the executive chairperson of a public company. I couldn't say anything about the board debates on the record. I asked a relative to help me find a reporter he trusted. This relative happened to be in a business in India that received a lot of media attention, so I knew he would have some trusted contacts. He put me in touch with a reporter, who then flew from Mumbai to Hyderabad to meet me. I did not want to be publicly seen with him, so I picked him up from the airport in a rented vehicle. Instead of driving somewhere, we just pulled off to the shoulder on a side road away from the airport and talked right there in the car.

He could see I was nervous. Indeed, I was second-guessing myself. Was this the right thing to do? It would hurt SKS, the company I founded and cultivated. SKS had already been reeling from a year-long political, bureaucratic, and media backlash. Would we survive a fight in the papers between the founder (albeit using off-the-record statements) and the board? What would happen to our members, our employees, our shareholders? On a personal level, I would have to be ready for the next tidal wave of press coverage headed my way. The day after Gurumani was dismissed, there was a huge article in the newspaper with his photo and a red-lettered stamp across his face that read *FIRED*. In fact, the August 16 *Economic Times* article—"SKS Microfinance Wants Vikram Akula to Step Down"— replete with anonymous sources, was the slow reveal of what awaited me. If I spoke to that reporter sitting next to me in the car, the board would surely up the ante.

As these questions swirled in my head, the reporter made small talk. I said nothing as I wrestled with my doubts about going through with the interview. During my long moments of silence, the reporter kept talking to fill the space, perhaps trying to ease my mind. He started talking about how off-the-record conversations helped journalists give a true picture of events.

"Everyone does it. I don't know why you are so hesitant," he said. And then he casually told me, "Your ex-wife had a whole lot of people giving off-the-record comments."

"Wait! What?" I blurted.

"Yes," he explained. "There were a number of people who would call us and tell us 'her side of the story.' Some were friends of hers. Some were her lawyers. But, Vikram, some were people you worked with, closely—even your CEO. How could you not have known that?"

Nope, I didn't know that.

The news coverage had not only affected me. It had affected my son. Over the prior year and a half, his name and face had been plastered across the media—TV, print, the internet. From the vernacular media to the most widely circulated English newspaper, *Times of India*, to the most prestigious Indian news channel, NDTV, no one had spared him. And the international media—NBC, the *New York Times*—uncritically picked up the narrative.

With that inadvertent bit of information, the reporter made the decision for me. My son had already been through so much. I couldn't subject him to more. And now that it had been confirmed to me that Rao had been egging on the groundswell of negative media coverage about me and my fight to get custody of my son, I could foresee what would happen if I took the step of an off-the-record interview about the internal struggles between the SKS board and me. I had neither the willpower nor the resources to match them. I knew it. And, I imagined, they knew it, too.

"I can't do this. I am sorry," I told the journalist. I drove him back to the airport.

So, having closed off that avenue, there was nothing left to do but resign.

But I could not get myself to resign. I just could not do it. There had to be a way to continue to fight for what I thought was best for SKS without the nuclear option of going public. My move—lukewarm though it may have been—was to send formal replies to the official missives from the board. I also sent a formal version of the email I had sent to the board on August 11. This time it was not from my personal email. There were no caveats, such as *draft: not for circulation*. This letter dove into the philosophy of microfinance, the path to success that SKS Microfinance had taken under my leadership, the problems with "cross-sell on a war footing," the problems with lending against gold, the suicide investigation by the private investigator. In more than 15,000 words, I laid out on the record what had gone wrong with SKS Microfinance. As a result, SKS could no longer pretend we had not contributed to the procedural lapses that led to over-indebtedness nor deny there were problems within our company.

Initially, I got the result I wanted—SKS hired a forensic auditor to delve into all the issues I raised. The board appointed Arpinder Singh, a partner at Ernst & Young, who went on to become the head of India and Emerging Markets, Fraud Investigation & Dispute Services at Ernst & Young.

Naturally, I was thrilled. I met with Arpinder Singh and his team, and I even pointed the audit team in the direction of some of SKS's larger transgressions. I had a laundry list. By the time the forensic audit took place, there were rumors within the management team that I would be resigning. A number of employees who were concerned about the changing culture at SKS surreptitiously reached out to me. I added their concerns to my own list and presented it to Singh and his team.

I was hopeful when I saw the forensic auditors show up and immediately seize some laptops of senior staff to download hard drives that they would then sift through. Meanwhile, I suggested areas to investigate to Singh and his team.

Perhaps the most dramatic moment was when Singh's team uncovered evidence of bribes that had been paid to police involved in suicide investigations. I had not known about such bribes when they occurred, but in the weeks prior to the audit a whistle-blower had alerted me to what had happened. As mentioned, the AP state government had accused SKS in seventeen cases of death that were allegedly suicides stemming from over-indebtedness. And as noted, many of these cases were falsely attributed to SKS; even the cases mentioned earlier do not, I believe, rise to the level of legal culpability.

But Rao was not taking any chances, especially since—as CEO of SKS—he was the prime accused in the cases filed under the AP Microfinance Act. It turns out that he had instructed branch managers in the respective districts to bribe police officers to conclude there was no probable cause for arrest. The bribe amounts were relatively small, ₹10,000 (about $200). But what was significant is that once our directors were made aware of this, they would have to take action against Rao, because it was clearly against the law to bribe police, not to mention that it was a fraudulent use of company funds.

The whistle-blower forwarded to me an email from the company secretary to Rao with a copy to Raj that asked for authorization of a payment. Now I needed corroboration. One of the regional managers involved in paying the bribes was J. S. Chalam, a longtime employee of SKS. He was on the email thread, which included an email from him documenting what transpired. I asked him to come to our headquarters to meet me. Like most of the employees outside of the senior management team, he was not aware of my struggle against the board or the forensic audit, so he probably did not think twice about my request to meet.

When Chalam arrived, my aide Sivani Shankar brought him directly into my office. After a bit of small talk, I said, "Forgive me, but can you give me your phone?" Chalam handed it to me, with a puzzled look. I then took him into the adjoining conference room, where Singh and his team were waiting to question him.

I knew that Chalam was scared, and I felt bad about treating him in this way, but I had to make sure Singh spoke with him before others at SKS could silence him. Upon Singh's questioning, Chalam revealed the bribing of the police officials in the branches under his purview. He affirmed the email thread I had shown Singh in which the company secretary sought Rao's authorization of the payment. Raj was copied. Chalam also affirmed that Rao had given the authorization, so he had paid the legal head. This was documented in a subsequent email in the thread.

While Chalam and I were inside the conference room with Singh and his team, others at the company were clearly in a panic. But there was nothing they could do. The next person to be called in was the legal compliance head. I am sure he was pressured to not reveal what had happened. But Singh had the damning email.

When Singh confronted him, the legal compliance head caved. I was in the room when he admitted to Singh, "Yes, we bribed the police." Singh now had clear evidence. This, I thought, was finally the smoking gun that would turn the tide in this internal struggle between Rao and me.

One would think our regular auditor would have been able to trace illegal payments to police. It's worth bearing in mind that SKS's CFO Dilli Raj had expertise in fraud, which I had not realized at the time he was hired. It came out some years later, in August 2016, when—during a late-night home raid by the federal government's Enforcement Directorate—Raj was arrested for his involvement in a ₹665 crore ($115 million) fraud in his previous company.[2] While yet to be tried, as of this writing, Raj had spent more than a year in jail because his bail was denied. When Raj joined SKS in 2008, Rao commented in the press: "We are very excited about Dilli Raj joining as CFO and Senior Vice President."[3]

The revelation of bribing police involved in suicide investigations caused me to wonder about the veracity of the report from the district superintendent of police that had appeared in the press and exonerated MFIs—the same report that Rao had shown to me in support of his claim that allegations of microfinance causing suicide were false. One of the cases included in the district superintendent's report was that of the beleaguered teenage girl I related in chapter sixteen. I had to wonder: Had Rao also bribed that police official?

In any event, once Singh had completed his work, I waited and waited for his report, only to find out that the board had arranged for the company's new law firm (not the company) to hire the forensic auditor. As such, whatever results and conclusions Singh and his team drew fell under attorney-client privilege. I was still chairperson of the board, so I should have had access to that document, but the company attorney refused to divulge any information. So once again, this time under the auspices of that privilege, the board appeared to stonewall me. My attempt to hold the board and the management accountable had been thwarted. The contents of that forensic audit have never been made public.

Interestingly, I had also met with Viren Mehta, the partner from Ernst & Young who oversaw SKS's annual audits. I shared the same material that I presented to the Ernst & Young Fraud Investigation team, but I also never saw any mention of the issues I had raised in the audit reports from Ernst & Young.

In my heart, I already knew I was going to be forced to leave. I knew my letters probably wouldn't change that. But what I hoped the letters would do, what I hoped the forensic audit would do, and what I hoped my discussion with Viren Mehta would do, was to get the board to respond to actual issues rather than seeming to focus on how to sweep it all under the carpet.

Now I had a final choice. I could leak the letters to the press. It would be a scorched earth approach, a hardball tactic. From what I knew, Rao, Raj, and the SKS board of directors were more than happy to play this game of hardball. In fact, they were much better at it than I was. They had made it clear that if this was a game of chicken, they were not going to blink. Complicating matters for me was the fact of my stock options. If I went through with this nuclear option and took the company down, not only would I be destroying my life's intellectual and professional work, but I would be acting financially irresponsibly toward my son, which of course impacted my decision making.

In a moment of clarity, I called Vinod Khosla one last time in late October 2011. I told him I had had enough of the fighting and that I was looking for a way out. I asked him to help me. For financial and personal reasons, I didn't want to get fired. Vinod helped me. He spoke with Sumir, who then spoke with me to work out terms of my departure.

I found it difficult to negotiate with Sumir. In our various conversations about the settlement, he did everything from humiliate me to ridicule me. Maybe it was a negotiating tactic, as I remember him once telling me that he'd had to fire a good number of entrepreneurs that he'd invested in. Regardless, it worked. I dreaded speaking to him about the settlement terms. I would get all worked up, both by the emotion of having to negotiate my exit from my own company and because Sumir always had some good excuse to give me less than what I wanted—less money, less time to exercise my stock options, more restrictions in my noncompete provision. Worse yet, he would never give me a firm answer when we spoke. There was always someone he had to check with—the other board members, the lawyers, and so on. I knew he was not being transparent. He had been given full authority by the board. But I had to suffer through it. He wore me down. When we finally, with Vinod's periodic intervention, came up with terms that were mutually acceptable, the lawyers pounded out a twenty-two-page separation agreement.

One of the aspects of the negotiation that Sumir would not budge on was staff. We were a big company, with 25,000 employees, many of whom had been with me and SKS from the beginning. I wanted to be able to at least take those employees with me. I asked to take 1,000 early field staff on the way out—I knew that if I left them behind they would be fired right away. I got 40 staff. The vast majority of the remaining 1,000 of my early field staff were fired soon after I left.

CHAPTER 22

ESCORTED OUT

I resigned on Wednesday, November 23, 2011, the day before Thanksgiving. I went to Paresh's Mumbai office, where our board meeting was being held in the same conference room where I had tried to present to the board back in July. The resignation itself took a long time. I had to hand over my company laptop and cell phone. I had to sign the lengthy separation agreement. My lawyer was present. The board's lawyer was present. A handful of board members was present, enough for a quorum.

My eyes welled up with tears as I signed the document. When it was over, and everyone else had left the conference room, I sat there alone and cried.

There was a swarm of media outside because rumors of my impending resignation were swirling on the news in what seemed to be a final attempt by Rao to humiliate me. I avoided the mob by walking out a back door and then darting across the street to the Trident Hotel in Nariman Point. One reporter saw me and escaped the crowd with me. She walked alongside me into the hotel, holding a recorder in her hand. I did not say anything.

Though my tears started when I signed my separation agreement, the real sadness began the day before. Since we were a public company,

I could not reveal to anyone that I was resigning. It had to be kept confidential because that news was the ultimate insider information. So I'd gone to the Hyderabad office around 9 PM on the day before to clean out my desk and take my personal belongings. The building was empty except for security guards. I went to my office and slowly, numbly, started putting my things in a small cardboard box. A bamboo reed mural made by one of our members, a wooden sculpture of a cow given to me by an early employee, a photo of my son, a photo of me with a group of our members in the field, the Ernst & Young Entrepreneur of the Year Award, the framed cover of *TIME* magazine when my picture was on the cover.

Once I packed everything in the box, I held it in two hands and walked out. Just as I was heading out the main door, one of the security guards walked up to me and took the box. I thought he wanted to help me carry it out to my car. Instead, he and another security guard started going through the box, noting each item in a notebook. I guessed that the guards had been instructed to check that I had not taken—stolen—anything from the office that did not belong to me. I imagine Rao had a hearty laugh when hearing of me standing there awkwardly, while the security guards were checking off the items in my cardboard box.

When it was done, they gave the box back to me and escorted me out to my car.

―――――――――――

The night of my resignation, I stayed at the Trident Hotel, across the street from the building where the board meeting had been held. It was too late to catch a flight back to Hyderabad. And frankly, I was too exhausted. I watched some of the news stories about my resignation that night, and the next morning I read about it on the front pages.

The SKS head of communications and I had prepared a press release for after I resigned. The content had been negotiated. I was to make some positive statements about the company, and they were to make some positive statements about me, which was in the spirit of Vinod's mandate to be "super cooperative." He had helped me with my financial settlement, so I owed it to him to listen.

That night's TV stories and the next day's newspaper stories carried my positive statements about the company. But there were scant positive statements from SKS about me. I suspected that the full press release was never sent by SKS, which I confirmed with some journalists. There wasn't much I could do about it. I couldn't run to Vinod with something so seemingly trivial.

The next few months were tough. In exchange for the financial settlement, I agreed to a three-year noncompete provision. I was not allowed to do anything in financial inclusion, the field in which I had spent my entire career. For me personally, staying in Hyderabad proved difficult. I was a recognizable figure in the city and, more generally, in India. News coverage of my resignation—negative news coverage, presumably curated by Rao and team—lasted through the new year, and it was difficult for me to carve out any new personal spaces in the city I had called home for more than twenty years. At the end of my son's school year in May 2012, we moved to New Jersey, close to my extended family and to a new existence in the United States. It was time for me to turn the page.

———

There's one more part of the SKS story that I'll tell you about here. It affected people other than me, and I find that deeply troubling. I earlier described how the board used the threat of firing me for cause ("conduct," as they put it in the aforementioned series of letters) to get me to back down on the strategic and ethical arguments I was making in the boardroom. Before I left for the States, I discovered that, as part of the campaign to oust me, Rao had pressured the executive management team to sign a statement to the board against me. The statement claimed that executive management were "victims of threats and inappropriate behavior" from me. The statement went on to say that I had been "tarnishing the image of the company." In the same statement, the executive management team urged the board to launch "loans against gold" by "floating a subsidiary." The statement ended with this: "We have bet our career on SKS . . . as days pass by with little progress, doubts are being raised if the bets were right."

The statement from the executive management team reminded me of Rao's and Raj's ultimatum against Gurumani before he was ousted.

The board had never shown me the statement. When I learned of it, naturally I was disappointed, in part because I never had the chance to respond and also because several of those executive management members were individuals whom I had recruited, groomed, taught, and then elevated to senior roles. They had become more than colleagues; they were friends. I was crushed when I saw their signatures on the statement. On the other hand, I also understood their situation. Taking a stand in my favor would have put their livelihood in jeopardy in a culture in which it was difficult to start over. I couldn't blame them for protecting their livelihoods and that of their families.

I also realized that even if there were executives who wanted to take a stand, they were in a work environment where it would have been difficult. Earlier I described how Rao would bully and intimidate staff, making it hard for anyone to go against him.

Another symbol of the toxic culture was daily *pai lagu*, meaning "touch your feet." It is a gesture of respect that is often used when greeting people who are older than you. Though this practice was traditionally a sign of deep respect, it has more recently been used by people trying to ingratiate themselves with a politician or local strongman. The behavior is encouraged by political figures, who tend to dole out favors to their followers who show such deference. The practice, unfortunately, has also crept into the business world.

Rao encouraged this. Senior management would stop in Rao's office every morning for pai lagu. The inner circle would stay on for a while and engage in an informal discussion. Rao would mock my American accent or some other characteristic of mine and everyone would laugh. This practice of pai lagu at SKS started after I left in 2008 in a moderate way and then increased in intensity after Gurumani was fired and Rao became CEO in 2010.

K.V. Rao, who was the head of field operations and who had formerly worked with Rao, epitomized the sycophancy. He not only touched Rao's feet daily but periodically even gave Rao foot rubs in full public view. This was not unlike a traditional village scene, in which a large landowner would hold court with his minions while a faithful supplicant massaged his foot.

I heard about all this secondhand after I resigned from SKS. But even when I was CEO, there were glimpses of the loyalist culture which I saw firsthand. For example, Rao smokes cigarettes. When he would leave the SKS building for smoke breaks, a coterie of his followers would trail after him to keep him company, even nonsmokers.

The loyalist work culture and the difficulty of taking a stand against Rao made me appreciate the courage of the one executive who refused to sign the statement. I've mentioned Ramesh Vautrey, the executive in charge of the Facilities and Administration department, who helped me when the investigator was interviewing the families in the suicide cases. He had joined SKS in February 2009. Trained as an engineer, Ramesh had worked in real estate and facilities management, including holding leadership roles in multinational corporations such as Jones Lang LaSalle and UBS Bank. He had read one of my interviews about financial inclusion and empowering poor women, and he wanted to leave his mainstream career to engage in work he found more meaningful. Financial inclusion was a perfect fit for him. He could use his skills and talents, yet not have to take on the bare-bones salary of a social worker. On our end, we had recruited him because SKS was growing at triple-digit pace, and we wanted someone who would be able to quickly steer the Facilities and Administration group to keep up with frenetic growth while maintaining quality and keeping costs down. Ramesh not only had the skills, talent, and experience to do this, but also the integrity. I mention this because, unfortunately, facilities and administration departments in any business in India are often rife with rampant kickbacks and corruption. In our references checks, particularly on this issue, Ramesh came out as having a reputation for integrity.

Indeed, his performance was excellent. Even Rao agreed. After all, Rao, to whom Ramesh reported, promoted Ramesh to executive vice president within a year of his joining.

But when Rao told him to sign the statement against me, Ramesh refused. Despite tremendous pressure from Rao and despite the fact that all other members of the executive management team acquiesced, Ramesh stood firm.

Rao physically accosted Ramesh and shouted obscenities at Ramesh in the hallway, probably in the hopes that the embarrassment would get Ramesh to cave. Ramesh did not.

Next Rao threatened to fire him and implicate him in false cases of embezzlement. But Ramesh continued to hold firm. He resigned one week after I did, on December 1, 2011. However, while I could walk away with a negotiated financial settlement, Ramesh could not. Per India business practices, Ramesh needed to be "relieved" officially, which involved getting his "experience certificate" and at least a neutral reference from SKS Human Resources to get another job.

Rao did not relieve him. Instead, he made Ramesh serve out his two-month notice period, during which he was made to sit in my former office, a cavernous chairman's executive office. No one would speak with Ramesh or even look at him for fear of getting caught in the crossfire. Just as I had a few months earlier, Ramesh walked around like a ghost at SKS. Then it got worse. To give Ramesh a negative reference (which would effectively blacklist him from getting any other job), Rao needed "cause," an incident showing some sort of misconduct. But with Ramesh, there were none. So one was concocted.

After days of letting Ramesh sit alone and sweat it out, isolated in my former office, on December 26, Rao; the head of human resources, Srini Reddy Vudumula; and a human resources manager, R. M. Murali, summoned a junior employee in the Facilities and Administration department. That employee, Kiran Raparthi, had worked under Ramesh and was responsible for making purchases from various vendors—everything from stationery to printing materials. Kiran, a slight young man, walked into the glass-enclosed fourth-floor conference room of the six-story SKS building. Sitting at the other side of the table were Rao and the two HR executives, Srini and Murali.

They told Kiran to sign a false statement about Ramesh having taken kickbacks, but Kiran refused. Srini tried to persuade him, saying something to the effect of, "If you do not sign this, you will be sacked and you will never be able to get a job." Kiran held firm, refusing to go against Ramesh. Then Srini and Rao left the room, and Murali remained alone with Kiran. Murali conveyed that this wasn't about Kiran nor even about Ramesh. "This is about Vikram," Murali said. "So just give the statement. I assure you that you will be taken care of."

Srini and Rao returned a few minutes later. Kiran still refused. Then all three left the conference room, locking Kiran inside and turning off the air conditioning. Kiran sat and sweated in that conference room for four long hours. They finally released him at 7 PM.

The next morning, Kiran was called into the conference room again. This time he was met by Srini and Murali. Srini screamed at Kiran to sign a statement against Ramesh or Srini would ensure that Kiran never get another job. He switched into the vernacular, Telugu, his voice still raised, and added words to this effect: "I will take a newspaper ad with your picture and the headline, 'Thief—do not hire,' and I will personally deliver it to your house, where your elderly parents will see it."

Just as on the previous day, they left the conference room and locked Kiran inside. This time, they also took his cell phone. Kiran sat there for hours. He could see people walking by the glass windows of the conference room, but everyone stayed clear.

At about 7 PM, Srini and Murali returned and demanded the statement. Kiran refused. Srini then left. He came back a few minutes later and handed his cell phone to Kiran, and said, "Talk. It's for you." On the other end of the line was Kiran's friend, Venkatesh Palvi. He worked at Satyam, where Srini had previously worked. Venkatesh pleaded with Kiran, "Please, sign the statement." Palvi explained that unless Kiran made the statement, his boss (a friend and former colleague of Srini) would fire Palvi. "Just do what they say," Palvi said. "Why do you have to get involved in the fight between powerful people?"

Kiran was moved by his friend's plight. It was now 8:15 PM. He had been in the conference room all day—no water, no bathroom break. He finally agreed to sign a statement but said he would only implicate himself, not anyone else. He signed it and was released.

The next day he was called into the conference room again and told that SKS legal counsel said the letter had to implicate Ramesh by name. Kiran refused. Srini said Kiran would be fired on the spot and that he would do all the things he'd promised—Kiran's friend would be fired, Srini would take an ad out in the paper, Kiran would be blacklisted.

Kiran continued to refuse. He was given a termination letter around 1 PM. His office laptop was taken, and he was paraded—in front of his former colleagues—out of the office by two security guards.

Kiran went straight to the Begumpet neighborhood police station to file a complaint. At the police station, Kiran narrated the three-day sequence of events to the sub-inspector (SI) of police. The SI said he would investigate. The SI went to SKS and came back a few hours later. To Kiran's shock, the SI tried to coax him into signing the statement implicating Ramesh.

"Kiran, you are a young man, and this is a huge company. Just sign the statement and get on with your life," the SI said. Perhaps the SI was bribed; perhaps he was just giving genuine advice to Kiran. Kiran said he would think about it and left.

A few days later, the SI called Kiran and asked him to come to the police station. When Kiran arrived, he saw Srini sitting at the desk of the SI. Srini said to Kiran, "Now you know my power. This police station is mine. There's nowhere you can go." Kiran listened but still refused to acquiesce and left the station. He spoke with a lawyer, who advised him to file a private petition in the local court office for wrongful confinement, wrongful restraint, and criminal intimidation. He did. SKS—with the backing of the SI—filed a countersuit against Kiran for cheating, misappropriation, and fraud.

The two cases were joined and the court proceeded. SKS was able to delay the cases. Finally, on June 5, 2017, more than five years later, and after more than one hundred court appearances, Kiran was finally cleared of all charges. During that time, Kiran received phone calls with death threats against him and his parents, and he was not able to get a job because he was blacklisted—receiving a negative reference—from SKS.

Meanwhile, Kiran's case against SKS is still pending as of the time of this writing. Rao is the prime accused, along with the board of SKS, Srini, and Murali. SKS has been successful in having the case delayed. SKS has hired E. Uma Maheswara, a lawyer who is famous for representing politician and former minister Gali Janardhan Reddy, who is implicated in a massive corruption scam and whose net worth is close to $1 billion.

Ramesh Vautrey was wrongfully terminated by SKS shortly after his notice period was completed, in early 2012. Before being terminated, Ramesh detailed all the events in a memo and sent it to the board chairperson, Ravikumar, then sought whistle-blower protection from the board. The memo not only highlighted the harassment of Kiran but also described the suicides investigation report (which

Ramesh had been coordinating and which I had submitted to the board the previous year) and the surveillance of me, including Rao ordering calls records and reading my texts and emails on the company server.

Ravikumar appointed CFO Raj as the investigating officer, which was farcical because Raj was part of the attack on Ramesh and because Raj also reported to Rao, against whom Ramesh was making his whistle-blower allegation. During the investigation, Ramesh received two death threats against him and his family. Eventually, Ramesh's whistle-blower complaint was rejected. Ramesh was terminated and then blacklisted in the form of receiving a negative reference from SKS. Subsequently, he was not able to find a job. In 2013, I reached out to both Ravikumar and Sumir personally, meeting Ravikumar in Mumbai and speaking with Sumir on the phone about the injustice meted out to Ramesh and Kiran. I told them, "Whatever gripe you have with me, take it out on me. But let these two individuals get on with their lives." Ravikumar did not act; Sumir did not act. They said handling the situation was in Rao's purview. To this day, Rao continues his rampage against Ramesh and Kiran.

I used my network to find Ramesh a suitable role, and he is currently the CEO of a nonprofit established by a relative of mine. The entity is Community Pure Water, which installs drinking water filtration systems in villages in India. Kiran also works there.

The attack on Ramesh and Kiran reminded me of the story of "big tobacco" and how they treated whistle-blower Jeffrey Wigand.

In the mid-1990s, after years of outrage about tobacco companies, especially about the "Joe Camel" marketing campaign that targeted teens, the U.S. Congress finally held hearings in 1994 in which the CEOs of the four major tobacco companies had to testify. All four CEOs claimed they did not *believe* that cigarettes were addictive or leading to fatal illnesses. Whistle-blower Jeffrey Wigand contradicted them, saying his company had long known that it was selling an addictive product that caused cancer. Wigand was harassed and received anonymous death threats. He was portrayed by Russell Crowe in the 1999 film *The Insider*.

The Justice Department tried to prosecute the tobacco CEOs for perjury. But because the four CEOs had crafted their answers carefully, presumably with help from attorneys, testifying what they "believed" allowed them to elude prosecution. I earlier shared a line from Ashish's statement to the press, when he was quoted as a former SKS board member, discussing suicides motivated by over-indebtedness. Here's more of that Associated Press article that appeared after I left SKS.

> "The growth was very rapid. That growth led to some suboptimal out-comes," said Ashish Lakhanpal, managing director of Kismet Capital, one of SKS's largest shareholders, who was on the SKS board until October 2010. "Were there lapses? Absolutely." While the board was concerned about fast credit growth, the company never believed it was harming borrowers, Lakhanpal said. "Mistakes were made, but I find it difficult to believe there was anything people did at a managerial level to encourage field officers to do that," he said.[1]

Consider further the statements in the same article by two others on the SKS board. The reporter wrote: "Ravikumar, who would become interim chairman when Akula resigned, said the board was never informed that SKS employees were implicated in any suicides, and denied Akula presented any such findings to the board."

As related earlier in this book, Ravikumar was the one who emailed me back and with whom I had a phone call after I sent him a soft copy of my July 26, 2011, presentation. Meanwhile, the same news article reports that Pramod replied by email: "Any issues raised to the board at various times were fully investigated by external parties and found to be unsubstantiated or without evidence or actions were taken on them where appropriate."

So Ashish said the board did not *believe* SKS did anything wrong. Ravikumar said the board was never informed SKS did anything wrong. Pramod said nothing went wrong or, if something did go wrong, "actions were taken on them where appropriate." The article also stated: ". . . the company stands by its September 2011 affidavit before India's Supreme Court. In that affidavit, chief executive M. R. Rao says SKS 'is neither the cause of nor responsible for any suicides in the state of Andhra Pradesh.'"

In contrast, Ramesh said in the article that he did not want "to be a part of a team abetting suicides . . . It is systemic failure. We have no right to kill anybody for our own business. Let's close down our business if we can't do it right."[2]

I don't necessarily agree with the statement that SKS was literally abetting suicide. I did agree with the spirit of what Ramesh was saying; we had to take moral responsibility for what SKS had catalyzed. Ramesh was ready to do that. Ashish, Ravikumar, Pramod, and Rao were not.

PART III
THE
RESURGENCE

CHAPTER 23

THE VIEW FROM NEW JERSEY

Six years have passed since I left SKS. I can tick off on one hand my reasons for resigning when I did: I was heartbroken over the loss of lives. I was worried about the plan to convert collateral-free loans to lending against gold. I was concerned about the dilution of training leading to more over-indebtedness. I was disturbed by the lack of transparency in our insurance products. I was uneasy about pushing ill-designed products as part of the "cross-sell on a war footing" strategy.

But I finally came to realize that I had been outmaneuvered at every turn. No matter what I did, the board seemed to spin it in a way that would not result in the concerns I had being addressed in a manner that would benefit our members—the poor women I had in mind when I founded SKS twenty years ago.

Swayam Krishi Sangam was built around the concept of "self-cultivation" nurtured by a supportive community. When that concept was set aside in favor of short-term self-interest, I felt that SKS had traded away its soul. As I write this chapter in late 2017, I am thankful that my worst fears were, in fact, not realized. Instead, what I had fought for when I was within the company ultimately materialized. Not because the SKS board had a change of heart. But because of

309

long-overdue regulations from the central bank, the Reserve Bank of India, and also because banks, the source of debt to MFIs, sobered up. Those RBI regulations were first announced in mid-2011, as I was in the final stage of my battle with the SKS board. They were finalized June 30, 2012, about seven months after I resigned.[1] Even though those regulations had been initially articulated before I resigned, my worry was that, even with regulations in place, the SKS board seemed ready to bend, and even break, the rules if doing so meant more profits.

In short, in 2011, during the throes of this battle with the board, all I saw ahead of me was a painful struggle to try to catch the management and board in what I saw as attempts to skirt regulations. Even if successful in such a game of cat and mouse, who would I run to if I found something? Vinod Khosla? The RBI?

In 2011, the multilateral organization the Consultative Group to Assist the Poor wrote an article on the 2011 RBI regulations that echoed this sentiment.[2] It pointed out a number of challenges in implementing the new policies and concluded: "It is difficult to design regulatory policy to meet all various and dynamic angles. The MFIs should invest in observing the spirit of regulation." From my perspective, SKS had no interest in observing the "spirit of regulation."

I do not think I was alone in my assessment. After I resigned, SKS inducted an independent director, Ranjana Kumar, on March 8, 2013. She was well suited to watchdog company operations, as she had been the constitutionally mandated Vigilance Commissioner for the federal government, the most senior official responsible for investigating government corruption. She also served as a director of several banks, including serving as the managing director of Indian Bank. She resigned from the SKS board in less than six months. Ravikumar, the board member who took over the chairperson role after I resigned, commented in the press: "She did not cite any reasons for her resignation."[3]

Despite the inner workings of the SKS board, thankfully and to my surprise, the regulations ended up working out well for the sector and kept SKS in check. Or it may well have been that the management team could not overcome the myriad challenges inherent in its strategy. They had clamored for a cross-sell on war footing tactic, but they never got it to scale. By October 2017, the latest figures available at the time of this writing, only 2.8 percent of SKS's income came from cross-selling.

SKS was also unable to execute on the gold loan strategy. It appears the company was never able to master the core competency needed. Moreover, the RBI completely removed lending against gold from priority sector lending in 2012.[4] SKS halted its lending against gold pilot initiative in January 2016, having achieved a portfolio of just ₹40 lakh ($63,000 at 2016 exchange rates). The thirty-nine gold loan branches were shut down in September 2017.

The Insurance Regulatory Development Authority of India (formerly IRDA, now known as IRDAI) came out with a policy in 2012 prohibiting MFIs from charging customers more than the actual costs of insurance. The policy stated: "NBFC-MFIs shall recover only the actual cost of insurance for group, or livestock, life, health for borrower and spouse. Administrative charges where recovered, shall be as per IRDA guidelines."[5] Moreover, it issued a show cause notice against SKS for seven different violations of its policies and fined the company ₹50 lakh ($92,000 at 2013 exchange rates) in 2013.[6] While not a relatively huge sum, the fine coupled with stricter regulations presumably was enough to deter SKS from trying to bend or break the rules further.

Perhaps the biggest thing that held SKS in check was simply that the industry stalled and the Wild West competitive environment leading up to SKS's 2010 IPO slowed down. The rogue MFIs faded away while the vast majority of mainstream regulated MFIs had to write off a huge amount of loans in Andhra Pradesh. The industry shrunk back to levels in line with 2005, and growth became slower and more systematic because of the RBI's new rule limiting the number of MFI loans to two per customer. In that muted environment, what was the best strategy for SKS (or, frankly, any MFI)? It was to go back to basics, as I had been wearily preaching.

And it was relatively easy for SKS to do this. The company simply stopped (or rather was forced by RBI regulations to stop) the extreme incentive structure that led to diluted group training, multiple loans, and over-indebtedness of borrowers. SKS did not need to create anything new. SKS did not need to innovate. SKS just went back to basics and grew once again with ease; after all, the competition had been wiped out. SKS was among the last ones standing. The turnaround was just a matter of time. By January 2018, the latest figures available at the time of this writing, SKS had a customer base of 6.6 million members spread across more than 100,000 villages and 335 districts in 16 Indian states, a loan portfolio of about a $1.8 billion (₹11,466 crore), and profits of $25.5 million (₹163 crore) in the last quarter of 2017—nearly back to its 2010 numbers. It had disbursed $12 billion in microloans since inception.

The broader environment also improved.

I saw this in dramatic fashion in December 2014. I was at the Ashok Hotel in Delhi, attending the Inclusive Finance India Summit—the annual flagship event for Indian microfinance—organized by ACCESS Development Services. It was the first industry event I had attended since leaving SKS. I had just flown in from New York, and I was in a suit and tie rather than my usual kurta. No one recognized me as I stood at the back of the plenary hall, where I had been on stage many times in past years. I listened to panelist after panelist speak—the deputy governor of the RBI, a start-up grassroots practitioner, the CEO of the largest MFI in the country, a Cabinet minister. One after another, they were all eloquently articulating ideas and themes very familiar to me: "We need to harness the market to work for the poor." "We have to innovate in the areas of micro-insurance and microsavings." "MFIs should become banks." The collective philosophy was the need to put forth and nurture a market that catered to the base of the pyramid.

I watched and listened, feeling quietly grateful. The concept of *Swayam Krishi Sangam* had taken root and flourished in India after all. That felt like a success.

There was a special buzz at that 2014 conference because earlier that year India had granted licenses to two new banks. It was the first time in ten years that a new bank was given a license in the country. One went to IDFC, an infrastructure financing company led by Rajiv Lall, who also had invested in a microfinance fund, Lok Capital. In fact, in 2004, I had taken Rajiv Lall—who was then a managing director of the private equity firm Warburg Pincus—on his very first microfinance field visit. He had not forgotten. Despite the people flocking around him at the conference, he saw me from a distance and carved out time for us to chat.

The second bank license was given to Bandhan, a microfinance institution that concentrated in the poorer, northeastern states of India. The news that Bandhan, an MFI, was issued a bank license was a tremendous boost for the sector. In 2010, Bandhan was the fourth largest MFI in India. But since the top three—SKS, Share, and Spandana—had large operations in Andhra Pradesh where the backlash occurred, Bandhan leapt to the top of the list by 2011. So, by 2014, it was well positioned to receive a bank license. While, naturally, I would have loved to have seen SKS become the first MFI in India to become a bank, I was delighted for the sector nevertheless. I was particularly happy because the founder of Bandhan, Chandra Shekhar Ghosh, was among the first generation of MFI leaders. He had been born into a poor refugee family and then joined the Bangladesh NGO BRAC before starting Bandhan, initially as a nonprofit.

In 2015, the RBI also issued ten small finance bank licenses. To everyone's surprise (mine included), the RBI did not select SKS for a small finance bank license. Again, naturally, I would have been delighted if SKS had received at least a small finance bank license, but I was nevertheless happy for the sector because ten new small finance banks meant microfinance had come of age. It was firmly part of the banking sector.

SKS Microfinance changed its name to Bharat Financial Inclusion in 2016.[7] In 2017, IndusInd Bank announced it was acquiring SKS for $2.4 billion. So what SKS did not achieve through the banking license route, it will achieve through being acquired; the announcement of that acquisition made SKS the most valuable microfinance company in the world. I am truly happy for SKS, its staff, shareholders, and, above all, the highly deserving member groups in India that will benefit.

Do I have any lasting regrets about leaving SKS when I did? No. The greatest benefit of leaving is that I have been able to make up for lost time with my son. When we came back to the United States in 2012, I got to be a full-time dad. I went to all his soccer games, basketball games, and tennis matches. I went to all his school concerts and parent–teacher meetings. I got to make him breakfast each morning, and we had dinner together each night. We went to Knicks games, Yankee Stadium, *Hamilton* on Broadway, the U.S. Open, the New York City ballet, even enjoying the occasional beach vacation and camping trip. He will be off to college soon, so I am cherishing the last year or so we have living together.

In the last six years, I have also had an opportunity to reflect on my experience at SKS. I have thought about the mistakes that I made and what I could have done differently. Initially, I was not ready to share my story publicly. I did, however, make an exception for social entrepreneurs because it was important for me share my experiences

with them so that other well-meaning entrepreneurs could learn
from my mistakes and, as a result, be in a better position to do things
better in their social enterprises. As such, I spoke at a handful of
closed sessions at carefully selected conferences in different parts
of the world—from China to Ethiopia to the United Kingdom to
Mexico, and, of course, India and the United States.

Admittedly, it has been difficult over these past six years not to
speak more openly, not to be able to fully contribute to public dis-
course on these important issues. It has been hard to stay quiet these
half-dozen years, knowing that a short list of people knew the true
events that took place inside SKS, but refused to acknowledge them.
Interestingly for me, the acquisition of SKS by IndusInd Bank allows
me to take the step of speaking publicly and writing this book. Until
the announcement of that acquisition, I was wary to tell the story. I
did not want to cause harm to SKS's members who were once again
able to get access to finance—once regulations were in place—or to
the many dedicated employees who remained with SKS following
my departure or to SKS shareholders, especially the retail shareholders: those individuals who believed in the mission of SKS and who
invested their hard-earned savings with the company. But with SKS
now under new ownership and the relevant facts being only of historical significance, I can finally speak openly without as much concern
of retaliation from SKS, and so I share my story with you, the reader.

I do so because my experience yielded important lessons, not
just for social entrepeneurs but for all entrepreneurs. I do so because
those lessons learned will be instructive for policy makers, not just in
India, but throughout the world. I do so because the mistakes that I
made have relevance not just for those involved in financial inclusion
but for all those trying to bring about inclusion across various sectors
and for different groups of marginalized people.

And so I close with thoughts on how all of us—from entrepreneurs to policy makers, from activists to investors—can make a better attempt to use markets to bring about greater inclusion.

CHAPTER 24

POVERTY AND PROFITS: MORAL RESPONSIBILITY IN BUSINESS

In the last chapter, I extolled the virtues of the microfinance regulations framed by the Reserve Bank of India in 2011 and implemented in 2012. Truly, that made all the difference for microlending endeavors in India.

Those regulations, however, came too late for borrowers unable to bear the weight of over-indebtedness. Was the SKS board at fault? I ask this question because many times during my debates with the SKS board, particularly over suicides linked to over-indebtedness, the common refrain was: "We have not broken any laws." I myself have said, in this book, SKS had no legal culpability for the deaths.

True, but I believe SKS had moral responsibility akin to that of Wall Street banks for the subprime mortgage crisis and its aftermath. Perhaps, at the corporate board level, you can't expect directors to see problems before they happen. For example, someone invents a complicated derivative, and a director can only know after the fact that it led to irresponsible risk-taking in subprime mortgage lending.

Someone cuts key elements of microfinance group training, and a director can only know after the fact that it led to over-indebtedness, group support morphing into group pressure, and some tragic cases of suicide.

What cannot be excused is lack of action after the fact is known. Mistakes happen, especially in frontier markets. When they do, admit it. Take moral responsibility. And then try to fix the problems. Johnson & Johnson did that with the tamper-proof Tylenol bottle because its leadership made the health and safety of its customers the top priority. I tried, unsuccessfully, to do that at SKS; thankfully, in the case of SKS, regulations emerged to ultimately achieve what I could not.

So far, so good, you might be thinking. Take moral responsibility after a tragic, unintended consequence. But what, if anything, can be done *before* a calamitous consequence? That question is of paramount importance for social entrepreneurs who are creating innovative for-profit models to solve social problems and, in so doing, are creating brand new industries where there may be few if any applicable regulations. (There are of course social entrepreneurs who use nonprofit models, but my focus is on the social entrepreneurs using for-profit models.) By definition, such entrepreneurs typically work in spheres where regulations have not yet emerged—whether that means for-profit provision of financial services for unbanked poor people in India in the late 1990s or other commercial initiatives to provide important products and services to marginalized individuals.

Moreover, the question of how to prevent a calamitous consequence before it happens also applies to entrepreneurs in any new sphere, even realms other than social enterprise. Consider social media, artificial intelligence, private space travel, the internet of things, crypto-currency, genetic cloning, and similar innovations. In such frontier markets, there will be a lag between pioneering innovations and regulations. Governments will be reactive, rather than proactive, as there are immense challenges in establishing laws and regulations to protect against unintended negative consequences that have not yet occurred.

How can Facebook anticipate and prevent Russian purchase of ads as a means of interfering in a U.S. election before it happens? How can Tesla anticipate the inability of its self-driving autopilot feature to tell the difference between a bright sky and a white truck and avert a driver fatality before it happens (albeit that the driver in this case did not heed a warning)? How can we prevent artificial intelligence from leading to a takeover of human civilization in what is, at the moment, the stuff of science fiction such as the 2004 movie *I, Robot*? These examples may seem far-fetched, but there are parallels in that when I started SKS I never could have imagined that the excesses of microfinance would contribute to suicides of borrowers.

When it comes to for-profit social enterprise, I believe Professor Yunus would say it is not possible to prevent calamitous consequences before they happen. His answer is to let only mission-driven people, mission-driven social investors, and mission-driven shareholders into a social enterprise. And at first glance, the SKS case seems to suggest he is right—when one mixes profit into a social enterprise, it morphs into something harmful. Nonetheless, I want to suggest a different interpretation. I am still a believer in using a for-profit model to scale a social enterprise, to fully harness the power of the market to make it work for the poor. It just has to be done more carefully and more thoughtfully than I have done it.

Professor Yunus expresses a zero-sum view of market forces: "Microfinance is in the direction of helping the poor retain their money rather than redirecting it in the direction of rich people."[1] In my view, it is not a question of the poor versus the rich. If microfinance is thoughtfully executed, you can accomplish both. For example, a borrower generates a surplus that she could not have created without access to finance. She gives a portion of that surplus in the form of interest to the company. She retains more value than before.

The investor earns a profit from the interest earned from millions of borrowers and makes more profit than before.

So, what happened? What went fundamentally wrong at SKS? More importantly, what would I have done differently to prevent the mistakes? Well, as I have explained, there are a number of things that could have prevented the crisis. Here are a few.

First and foremost, if the MFI sector had been able to self-regulate and keep in check rogue MFIs (and concomitantly incumbent MFIs that strayed), things might have been very different. But as noted, we did not, and perhaps—given the raw nature of the top MFI leadership (myself included)—we could not. We needed some adults in the room. Where Google had Eric Schmidt or Facebook had Sheryl Sandberg, we did not have the depth of experience and expertise in our ranks; or at least we did not listen to the voices of the few elders in the sector.

Second, it would have been great if the Reserve Bank of India had set up regulations early on and not left a vacuum. Within that vacuum, the industry ended up engaging in unbridled growth and diluting key processes, giving a foothold to powerful vested interests that were champing at the bit and that unleashed the Andhra Pradesh juggernaut.

Of course, payments could have been made to corrupt politicians and extortionist local-language media, as is routinely done in other Indian industries. It may have cost $10 to $20 million, but it may well have saved a billion dollars in loan write-offs and perhaps more than that amount in shareholder value of the stock held in SKS, let alone stock in the banks that lent to the microfinance industry. However, paying bribes would not have solved the process dilution. Borrowers would have continued to take on too much debt. Yes, presumably regulations would have eventually been enacted, though perhaps not as quickly as was done due to the intensity of the political backlash. But I declined to pay bribes and, frankly, no genuine social entrepreneur would (or should). As mentioned, corruption is not only morally wrong; a system of corruption hurts those who cannot afford to pay bribes, precisely the people microfinance is trying to help—the poor and the vulnerable. In pursuing that noble end, there is no room for paying bribes, whether $1 or $10 million.

So, looking backward, if I wanted to harness the power of the market to scale microfinance, but government was slow to regulate and I would not bribe politicians, what could I have done differently within the area under my purview?

On an institutional level, I believe I should have made sure I selected investors who were more aligned with our social enterprise mission—those who were both committed to creating a social impact *and* committed to using a for-profit model to do this. My error was, at the early stage, picking investors who leaned more toward the latter and then effectively ceding control to the affiliated board nominees. I should have more carefully vetted investors and board members to make sure that they were aligned with the mission. I wish I had been more careful.

But I really don't want you to look back at the last few paragraphs and tease out a list of the seven principles of highly success-ful social enterprises. It's not as much about specific things as it is about an ethos. What is that ethos and how do you create it? I don't have definitive answers, but here are some pertinent thoughts. The first decade of SKS provides some insight. We disbursed our first loan in June 1998 and until 2008, there was positive impact. And there was scale. By the end of fiscal year 2008–09, we had reached almost 4 million members and had a cumulative disbursement of $4.5 billion in loans over those eleven years. In 2008–09, SKS also had profits of $15.7 million and a return on equity of 19.2 percent. More importantly, there were no allegations of over-indebtedness, let alone allegations of group pressure leading to suicide. There were as yet no rogue MFIs. Politicians left us alone. Bureaucrats left us alone. The local media left us alone. And in that placid environ-ment, for more than a decade, poor women got access to billions of dollars in finance and made profits. Investors earned profits. An industry was born.

What was SKS like back then? It was a company that, absolutely, had profit as one overarching goal, but that goal was confined to board discussions and did not trickle down to the frontline staff. What did that look like? It paralleled morality. Let me explain.

Morality dictates that people do things because it is right. For example, we should not steal (even when we are positive we can get away with it). If everyone followed this moral rule, society would be safer and better off. An individual may follow a moral rule because of its intrinsic value, but from a broader perspective, if everyone follows a moral rule, society as a whole is better off. This works because not stealing is part of the moral code. The majority of people don't go around thinking, *Hmmm, even though I could get away with it, I should not shoplift because if everyone did that, society would be chaotic.* In other words, we don't necessarily think through the instrumental value of not stealing. Of course, there are exceptions (criminals) and even for the rest of us, all moral decisions have a layered and complicated set of considerations in play. But, for the most part, we simply act morally for the sake of acting morally. Full stop.

Likewise, in our first decade, I am confident that SKS field staff acted in the best interests of our members because they felt it was right to do so. They didn't go around thinking, *Hmmm, even though I could give a larger loan and still get a repayment, despite some difficulty for the borrower, I am not going to do that because we want to do right by the customer so that the customer stays with us in the long run.* Within the culture of SKS, the loan officers did not think through the instrumental value. He or she just acted in the best interests of the customer. Full stop.

We need to fashion corporations—especially those in unregulated frontiers—where the frontline staff feel the same way. Perhaps the most famous example is the often-told story of a customer returning a couple of tires to Nordstrom, the luxury department store. The customer was apparently confused; Nordstrom does not sell tires. But the salesperson took the return anyway because the company's customer service culture reinforced the mantra that the customer is always right. Such an act, no doubt, would not help profits in the short term. But the sales ethic woven into the anecdote models the sales ethic for which Nordstrom is known and that has created broad customer loyalty.[2]

One may wonder just how an example from a U.S.-based luxury department store translates to microfinance in India or elsewhere. In the early days of SKS, the company was structured to make sure every action was in the best interests of the customer. There were no incentives for group formation that would lead to poor quality training. There were no incentives to increase loan size. We lent money—whether that was ₹1,000 ($20) or ₹20,000 ($400)—in a way that worked for our members. Our field staff—many from the same social milieu as our members, basically sons and daughters of members—saw their work as giving back to their communities. They were guided by the intrinsic value in doing what was best for their customer. SKS was fashioned to make sure every action was in the best interests of the customer.

I am not saying that we can expect to create moral corporations with saint-like investors and angel-like staff. Let's be realistic. What I am saying is that the frontline staff, the field force, have to be encouraged via training and example by leadership to do what is best for customers because of the intrinsic value of the action. Let me take a risk here and say that, for me, this notion is rooted in the philosophy of Mahātmā Gandhi. I know that on the surface it seems absurd to invoke Gandhi when discussing for-profit money lending. But let me explain.

On one of my childhood visits to India, I went to Raj Ghat, the memorial dedicated to Gandhi in Delhi. There, I read his talisman.

Whenever you are in doubt, or when the self becomes too much with you, apply the following test. Recall the face of the poorest and the weakest man [or woman] whom you may have seen, and ask yourself, if the step you contemplate is going to be of any use to him [or her]. Will he [or she] gain anything by it? Will it restore him [or her] to a control over his [or her] own life and destiny? In other words, will it lead to swaraj [freedom] for the hungry and spiritually starving millions?[3]

I don't presume to say that I have been able to live my life in a way that is true to Gandhi's words. Far from it. But in the early days of SKS, I tried to set up the company with this principle in mind. Yes, SKS microfinance, once it scaled, achieved profits—even huge profits. But that's not what our field staff were thinking when they would rise at 6 AM, brave monsoon rains, and sit on the muddy ground to deliver a ₹1,000 ($20) loan to some poor woman in some remote village. They did it because it was good for her, the poor, marginalized woman who otherwise might need to scour the floor for a few grains of rice. That's why SKS became a success. That was our foundation. That was our culture. And that's what our early funders—from social investors to our first for-profit investor, Vinod Khosla—believed. They understood the importance of doing right by the microfinance customer over any short-term profit maximization.

Over time, that changed. When SKS brought in short-term, profit-oriented investors like Sequoia and Kismet and Sandstone, they pushed to incentivize the field force based on activities that would generate quick profits. With such incentives in place, the field staff, who once would take the time to patiently train a borrower on the principles of group support, ended up failing to deliver high-quality training because they wanted to quickly move to the next group, the next target. The ethic of doing what's best for the customer was lost. And yes, I have by no means forgotten that I brought in Sequoia, and, yes, all of this happened under my watch as chairperson. I am a culprit, too.

But I am still a believer. I still want to harness market forces to work for the poor. And my thought is that if an enterprise can keep the discussion of profits confined to the boardroom and not let it percolate down to the field staff, then outcomes can be different. We saw that in the first decade of SKS.

In other words, do not impose the instrumentality of actions on the frontline team; let them be motivated by and rewarded for the intrinsic value of serving the customer. You can easily incentivize staff to do what is best for the customer. I am arguing this not only because such a focus will help avert tragic, unintended consequences, but also because it makes business sense; in the microfinance context, such an ethic creates loyal members who will stay with the company as they move up the economic ladder. This approach will create greater long-term shareholder value than a short-sighted approach. As Amazon CEO Jeff Bezos once said: "We're not competitor obsessed; we're customer obsessed. We start with what the customer needs and we work backwards."[4] Or consider the words of Warren Buffett, when asked about the most important piece of advice for entrepreneurs: "If there's one thing to remember: Delight your customer . . . [Entrepreneurs should] write this on their mirror so that they [see] it in the morning when they [get] up every day." He added: "If you've been treated well and honestly, if you've been delighted by the person you're doing business with, you're going to return to that person."[5]

That's what we did in the first decade of SKS—we knew there was *instrumental* value in treating our members well. But staff treated our members well for the *intrinsic* value, because it was the right thing to do. That message was part of virtually every communication from the head office to the field.

When I brought in senior executives and board members from the banking and finance worlds, things changed at SKS. The board and top executives were guided by the view that they had a fiduciary duty to shareholders to maximize both profits and investor returns.

In the heat of debate, directors would often say to me, "We have a fiduciary responsibility," and that's why we can't spend $10 million on retraining groups, or that's why we have to get into lending against gold. Let me leave aside whether lending against gold was actually more profitable. Let's assume it was more profitable. Do I have a duty as a director to support lending against gold even if I feel it is predatory and exploitative, albeit not against the law? Certainly, that is how the board of American tobacco companies felt when it came to marketing cigarettes to teens. Perhaps that is how the board of Wall Street banks felt when they dealt in subprime mortgage loans with teaser rates.

But there has to be a better way. Otherwise, corporations—especially those defining new industries—will continue to create unintended, devastating consequences and regulators will keep trying to catch up after the fact. Again, is there anything that can be done to give corporations—or entrepreneurs who founded them—a chance to prevent tragedies before they happen?

There is.

Over the last decade or so, ideas about capitalism have evolved. Conscious capitalism, compassionate capitalism, creative capitalism, and stakeholder capitalism—these new philosophies posit that boards and executives of corporations should have more than just a fiduciary duty to maximize profits. They argue that there should also be a duty to achieve higher standards of social and environmental performance, accountability, and transparency than exist in mainstream corporations.

This new form of capitalism has been codified in law, beginning in 2010. Today, the majority of U.S. states as well as Italy have such laws.[6] In these jurisdictions, a for-profit company can be incorporated as a benefit corporation, which means that the company includes making a positive impact on society, workers, the community, and the environment—in addition to profit—as its legally defined goals. In other words:

The major characteristics of the benefit corporation form are: 1) a requirement that a benefit corporation must have a corporate purpose to create a material positive impact on society and the environment; 2) an expansion of the duties of directors to require consideration of non-financial stakeholders as well as the financial interests of shareholders; and 3) an obligation to report on its overall social and environmental performance using a comprehensive, credible, independent and transparent third-party standard.[7]

Even companies that are not benefit corporations are talking about similar ideas. Larry Fink, CEO of BlackRock, a fund that manages $1.7 trillion in assets, wrote in a recent open letter: "Society is demanding that companies, both public and private, serve a social purpose. To prosper over time, every company must not only deliver financial performance, but also show how it makes a positive contribution to society. Companies must benefit all of their stakeholders, including shareholders, employees, customers, and the communities in which they operate."[8]

Well, whether formally a benefit corporation or not, the non-profit entity B Lab certifies corporations committed to these principles in a similar fashion to the way that UL, the global safety certification company, certifies the safety of products. As of December 2017, B Lab had certified 2,300 "B Corporations" in more than 50 countries across 130 industries. Those companies range from eyeglass maker Warby Parker to the outdoor apparel manufacturer Patagonia to ice cream maker Ben & Jerry's. My new financial inclusion company, Vaya Finserv,[9] is in the process of B Lab certification, which exists even in countries that do not have benefit corporation legislation in place.

I started Vaya after my three-year noncompete period ended in 2014. As a capstone of my twenty-year journey in financial inclusion, Vaya owes part of its heritage to SKS. The Sanskrit word *vaya* means "power" or "strength." It is a feminine gender word. I chose the name for the new entity because it embodies what Vaya—and SKS before it—strives to do: build on the strength of women.[10] It is microfinance 2.0 in the sense that Vaya blends the agility of a start-up with the deep experience of my team, many of whom are part of the seasoned team that came over from SKS when I left. Vaya implemented the first tablet-banking solution for rural India. It was the first business correspondent to have 100 percent electronic identity verification using the government of India's unique identification card as well as the first to have 100 percent cashless disbursements. By early 2018, Vaya was serving 350,000 members across six states, had a loan portfolio of $85 million, and was profitable. With a three-year track record, Vaya hopes to apply for a small finance bank license in the next round of applications.

Most importantly, at Vaya we are also using benefit corporation frameworks, even though such legislation does not yet exist in India. So, we are also exploring ways to parallel the effect of that legislation, such as creating "golden shares." These would be held by a founder and allow the founder to exercise veto rights on major decisions that could result in mission drift. Other alternatives include using two classes of share capital that reserve rights related to the mission to one of the two classes. These ideas are not unheard of and have precedents in the tech world. While the norm is that companies operate according to a one-share, one-vote principle, it is common knowledge that "several high-profile technology companies, including Google, Facebook, and Snap, give extra per-share voting rights to founders and early investors."[11] As such, in companies such as Google, the founders retain a majority of the voting power although owning far less than 50 percent of the company's shares.

While we are looking into this approach at Vaya as we are about to raise our first external equity investment, we are also focusing on instilling the ethos of what the early SKS field staff were like. Vaya loan officers are called sangam mitras, friends of the lending center. For those not directly involved in interacting with our members, we have an "I am sangam mitra" program, in which staff, including middle and senior managers, go to the field once a quarter. We have a dedicated human resources specialist who anchors this program, maintains records of field visits, and seeks opportunities to send staff to the field. Vaya sangam mitras also come to the head office each quarter to share their field experiences. The goal is to get the head office staff close to the field and therefore ensure a better understanding of our members.

I also hope to bring these principles to a fintech venture for financial inclusion in which I have invested. The start-up is called ArthImpact, and it uses an app to provide credit to the "missing middle"—small merchants who are above the threshold of microfinance yet still not large enough to garner the attention of mainstream banks.[12] I think of these small merchants in India as modern-day versions of my grandfather—who had to drop out of school in the fourth grade in order to support his family and who then worked as an assistant in a clothing shop for a few years before being able to get a loan to start his own sari shop.

Since I have invoked Mahātmā Gandhi in this concluding chapter, let me remind you that when I first met Professor Yunus, I promised to write my autobiography and call it *The Story of My Experiments with Grameen*. At the time, Professor Yunus just smiled, no doubt amused at the hubris of a twenty-something upstart who had yet to distribute a single loan from his own organization. Well, I have completed my experiments with Grameen. They did not go exactly as I had wanted. My hope is that the next generation of social entrepreneurs can learn from my mistakes and have greater success when they do their own experiments.

I would like to thank you for spending your time reading this book. My sincere hope is that, by using principles that characterize the benefit corporation movement, and taking lessons from moral systems, this new generation of social entrepreneurs will have a chance to succeed where I came up short. My hope is that the experiences—some painful, some joyful—that I have shared in this book will help upcoming social entrepreneurs better harness market forces to massively scale a social enterprise and yet retain the *social* character of that enterprise. My hope is that this generation can both do well *and* do good or, better yet, they can do well *by* doing good. This is my hope.

APPENDIX

DOES MICROFINANCE WORK?

Spoiler Alert: Please read Part II of this book before you read this appendix, as I refer to events that take place in Part II.

ecent studies of the impact of microfinance have used randomized evaluations that attempt to mimic randomized controlled trials (RCTs) used in scientific experimentation. Two researchers who pioneered this approach are MIT economists Abhijit Banerjee and Esther Duflo. In their 2011 book, *Poor Economics: Rethinking Poverty and the Ways to End It*, they described their approach as one in which "individuals or communities are randomly assigned to different 'treatments'—different programs or different versions of the same program. Since the individuals assigned to different treatments are exactly comparable (because they were chosen at random), any difference between them is the effect of the treatment."[1]

The merits of using RCTs to understand the impact of a development initiative has been hotly debated. I wish to contribute to this debate by discussing the RCT done in India on the microfinance institution (MFI) Spandana, entitled "The Miracle of Microfinance? Evidence from a Randomized Evaluation."[2] Among the major RCT evaluations of microfinance, this study was the "first and longest running evaluation of the standard group-lending loan product" (2015:51). It was authored by Banerjee and Duflo, along with two other economists, Rachel Glennerster and Cynthia Kinnan.

The work of Banerjee and Duflo is influential. In fact, I was invited to debate Duflo at Harvard Business School in 2014. To prepare, I called a friend, an economics professor, for help. I had been expecting him to suggest the latest articles I might read so that I could sharpen my argument. Instead, he looked at me, paused, and said, "You should drop out; just say you are sick or something." The statement was not tongue-in-cheek, and it gives you a sense of the stature of Banerjee and Duflo among academics.

This research and the research of others who take similar approaches have been deemed to show that microfinance has a limited impact on poverty alleviation. The 2015 Banerjee et al. study examined the MFI Spandana in Hyderabad in the time period between 2005 and 2010. The authors conclude that "monthly consumption, a good indicator of overall welfare, does not increase for those who had early access to microfinance, either in the short run . . . or in the longer run" (2015:51).

The authors indicate there are some positive aspects of microfinance, such as the finding that borrowers "invest in home durable goods and restrict their consumption of temptation goods and expenditures on festivals and parties" and that microcredit "expands households' abilities to make different intertemporal choices, including business investment" (2015:52). But the conclusion is that microfinance does not make much of a difference in terms of increased incomes.

This assessment of microfinance was covered widely in the press—from NPR to the BBC to the *Wall Street Journal*—with often simplified reports. A 2016 NPR report on the Banerjee et al. study and several other studies, for example, said, "about a dozen randomized controlled trials of microloan programs in multiple countries have been conducted . . . In each case they compared a randomly selected group of people who had been offered the loans to an otherwise identical group that had not . . . in none of the studies did the average microloan borrower end up significantly increasing income relative to the control group."[3] Many journalists have interviewed me about what I thought of the Banerjee et al. study.

So, here are a few comments about the study of Spandana.

First, I have a concern about relying on surveys done by a third party; the survey entity was not the Indian research partner but a "market research company." I worry about the accuracy of data if the study relied on standard market research surveys, which typically involve brief and hurried surveys in which researchers scurry around—clipboards in hand—trying to collect specific details from borrowers such as household expenditure as well as revenue and expenses of their businesses. The authors themselves noted that the "baseline survey had to be conducted very rapidly to gather some information necessary for stratification before Spandana began their operations" (2015:31).

This concern about data accuracy is not specific to RCTs. But in my experience with India's poor people, such surveys often intimidate them, so borrowers may end not up giving accurate information, let alone the question of whether they are accurately able to recollect revenue and expenses in the manner in which the surveyor would need to record it. As mentioned in chapter three of this book, this was an important lesson from my three years of field work with the grassroots Deccan Development Society and my reading of Robert Chambers's *Rural Development: Putting the Last First.*[4]

Aside from that general concern about accurate data collection, there are other methodological problems with this specific RCT. First, it should be noted that the "treatment" was defined as the mere presence of a Spandana branch in a neighborhood, not the actual receipt of loans. Even households that did not take a Spandana loan were included as part of the "treatment communities" (2015:36). That is, this is not a study about borrowing; it is about being able to borrow. This is equivalent to trying to determine the impact of a health clinic or school on households' health or education by examining the mere access to the clinic or school, regardless of how many people actually use it. In the case of Spandana, only 26.7 percent of households borrowed by the end of the first endline and that increased to 38.5 percent by the second endline. But the study is examining the impacts of microfinance on an entire area, even though only 38.5 percent of the households took a loan (2015:24). That's akin to examining the impact of a health clinic or school on *all* residents in an area when only 38.5 percent use the clinic or school. This is an odd approach even when trying to assess interventions with a direct impact on health and education, let alone assessing MFIs that have indirect impacts on outcomes. In short, Banerjee et al. are not making claims about microfinance, which many popularly understand as the actual use of loans; they are instead making claims on the impact of having access to a microfinance branch.

Second, the study does not have a proper control group because before the first endline survey (in 15–18 months), other MFIs began lending within the no-lending control area. The authors admit that this happened. They wrote, "Other MFIs had also started their operations in both treatment and comparison areas . . . (26.7 percent borrowers in treated areas versus 18.3 percent borrowers in comparison areas)" (2015: 24). Along the same lines, one of the authors elsewhere explained: "[I]n the early stages of our evaluation of Spandana's microcredit product we became aware that credit officers from Spandana were going into some control areas to recruit microcredit clients."[5] The authors, however, note "this was stopped relatively rapidly" (2015:31–32).

Worse yet, after the second endline survey (two years after the first endline), other MFIs *and* Spandana started lending in no-lending control areas. The authors wrote that two years after this first endline survey, when the same households were surveyed once more, "Both Spandana and other organizations had started lending in the treatment and control groups, so the fraction of households borrowing from microcredit organizations was not dramatically different (38.5 percent in treatment and 33 percent in control)" (2015:24). As such, researchers had to amend their research goal. Instead of a comparison between a treatment group that received MFI loans and a control group that did not, they ultimately compared two different borrower groups, ". . . those who borrow for longer versus those who borrow for a shorter time, rather than those who do and those who do not borrow at all" (2015:24).

A third problem is that the study could not use the original baseline survey because it was not done randomly. The authors wrote: "The households were not selected randomly from a household list: instead field officers were asked to map the area and select every nth house, with n chosen to select 20 households per area. Unfortunately, this procedure was not followed very rigorously by the market research company, and we are not confident that the baseline is representative of the slum as a whole" (2015:31). The authors commented, "Since we lack a rigorous baseline sample that was systematically followed, a potential worry is that the sample that was surveyed at endline may not be strictly comparable in treatment and control areas, if there was differential attrition in treatment and in control groups" (2015:33).

The authors attempted to compensate for this error by taking a new census in each area "to create a proper sampling frame for the endline," this time with the census being conducted by the research partner in India and not by the market research company (2015:32). The census was done one year after lending had already started, which is problematic.

In addition, the first endline was done only one year after the new census. The authors wrote, "The first endline survey was conducted at least 12 months after Spandana began disbursing loans within a given area, and generally 15 to 18 months after" (2015:32). It is not clear whether that would be sufficient time to see any impact at the first endline. This is especially true if Spandana followed the typical group-lending model in India in which there was staggered disbursement of loans; that is, in treatment areas, borrowers would not have received loans up front but would receive them in a staggered manner over the course of 12 to 18 months, depending on how fast Spandana formed new groups. The authors admit that the new census to create a "proper sampling frame for the endline" was inadequate: "In retrospect, it was a clear mistake not to attempt to systematically re-survey at least a fraction of the baseline sample, even though the baseline sampling frame was weak" (2015:32–33).

There is also a selection bias in that the study was conducted in an area Spandana considered "marginal" neighborhoods in which it had a limited interest. The area was poorer; neighborhoods, smaller. As the authors admit, the study locations were "those Spandana was indifferent about working with at the outset—and the impacts may have been different in the neighborhoods they chose to exclude from randomization." Another problem was that the "evaluation was run in a context of very high economic growth, which could have either decreased or increased the impact of microfinance" (2015:25). The authors recognize these and other problems in the study.

The researchers then make reference to studies elsewhere, which may be of limited comparative value. "Thus, it is an important reassurance that our results find a strong echo in five other studies that look at similar programs in different contexts," the authors wrote (2015:25). This statement seems odd given that the other MFIs referenced are not "similar programs." The MFI in Ethiopia combined microfinance with family planning programs to encourage contraceptive use. The borrowers in Bosnia-Herzegovina were categorized by the microlenders in the area as "risky" and "unreliable," not to mention that the study was done at the height of the 2008–2009 financial crisis, which strongly affected the country, and the country came out of a bloody war in the mid-1990s. The example in Mongolia is from a country that is the second least densely populated country in the world, after Greenland; India is the among the most densely populated countries. The MFI in Morocco gave loans that were 25 percent of gross national income (GNI), not the 8 percent of GNI that characterized Spandana loans. And the MFI in Mexico had interest rates that were extraordinarily high (110 percent) compared to Spandana's (24 percent); plus, the region of the study in Mexico is an area known for cartel violence.

In addition, not all of the other MFIs target exclusively women, as Spandana does. The MFI in the Bosnia-Herzegovina study had both men and women. The Moroccan MFI had both men and women. The study of the Ethopian MFI was majority men. These differences are important because, in India, gender is an important dimension to microlending, perhaps more than in other countries.

It is not clear how the conclusions from such studies compensate for the flaws in the Spandana study. The very term "microfinance," as used by the authors, seems to indicate a wide range of program types. Lumping together these diverse MFIs as "similar programs" requires justification—especially when they are being cited as support for conclusions in a study of Spandana that the authors readily admitted has a number of methodological flaws.

Worse yet, the authors extrapolated from Spandana to other MFIs in India to make a broad, sweeping claim about the impact of microfinance in India. This is problematic because the microfinance industry in India between 2005 and 2010 was incredibly diverse. In 2007, the industry network Sa-Dhan had 129 MFIs.[6] The top 30 MFIs had a total member base of 10.5 million. Spandana was the second largest with 916,000 members. But it had only 8.7 percent of the total members in India.

Spandana was also different from other MFIs in significant ways. Insisting that loans be used for income generation is a core part of the "Grameen Essentials."[7] Several of the top MFIs in India—including SKS—were Grameen replicators and followed this fundamental tenet. Even MFIs that were not Grameen replicators also followed this principle.

But Spandana did not.

This is important because only if a borrower invests in an income-generating activity (a small business), whether that be existing or new, will a borrower have a chance to increase her household's income. If a borrower does not invest in a business and instead uses a loan for consumption, there is little chance that the loan will generate surplus income. Assuming a poor borrower will use an unrestricted loan to invest in a business is like assuming a person who gets a credit card will use it to start a business. It is possible but highly unlikely, which is especially true if you face the daily economic pressures that poor people in India face. If they have cash in hand, they are more likely—and understandably so—to spend it on everyday, basic needs such as food, clothing, shelter, and school fees.

At SKS we conducted strict loan-utilization visits to verify that the funds were being used for income-generating activities. In chapter five, I described how important this protocol was at SKS, at least in the first decade of SKS before changes—explained in Part II of this book—occurred. (Remember my account of arguing with a borrower about the color of her goat to determine how she had used her loan.) As mentioned, this fundamental precept of insisting on income-generating activities was also adopted by the vast majority of MFIs in India at that time—again, with the caveat that things changed across the industry in its later stages.

This is not to say that at SKS there was no leakage of funds. But because field staff visited borrowers at their places of business, whether at home or in the field, one week after a loan was disbursed to confirm they had invested in a business (and staff also did quarterly follow-up visits), leakages were low, perhaps 5 to 10 percent of the loan amount.

Some may argue that loan utilization visits do not adequately counter the argument about money being fungible. That is, some may argue that even if there were loan utilization visits, borrowers would simply divert existing spending on businesses (for which they would use the new loan funds) to spending on consumption. The problem with this argument is that it assumes that borrowers are already spending on businesses at the maximum of their capacity. If so, it would be true that money is fungible, and new loan funds for business would free up funds for consumption. But, if borrowers are systematically underspending on their business and then getting new loan funds that they can only spend on business, there is little possibility for diverting funds—subject, of course, to robust loan utilization visits.

So, the question becomes, do poor borrowers underspend on their businesses? Typically, they do. Consider a typical micro-business, a home-based activity such as being a cobbler or a seamstress. Since such micro-enterprises use family labor, new loan funds do not enable a borrower to redirect family labor to consumption. Family labor is not fungible. Paid wage labor would allow for fungibility, but that is not the nature of home-based micro-enterprises. Consider even the purchase of raw material. Typically, a poor borrower would have bought raw material (say leather or cloth) on credit from a middleman. There is no cash expenditure up front. So, if the borrower gets a loan from an MFI and buys raw material in cash (at a lower price than what it would have cost with credit), she is not able to divert any funds to consumption. She did not have those funds in the first place.

For these reasons, it is significant if an MFI insists on lending exclusively for income-generating activities, as SKS did.

Spandana, on the other hand, did not require an investment in business. Their loans were initiated as consumption loans. Therefore, it is not surprising that the study found that Spandana borrowers did not start or expand businesses and, as a result, did not increase income. More to the point, the fact that the authors found that Spandana's loans to borrowers did not increase income does not permit any conclusion about SKS or any other MFI that insisted on income-generating loans, which was more the norm at the time of the study than was Spandana's practice of giving unrestricted loans.

There are other important differences between Spandana and other MFIs, such as SKS. SKS lent primarily in rural areas; the Spandana study was conducted in the metropolitan city of Hyderabad. The group size at Spandana was much larger, ranging from six to ten members per group, which would make implementing the rigorous group training that I described in chapter five difficult. Without rigorous group training, there would be no right-sizing of loans and no group incentive to ensure each loan was invested in a business.

Spandana also had centers that were much larger than SKS's, making center dynamics difficult. According to the authors, Spandana centers were composed of 150 to 450 women (2015:26). That is incorrect; it would be hard to even find a meeting place in an urban slum that would accommodate that many women. Having said that, it is nonetheless true that Spandana centers were much larger than SKS's. At that time, SKS had centers with a maximum of 50 members and an average of about 30. Centers with more than 50 members make the dynamics of group lending difficult.

The study also ignores the results of a natural experiment resulting from the microfinance crisis in the Indian state of Andhra Pradesh. As described in Part II of this book, the AP government effectively banned microfinance on October 14, 2010, when it passed the AP MFI Ordinance, which later became an Act. As such, there was a natural "control" (Andhra Pradesh) and a natural "treatment group" (the rest of India, which still had access to microfinance). Economists have written about the natural experiment and examined consumption data a year before and a year after the ban, using panel data from the Centre for Monitoring Indian Economy (CMIE).[8] The CMIE data was from 150,000 households while the Spandana study involved 6,850 households. The CMIE data revealed that the average household expenditure dropped by 19 percent in Andhra Pradesh compared to those who continued to have access to microfinance in the rest of the country. Notably, the largest decrease was in expenditure on food. This information, however, is not mentioned by Banerjee et al.

The other reason it would have been important to address this natural experiment is that scale matters. If one randomizes across all of India, that would be potentially stronger than randomizing across all of Andhra Pradesh. Similarly, randomization across all of Andhra

Pradesh would be stronger than randomizing in just Hyderabad. Randomization across all of Hyderabad would be stronger than randomizing across just a subset of neighborhoods. This is not to say that the natural experiment had systematic randomization. But it does raise the importance of scale—the importance of the unit of analysis. Banerjee et al. do not address that.

For the aforementioned reasons, the study's conclusions need to be questioned. Banerjee and Duflo do not stop there. In their book, *Poor Economics,* they criticize MFIs for being "reluctant to gather rigorous evidence to prove their impact" (2011:169). Their implication is that had we done so, we could have possibly stopped the political juggernaut against microfinance in Andhra Pradesh. After reading this book, you can judge for yourself whether "rigorous evidence" (let's assume for a moment that it was RCT evidence that proved microfinance increased incomes) would have made a difference. I hope I have shown in these pages that the vested interests against microfinance would likely not have been moved by "rigorous evidence." The attack against microfinance in 2010 in Andhra Pradesh was much more complex.

I did end up going to that 2014 debate at Harvard Business School with Esther Duflo. She made her comments. I made mine. At the end of our panel, she had to leave for another commitment. The next speaker opened his comments by thanking me for scaring Duflo off. It was a tongue-in-cheek remark, but I appreciated the nod that, as a practitioner, I was able to raise some important questions about the Spandana study. My hope is that the comments on that day and here may prompt a rethinking of the Banerjee et al. study's conclusions about the lack of impact of microfinance.

MAP OF INDIA

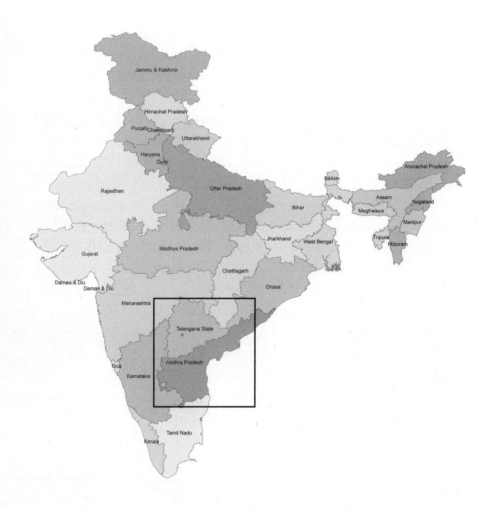

Andhra Pradesh and Telangana (jointly Andhra Pradesh until 2014)
are where the political attacks on microfinance occurred in 2010.

ACKNOWLEDGMENTS

There are many people who have helped achieve what has been captured in this book.

First and foremost are the microfinance borrowers at SKS and at Vaya. They are extraordinary women who struggle to overcome myriad challenges to make better lives for themselves and their families. I am constantly inspired by what they have been able to accomplish. I have learned a lot from them and continue to do so.

Second, I thank our field staff at SKS and at Vaya. I have had the privilege of working side by side with many of them over the past twenty years. They are my teachers, and they have made me a better person.

Third, I am grateful to my family. I know that I follow in the footsteps of my paternal grandmother, Akula Ranganayakamma, and my paternal grandfather, Akula Venkatramiah. My maternal grandmother, Dhaduvai Shakunthala, gently guided me during my post-college years in India. Though my maternal grandfather, Dhaduvai Kishtaiah, passed away when I was young, it is wonderful to know that I probably have walked along many of the same Telangana village roads that he once did. There is, of course, my large, boisterous, extended immigrant clan spread across the United States. Through the years, we have had philosophical differences, fierce family debates, and tons of fun. At every stage and with every turn, my family has been there. My parents, Akula V. Krishna and A. Padma Krishna (who list their surnames first, as is the custom in India), have been pillars of strength. My brother Gautham Akula and cousin Prashant

Mitta are my closest confidants. I could not have survived in India without my cousin Chandana Gadwala; her parents, G.V. Ramana Babu and G.V. Kalpana, guided me in the early SKS days. I have also had financial support from each of my paternal uncles and their wives in India (and home offices in their homes): A.V. Panduranga Rao and A. Shakunthala, A.V. Hanumanth and Vijaya Laxmi Rao, and A.V. Mohan and Vidya Rao. I thank my son, Tejas, for the love and joy we have shared—and for laughing at my "dad jokes."

Every member of my extended family contributed money to help get SKS started, including Ravi Reddy and Pratibha Reddy, Jagdish and Shanta Chandra, Srinivas and Swatantra Mitta, Satyamurthy and Sashikala Abkari, Ashok and Swarup Pilly, Ameresh and Swarnakala Kura, Govind and Jyothi Rao, Janardhan and Kumuda Reddy, the late Chandrashekhar Thunga and Vijaya Thunga, Raghuveer Thunga, and Ashish Prasad. All my cousins contributed and some, such as Suma Reddy, even came to India to work with me.

Meanwhile, many friends have also contributed generously, including Sanjiv Sidhu, Lekha Singh, Srikanth Ravi, Sudhakar Ravi, Phil Smith, and George Kaiser. Other funders include the Echoing Green foundation, led by Cheryl Dorsey; the India Development Service; Friends of Women's World Banking, led by Vijaya Lakshmi Das; Grameen Foundation USA, founded by Alex Counts; Unitus, led in its early days by Mike Murray and Geoff Davis; and the great team at the Small Industries Development Bank of India, including former director Brij Mohan and former chairperson R.M. Malla.

I cannot list all the colleagues who have helped along the way, but let me make a special mention of Patlolla Niroop, Krishna Kumar, Biksham Gujja, Bala Krishnamurti, Praseeda Kunam, Gautam Ivatury, Chris Turillo, Manish Kumar, Anu Pillai Mitta, Vijay Thamban, Paul Breloff, Anna Somos Krishnan, Sanjay Dharba, G.S.V. Ramu, Monica Verma, Amee Patel, Kiran Kumar, Amy Yee, and Saheba Sahni. At Vaya, I have had the privilege of working with Jagadish Ramadugu, Lakshminarayan Subramanyam, Megha Nainani, A.V. Sateesh

Kumar, Sivani Shankar, Narender Reddy, Pushkar Parashar, Vijay Kumar, Rajeev Ranjan, and G.V. Surya Kumar.

I am also grateful to Sandhya Rani, J. Srinivas, B. Ashoka Chakravarthy, M. Sangaiah, S. Ramulu, B. Baswaraj, S. Vinod Rao, Raheem Pasha, Y. Peeraiah, Sudhakar Reddy, B. Dilip Kumar, P. Srinivas, P. Bhaskar, B. Rupesh, Sher Ali, Hruday Ranjan Sahoo, Anil Kumar, Venkat Jade, E.G. Rajashekar, M. Ramesh, Gnaneswar Rao, D. Raju, Brajesh Patel, Mohammed Yaseen, Tapaswini Lenka, Jagannath Behara, Bibudatta Biswal, Parsuram Hota, Madan Madhu Kumar, V. Srinivas Rao, Ullas Kumar Pradhan, K. Sailu, K. Nirmala, Donald Thomas, Rakesh Sarkar, and the late Madaram Bharathi.

Several of the people mentioned above have given me helpful comments on drafts of this book. Other reviewers are Shankar Ramaswami, Jessica Rubenstein, Barbara Magnogni, Meryl Fell, Bhavna Dalal, Shabri Mitta, and Mahathi Gottumukkala.

A special thanks to attorneys David Carpenter and Marc Kadish of Mayer Brown LLP and Michael DiDomenico of Lake Toback DiDomenico.

Finally, I am grateful to Laurel Leigh for all her editorial help, to Glenn Yeffeth and the great team at BenBella Books, and to my agent Howard Yoon.

ENDNOTES

CHAPTER 2: MY UNEXPECTED QUEST TO END POVERTY THROUGH PROFITABILITY

1. The Constitution of India lists twenty-two official languages. English is the twenty-third. *See* Government of India, Ministry of Law & Justice, *The Eighth Schedule of the Constitution of India, as of 1 December 2007*, 330. lawmin.nic.in/coi/coiason29july08.pdf.

2. In fact, the South Asia region sits alongside sub-Saharan Africa as the most poverty-stricken region in the world. *See* the World Bank's "Poverty & Equity Data Portal": povertydata.worldbank.org/poverty/country/IND.

CHAPTER 4: THE STORY OF MY EXPERIMENTS WITH GRAMEEN

1. *See* "Monthly Report: 2017-11 Issue 455 in USD." Grameen Bank (website), December 5, 2017. www.grameen.com/data-and-report/monthly-report-2017-11-issue-455-in-usd/.

CHAPTER 5: RANGOLI POWDER AND A HANDFUL OF SEEDS

1. "Boss' Day Out: Vikram Akula of SKS Microfinance (Aired May 2007)," YouTube video, 11:35. Posted by NDTV, January 30, 2014. www.youtube.com/watch?v=Lqo45GX5p98.

2. Morduch, Jonathan. "The Role of Subsidies in Microfinance: Evidence from the Grameen Bank." *Journal of Development Economics* 60 (1999): 229–48. www.scribd.com/document/227420635/Role-of-Subsidies. Morduch also explained, "To reach full economic sustainability between 1985 and 1996, Grameen would have had to increase average interest rates by about 65 percent to a rate of 26 percent per year." Morduch added, "If Grameen had to rely on the open capital market to obtain all funds for on-lending . . . Grameen would have to charge its borrowers nominal interests on general loans of at least 40 percent per year."

3. Cull, Robert et al. "Financial Inclusion and Development: Recent Impact Evidence." Consultative Group to Assist the Poor (CGAP), *FocusNote* 92, April 2014. www.cgap.org/sites/default/files/FocusNote -Financial-Inclusion-and-Development-April-2014.pdf.

CHAPTER 6: MCDONALD'S OF MICROFINANCE

1. Bellman, Eric. "Entrepreneur Gets Big Banks to Back Very Small Loans." *Wall Street Journal*, May 15, 2006. www.wsj.com/articles /SB114765489678552599.

CHAPTER 8: GOAT ECONOMICS

1. *See* "At the Crossroads." *Forbes*, September 27, 2009. www.forbes .com/2009/09/25/crossroads-vikram-akula-sks-microfinance-suresh -gurumani-forbes-india.html#3907370139b6.

2. The entity that managed the investments was Sequoia Capital India, and investments were held by a number of subentities, such as Sequoia Capital India Growth Investments I and Sequoia Capital India II, LLC. Also, Sumir Chadha left Sequoia Capital India in February 2011 and joined WestBridge Capital Partners, so some investments became a part of WestBridge Ventures II, LLC. For ease of reading, I refer to the various entities as Sequoia and to Sumir as representing Sequoia.

3. Bruck, Connie. "Millions for Millions." *The New Yorker*, October 30, 2006. www.newyorker.com/magazine/2006/10/30/millions-for -millions.

4. Rosenberg, Richard. "CGAP Reflections on the Compartamos Initial Public Offering: A Case Study on Microfinance Interest Rates and Profits." Consultative Group to Assist the Poor (CGAP), *FocusNote* 42, June 2007. www.cgap.org/sites/default/files/CGAP-Focus-Note -CGAP-Reflections-on-the-Compartamos-Initial-Public-Offering -A-Case-Study-on-Microfinance-Interest-Rates-and-Profits -Jun-2007.pdf.

5. *See* "Online Extra: Yunus Blasts Compartamos." *Bloomberg Businessweek*, December 13, 2007. www.bloomberg.com/news/articles/2007-12-12 /online-extra-yunus-blasts-compartamos.

6. Morduch, Jonathan. "The Role of Subsidies in Microfinance: Evidence from the Grameen Bank." *Journal of Development Economics* 60 (1999): 229–48.

7. Basu, Priya. *Improving Access to Finance for India's Rural Poor.* Washington, DC: The International Bank for Reconstruction and Development/The World Bank (2006): 23. siteresources.worldbank.org

/INTTOPCONF3/Resources/364480PAPER0IN101OFFICIAL
0USE0ONLY1.pdf.

CHAPTER 10: BRINGING IN THE BANKERS

1. The entity that managed the investments was Kismet Capital LLC, and investments managed were held by a number of subentities, such as Kismet Microfinance and Kismet SKS II. For ease of reading, I refer to the various entities as Kismet.

CHAPTER 11: AKULA VERSUS THE U.S. STATE DEPARTMENT

1. For an example, *see* "A Letter from the Former Wife of SKS Microfinance's Vikram Akula." *Moneylife News & Views*, October 12, 2010. www.moneylife.in/article/a-letter-from-the-former-wife-of-sks -microfinancersquos-vikram-akula/9924.html.

2. *See* "Custody Battle: A Child's Wait for Justice." *NDTV*, March 26, 2010. www.ndtv.com/india-news/custody-battle-a-childs-wait-for -justice-413607.

3. *See* "Hoffman Estates Mom Fighting to Bring Son Home from India." *Daily Herald*, March 8, 2010. prev.dailyherald.com/story/?id=364372. *See* "The Mother Is a Lawyer in Hoffman Estates. The Father Is a Powerful Entrepreneur in India. She Won Custody of Their Son in Illinois After Their Divorce; He Won the Right to Keep the Boy in India. Where Does Tejas Belong?" *Daily Herald*, March 9, 2010. www .highbeam.com/doc/1G1-220716058.html.

4. *See* "Boy Caught Up in International Custody Battle." NBC 5 Chicago, March 9, 2010. www.nbcchicago.com/news/local/cook-county-india -custody-battle-87175412.html.

5. Strom, Stephanie and Vikas Bajaj. "Amid Celebrity, a Long Legal Battle Over a Child." *New York Times*, July 29, 2010. www.nytimes .com/2010/07/30/business/30microbar.html.

6. Ibid.

CHAPTER 12: BIG BANG IPO

1. *See* "No Paper Tigers: Over 60 SKS Staffers Join Millionaire Club." *Economic Times*, October 29, 2010. economictimes.indiatimes.com /news/company/corporate-trends/no-paper-tigers-over-60-sks-staffers -join-millionaire-club/articleshow/6832201.cms.

CHAPTER 13: THE BACKLASH

1. The Bombay Stock Exchange changed its name to BSE Limited in July 2011.

2. Per an article in the *Economic Times*, 70 MFI-linked cases were reported between March 1 to November 19, according to information from the Society for Elimination of Rural Poverty, Hyderabad. *See* "Suicides Reveal How Men Made a Mess of MFIs." *Economic Times*, January 5, 2011. economictimes.indiatimes.com/industry/banking/finance /suicides-reveal-how-men-made-a-mess-of-mfis/articleshow /7219687.cms.

   The Associated Press reported that there were more than 200 MFI-linked cases. This AP-generated article appeared on several news sites, including the *San Diego Union-Tribune*. *See* Kinetz, Erika. "AP IMPACT: Lender's Own Probe Links It to Suicides." *San Diego Union-Tribune*, February 24, 2012. www.sandiegouniontribune.com/sdut-ap -impact-lenders-own-probe-links-it-to-suicides-2012feb24-story.html.

3. Bateman, Milford. "Milford Bateman on the Andhra Pradesh Microfinance Crisis in South India." *India Microfinance* (blog), 2010. indiamicrofinance.com/milford-bateman-andhra-microfinance-crisis -273203821.html.

4. "Indian Microfinance: Looking Beyond the AP Act and Its Devastating Impact on the Poor." Legatum Ventures (white paper), March 13, 2012. www.legatum.com/news/looking-beyond-the-ap-act-and-its -devastating-impact-on-the-poor/.

CHAPTER 14: CULPRIT NUMBER ONE: THE MICROFINANCE INDUSTRY

1. Ashta, Arvind et al. "Is Microfinance Causing Suicides in Andhra Pradesh? Recommendations for Reducing Borrowers' Stress when Lending to the Poor." *European Microfinance Platform* (blog), May 8, 2015. www.e-mfp.eu/blog/microfinance-causing-suicides-andhra -pradesh-recommendations-reducing-borrowers-stress-when.

2. Polgreen, Lydia. "Suicides, Some for Separatist Cause, Jolt India." *New York Times*, March 30, 2010. www.nytimes.com/2010/03/31/world/asia /31india.html.

3. Bellman, Eric. "India Journal: Microfinance by the Numbers." *Wall Street Journal* (archival post), November 15, 2010. blogs.wsj.com /indiarealtime/2010/11/15/india-journal-microfinance-by-the -numbers/.

4. Polgreen, Lydia. "Suicides, Some for Separatist Cause, Jolt India." *New York Times*, March 30, 2010. www.nytimes.com/2010/03/31/world /asia/31india.html.

5. As noted, peer-group lending contrasted with conventional banks, which insisted on physical collateral. Since the poor don't have such collateral, they could not get a loan. Also, a bank could not give out unsecured loans because—in the absence of a group appraisal and joint responsibility—conventional banks simply didn't think it was worth the risk or the high cost of appraising a tiny loan. By having a group lending model with a group guarantee, microfinance was able to overcome that problem.

6. To illustrate, I am using the maximum interest SKS charged, which was 36 percent during the period 1998 to 2000. As noted in Chapter 5, as SKS grew and benefited from economies of scale, it dropped its interest rates from 36 percent to 28 percent to 24 percent, and then to 19.75 percent in 2017, which was in line with unsecured loan rates for middle-class Indians with average credit scores.

7. Shankaran, Sanjiv. "Maoists, Mafia, MLAs and Moneylenders: They Are External, Extortionist Threats." *LiveMint* (HT Media Ltd.), July 16, 2010. www.livemint.com/Companies/BtFdgqlsEzt0XGKk3ddtEM /Maoists-mafia-MLAs-and-moneylenders-they-are-external-ex.html.

8. The CyberBullyHotline published figures in 2012 indicating an alarming number of teen suicides in the United States linked to cyber bullying. *See* "Cyberbullying Rampant on the Internet." *CyberBullyHotline*, July 10, 2012. www.cyberbullyhotline.com/07-10 -12-scourge.html.

CHAPTER 15: CULPRIT NUMBER TWO: VESTED INTERESTS

1. Robinson, Marguerite S. *The Microfinance Revolution*. Washington, D.C.: The International Bank for Reconstruction and Development/ The World Bank (2001): 178–9. http://documents.worldbank.org/ curated /en/226941468049448875/pdf/232500v10REPLA18082134524501 PUBLIC1.pdf.

2. Qazi, Moin. "Inside the World of Indian Moneylenders." *Diplomat*, March 31, 2017. thediplomat.com/2017/03/inside-the-world-of -indian-moneylenders/. Qazi is the author of *Village Diary of a Heretic Banker* (Chennai, India: Notion Press, 2014).

3. Robinson, *The Microfinance Revolution*, 184.

4. *See* "Koppula Raju: Know More About the Ex-Bureaucrat in Rahul Gandhi's Team." *Babus of India* (blog), September 18, 2013. www

.babusofindia.com/2013/09/koppula-raju-know-more-about-ex
.html; and "Koppula Raju Named Congress SC Cell Chief." *Hindu*,
August 27, 2013. www.thehindu.com/todays-paper/tp-national
/tp-andhrapradesh/koppula-raju-named-congress-sc-cell-chief
/article5063542.ece.

5. Polgreen, Lydia, and Vikas Bajaj. "India Microcredit Faces Collapse
    from Defaults." *New York Times*, November 17, 2010. www.nytimes
    .com/2010/11/18/world/asia/18micro.html.

6. Basu, *Improving Access to Finance for India's Rural Poor*, 23.

7. The rupee amount for each is as follows: Sequoia and affiliated
    entities earned ₹6,050,521.952 or ₹605 crore; Kismet and affiliated
    entities earned ₹3,991,967,185 or ₹399 crore; Sandstone earned
    ₹1,680,213,329 or ₹168 crore. Due to exchange rate changes between
    2010 and 2017, the dollar value stated above is only an approximation.
    Carry description and percentage from Alex Iskold, "8 Things You
    Need to Know About Raising Venture Capital," *Entrepreneur.com*,
    July 15, 2015. https://www.entrepreneur.com/article/248377.
    Sequoia information from Sumir Chadha, personal communication
    in 2008, and from Jason Calacanis, "according to VentureWire Sequoia
    Capital commands 2.5% management fee and 30% carry. Impressive,
    well earned," *Calacanis.com*, December 21, 2009, http://calacanis.
    com/2009/12/21/according-to-venturewire-sequoia-capital
    -commands-2-5-management-fee-and-30-carry-impressive-well
    -earned.

8. *See* "Satyam Fudged FDs, Has 40,000 Employees: Public Prosecutor."
    Times of India, January 22, 2009. timesofindia.indiatimes.com/India
    _Business/Satyam_fudged_FDs_has_40000_employees_Public_
    prosecutor/articleshow/4015830.cms; "Satyam's Chairman Ramalinga
    Raju Resigns, Admits Fraud." *Times of India*, January 7, 2009.
    timesofindia.indiatimes.com/business/india-business/Satyams
    -chairman-Ramalinga-Raju-resigns-admits-fraud/articleshow
    /3946088.cms; and "Full text of Raju's resignation letter to the Board."
    Times of India, January 7,2009. https://timesofindia.indiatimes.com
    /business/india-business/Full-text-of-Rajus-resignation-letter-to-the
    -Board/articleshow/3946538.cms.

9. Das, Gurcharan. *The Difficulty of Being Good: On the Subtle Art of
    Dharma*. New Delhi: Oxford University Press, 2009:278.

10. Timmons, Heather and Jeremy Kahn. "Past Graft Is Tainting New
    India." *The New York Times*, January 19, 2009. http://www.nytimes
    .com/2009/01/20/business/worldbusiness/20corrupt.html.

11. Sekhar, A. Saye. "Riding a Tiger Without Knowing to Get Off: Raju."
    The Hindu, January 8, 2009. http://www.thehindu.com/todays-paper

/tp-business/Riding-a-tiger-without-knowing-to-get-off-Raju/article
16348024.ece.

12. The report for 2010 is available at https://www.transparency.org/cpi
2010. The report for 2014 is available at https://www.transparency.org
/cpi2014.

13. Benbabaali, Dalel, Abhijit Banerjee, et al. "Dominant Caste and
Territory in South India: Migration and Upward Social Mobility of the
Kammas from Coastal Andhra." https://www.academia.edu/2505857
/Dominant_Caste_and_Territory_in_South_India_Migration_and
_Upward_Social_Mobility_of_the_Kammas_from_Coastal_Andhra.

14. Vanita Kohli-Khandekar. "When Politicians Own the Media." *Business
Standard*, January 24, 2013. www.business-standard.com/article
/opinion/vanita-kohli-khandekar-when-politicians-own-the-media
-112070300063_1.html.

15. Ramana, K.V. "86-Yr-Old Andhra Governor Targeted in Sleaze CDs."
Daily News & Analysis (*DNA*), December 26, 2009. www.dnaindia
.com/india/report-86-yr-old-andhra-governor-targeted-in-sleaze
-cds-1327605.

16. *See* "Don't Repay Microfinance Loans: TDP." *Indian Express*, November
2, 2010. archive.indianexpress.com/news/dont-repay-microfinance
-loans-tdp/706093/.

17. Mahapatra, Dhananjay. "2G Loss? Govt Gained Over ₹3,000cr: Trai."
Times of India, September 7, 2011. timesofindia.indiatimes.com/
india/2G-loss-Govt-gained-over-Rs-3000cr-Trai/articleshow/9890803.
cms?referral=PM.

18. *See* "Andhra Pradesh Issues Ordinance to Regulate Microfinance
Sector." *Information Company* TIC (India's online business daily),
October 15, 2010. www.domainb.com/finance/financial_services
/20101015_microfinanc_esector.html.

19. Based on typical exchange rates in 2011 (₹45 = USD $1).

20. Bandyopadhyay, Tamal. "Can India's MFI industry be saved?"
Livemint. January 15, 2012. http://www.livemint.com/Opinion/
f62emJdhiz7UmkCG3lQydL/Can-india8217s-MFI-industry-be
-saved.html; Sridhar, G. Naga. "Micro-lenders May Have to Write
Off ₹7,000 Crore in AP." *Hindu BusinessLine*, July 9, 2011. www
.thehindubusinessline.com/todays-paper/microlenders-may-have
-to-write-off-rs-7000-crore-in-ap/article2215643.ece; and Chintala,
Prashanth. "Has SKS Moved on from the Andhra Crisis?" *Business
Standard*, December 25, 2012. www.business-standard.com/article
/finance/has-sks-moved-on-from-the-andhra-crisis-112122502015
_1.html. (Typical exchange rate in 2011: ₹45 = USD $1.)

21. Ibid.

22. Bandyopadhyay, Tamal. "Microfinance Crisis Leads to Loss of 35,000 Jobs." *Livemint*. October 22, 2013. http://www.livemint.com /Companies/99un1M17pdKE1O6BOAB1qJ/Microfinance-crisis -leads-to-loss-of-35000-jobs.html.

23. Ramana, K.V. "86-Yr-Old Andhra Governor Targeted in Sleaze CDs."

24. *See* "Moneylenders Cater to 50% of Credit Needs in Telangana." *Hindu BusinessLine*, May 14, 2017. www.thehindubusinessline.com/news /national/moneylenders-cater-to-50-of-credit-needs-in-telangana /article9697788.ece.

25. The figure was $280 million based on the fact that SKS wrote off ₹1,362 crore between the period December 31, 2010, to June 30, 2012, at an average exchange rate of 48.54. *See* "SKS Microfinance Earnings Update—Q2 FY13," October, 2012. www.bfil.co.in/wp-content/themes /sks/public/downloads/Q2-FY13_Earnings_update.pdf; exchange rate per Reserve Bank of India's Reference Rate Archive: www.rbi.org.in /scripts/referenceratearchive.aspx.

CHAPTER 16: CULPRIT NUMBER THREE?

1. Thirani, Neha. "'Yunus Was Right,' SKS Microfinance Founder Says." *New York Times*, February 27, 2012. india.blogs.nytimes. com/2012/02/27/yunus-was-right-sks-microfinance-founder-says/.

CHAPTER 17: *SANGAM MITRA*

1. Markel, Howard. "How the Tylenol Murders of 1982 Changed the Way We Consume Medication." *PBS NewsHour*, September 29, 2014. www .pbs.org/newshour/health/tylenol-murders-1982.

2. Sridhar, G. Naga. "MFIs Now 'Default' on Payment of Life Insurance Claims of Poor." *Hindu BusinessLine*, April 21, 2011. www.thehindu businessline.com/money-and-banking/mfis-now-default-on-payment -of-life-insurance-claims-of-poor/article1715701.ece.

3. Ibid.

CHAPTER 18: BATTLE IN THE BOARDROOM

1. *See* "Akula Admits to Lapses at SKS." *Times of India*, May 11, 2011. timesofindia.indiatimes.com/business/india-business/Akula-admits-to -lapses-at-SKS/articleshow/8235429.cms.

2. Nandakumar, V. P. "The Social Relevance of Gold Loans." Manappuram Finance Limited (web page), accessed January 13, 2018. www.manappuram.com/company/social-relevance.html.

CHAPTER 19: ROUND TWO: BACK IN HYDERABAD

1. By 2013, the Indian Companies Act was changed to prohibit a company from providing stock options to independent directors. Under the new Act, independent directors had to buy options themselves, and they were restricted to only 2 percent.

2. *See* Kinetz, Erika. "AP IMPACT: Lender's Own Probe Links It to Suicides." *San Diego Union-Tribune*, February 24, 2012. www.sandiegouniontribune.com/sdut-ap-impact-lenders-own-probe-links -it-to-suicides-2012feb24-story.html.

3. For the full text of the news article, *see* Ghosh, Sugata. "After Suresh Gurumani Termination, SKS Microfinance Wants Vikram Akula to Step Down from Executive Chairman Post." *Economic Times*, August 16, 2011. economictimes.indiatimes.com/articleshow/9617437. cms?utm_source=contentofinterest&utm_medium=text&utm_ campaign=cppst.

CHAPTER 20: SHOWDOWN AT THE ROSEWOOD HOTEL

1. Cowley, Stacy, and Jennifer A. Kingson. "Wells Fargo to Claw Back $75 Million from 2 Former Executives." *New York Times*, April 10, 2017. www.nytimes.com/2017/04/10/business/wells-fargo-pay-executives -accounts-scandal.html.

CHAPTER 21: IF YOU SCORCH THE EARTH, YOU MIGHT GET BURNED

1. *See* "Draft Red Herring Prospectus." SKS Microfinance Limited, March 25, 2010, 35. www.credit-suisse.com/media/ib/docs/in/ipo/sks -microfinance-drhp.pdf.

2. Vaitheesvaran, Bharani. "First Leasing Scam: ED Arrests Former Top Finance Execs Dilli Raj, Sivaramakrishnan." *Economic Times* (blog), August 1, 2016. blogs.economictimes.indiatimes.com/et-commentary /first-leasing-scam-ed-arrests-former-top-finance-execs-dilli-raj -sivaramakrishnan/; and Antony, Anto. "Bharat Financial President S Dilli Raj Arrested, Stock Falls." *LiveMint* (HT Media Ltd.), August 2, 2016. www.livemint.com/Companies/xBnwAbSeQHh2z5lu6y3anN /Bharat-Financial-president-S-Dilli-Raj-arrested-stocks-fall.html.

3. Bharat Financial Inclusion Limited. "Bharat Financial Inclusion Limited Appoints Mr. Dilli Raj as Chief Financial Officer," March 4, 2008. http://www.bfil.co.in/media/sks-microfinance-appoints-mr -dilli-raj-as-chief-financial-officer.

CHAPTER 22: ESCORTED OUT

1. *See* Kinetz, Erika. "AP IMPACT: Lender's Own Probe Links It to Suicides." *San Diego Union-Tribune*, February 24, 2012. www.sandiegouniontribune.com/sdut-ap-impact-lenders-own-probe-links-it-to-suicides-2012feb24-story.html.
2. Ibid.

CHAPTER 23: THE VIEW FROM NEW JERSEY

1. *See* "Introduction of New Category of NBFCs: Non Banking Financial Company–Micro Finance Institutions (NBFC-MFIs)—Directions," Reserve Bank of India (Master Circular), July 2, 2012. www.rbi.org.in/scripts/NotificationUser.aspx?Id=7392&Mode=0.
2. Srinivasan, N. "Regulation at Last for Indian MFIs." Consultative Group to Assist the Poor (CGAP) (blog), May 8, 2011. www.cgap.org/blog/regulation-last-indian-mfis.
3. *See* "SKS Microfinance Independent Director Ranjana Kumar Resigns." *LiveMint* (HT Media Ltd.), September 25, 2013. www.livemint.com/Companies/ZPiQbFxQzKfZDR85oAVKVJ/SKS-Microfinance-independent-director-Ranjana-Kumar-resigns.html.
4. *See* Reserve Bank of India's Notification post entitled "Priority Sector Lending: Targets and Classification," July 20, 2012. rbi.org.in/scripts/NotificationUser.aspx?Id=7460&Mode=0.
5. *See* "Master Circular-'Non-Banking Financial Company-Micro Finance Institutions' (NBFC-MFIs)—Directions." Reserve Bank of India (Master Circular). https://www.rbi.org.in/scripts/BS_ViewMasCirculardetails.aspx?id=9827.
6. M. Saraswathy. "IRDA Slaps Rs 50-lakh Penalty on SKS Microfinance, Microfinance institution levied a charge on members, that exceeds the premium and violates regulations." *Business Standard*, February 2013. http://www.business-standard.com/article/finance/irda-slaps-rs-50-lakh-penalty-on-sks-microfinance-113022000850_1.html.
7. *See* "SKS Microfinance renamed Bharat Financial Inclusion." *Economic Times*, June 13, 2016. economictimes.indiatimes.com/industry/banking/finance/sks-microfinance-renamed-bharat-financial-inclusion/articleshow/52734652.cms.

CHAPTER 24: POVERTY AND PROFITS: MORAL RESPONSIBILITY IN BUSINESS

1. DealBook. "SKS I.P.O. Ignites Microfinance Debate." *New York Times*, July 29, 2010. dealbook.nytimes.com/2010/07/29/sks-i-p-o-sparks-microfinance-debate/.

2. Conte, Christian. "Nordstrom Customer Service Tales Not Just Legend." *Jacksonville Business Journal*, September 7, 2012. www .bizjournals.com/jacksonville/blog/retail_radar/2012/09/nordstrom -tales-of-legendary-customer.html.

3. *See* "Gandhi's Talisman." *Bombay Sarvodaya Mandal/Gandhi Book Centre* (web page) www.mkgandhi.org/gquots1.htm.

4. Morris, Patrick. "Importance of Treating Customers Well." *Motley Fool*, June 1, 2014. www.fool.com/investing/general/2014/06/01/warren -buffett-reminds-us-of-the-critical-importan.aspx.

5. Belanger, Lydia. "Warren Buffett's 3 Top Pieces of Advice for Entrepreneurs." *Entrepreneur*, August 30, 2016. www.entrepreneur.com /article/277648.

6. Benefit corporation jurisdiction description confirmed by B Lab, New York, January 16, 2018.

7. Clark Jr., William H. et al., "The Need and Rationale for the Benefit Corporation: Why It Is the Legal Form That Best Addresses the Needs of Social Entrepreneurs, Investors, and, Ultimately, the Public." Benefit Corporation, January 18, 2013. benefitcorp.net/sites/default/files /Benefit_Corporation_White_Paper.pdf.

8. Fink, Larry. "A Sense of Purpose: Larry Fink's Annual Letter to CEOs." BlackRock (web page), accessed January 19, 2018. www.blackrock.com /corporate/en-us/investor-relations/larry-fink-ceo-letter?cid=twitter :larryslettertoceos::blackrock.

9. To learn more about Vaya, visit vayaindia.com.

10. Watch Vaya borrower and employee stories at http://vayaindia.com /video-stories#.

11. Lee, Timothy B. "Shareholders Force Zuckerberg to Give Up Plan for Non-Voting Shares." *ArsTechnica*, September 22, 2017. arstechnica.com /tech-policy/2017/09/shareholders-force-zuckerberg-to-give-up-plan -for-non-voting-shares/.

12. The pursuit of *arth* (अर्थ) is considered an important aim of life in traditional Hindu philosophy. ArthImpact enables economic prosperity and wealth creation for small businesses. www.arthimpact.com.

APPENDIX: DOES MICROFINANCE WORK?

1. Banerjee, Abhijit V., and Esther Duflo. *Poor Economics: Rethinking Poverty and the Ways to End It*. Noida, UP: Random House India, 2011: 14 (hereafter page numbers are cited in text).

2. Banerjee, Abhijit et al. "The Miracle of Microfinance? Evidence from a Randomized Evaluation." *American Economic Journal: Applied Economics* 7, no. 1 (2015): 22–53 (hereafter page numbers are cited in text).

www.povertyactionlab.org/sites/default/files/publications/44_275%20
Miracle%20of%20Microfinance%20AEJ.pdf.

3. Aizenman, Nurith. "You Asked, We Answer: Can Microloans Lift
   Women Out of Poverty?" *Goats and Soda* (NPR blog), November 1,
   2016. www.npr.org/sections/goatsandsoda/2016/11/01/500093608
   /you-asked-we-answer-can-tiny-loans-lift-women-out-of-poverty;
   Bellman, Eric. "Calls Grow for a New Microloans Model." *The Wall
   Street Journal*, March 17, 2015. www.wsj.com/articles/calls-grow
   -for-a-new-microloans-model-1426627810; and Morris, Madeleine.
   "Microcredit 'Not the Silver Bullet' for Poverty." *BBC News*, January 24,
   2011. news.bbc.co.uk/2/hi/programmes/newsnight/9369880.stm.

4. Chambers, Robert. *Rural Development: Putting the Last First*. New York:
   Routledge, 2013. (Chambers's book was first published in 1983.)

5. Glennerster, R. "The Practicalities of Running Randomized
   Evaluations: Partnerships, Measurement, Ethics, and Transparency"
   in *Handbook of Economic Field Experiments* 1, ed. Abhijit Banerjee and
   Esther Duflo. Oxford, England: Elsevier B. V.: 2017.

6. Ghate, Prabhu et al. *Microfinance in India: A State of the Sector Report,
   2007*. New Delhi: Microfinance India, 2007: 180. www.microfinance
   gateway.org/sites/default/files/mfg-en-paper-microfinance-in-india-a
   -state-of-the-sector-report-2007-2007.pdf.

7. Alam, Mohammad Nurul, and Mike Getubig. *Guidelines for
   Establishing and Operating Grameen-Style Microcredit Programs*.
   Washington, D.C.: Grameen Foundation and Grameen Trust,
   2010. www.grameenamerica.org/sites/default/files/Grameen%20
   Replication%20Guidelines.pdf.

8. Sane, Renuka, and Susan Thomas. *The Real Cost of Credit Constraints:
   Evidence from Micro-finance*. Mumbai: Indira Gandhi Institute of
   Development Research, July 2013. www.igidr.ac.in/pdf/publication
   /WP-2013-013.pdf.

INDEX

on borrower suicides, 305–306
forced resignation by, 286–287
interest in SKS, 264
as investor, 139
profit shares, 188
Lall, Rajiv, 313
Lauren, Ralph, 115
Laxmi, Rama, 54, 80–81
laziness, and poverty, 33
legal liability, 258, 316
Legatum Ventures, 167
Lehman Brothers, 138, 266
lending cap, 176–177
LIC (Life Insurance Corporation of India), 111
livestock fraud, 64–65
loans, Grameen Bank, 47–48
loan sharks, 125, 182–183
loans size, 173–174
loan training, 58
Loan Utilization Checks, 220
loan-utilization visits, 340–341
LongWealth, 143
Lopez, Jennifer, 115
loyalist culture, 299
loyalty, 324

M

Madiga caste, 215
mahajan, 182
Mahajan, Vijay, 171–172, 200
Malegam, Yezdi Hirji, 204
Manappuram, 245–247
mangalsutra, 246
manual accounting, 49
Maoist guerillas, 105
Mayer Brown, 90–91
MBA hires, 108–109, 114
McDonald's, 77–79, 108
McKinsey & Company, 92, 110–111
McNealy, Scott, 100
Meals on Wheels, 19
media, 190–194, 287–288
Mehta, Viren, 293

Member of the Legislative Assembly (MLA), 198
Metro Cash & Carry, 130
Mexico, 338–339
MFIN. *see* Microfinance Institutions Network
"MFIs Now 'Default' on Payment of Life Insurance Claims of Poor," 231
microcredit, 122
Microcredit Summit, 45–46
microenterprises, 118
micro-enterprises, 341
microentrepreneurs, 118
microfinance
    assessment of, 333–343
    backlash to, 182–186
    banning, 195–196
    benefits of, 10
    crisis in, 206–207
    emergence of, 37–38, 115–116
    for-profit industry backlash, 121–123
    improving practice of, 41–42
    member concerns in, 245
    model of recruiting, 108–109
    moral responsibility in, 316–329
    new practitioner in, 171–172
    as poverty relief effort, 36
    power in, 41
    problems with, 38–41
    profits in, 187–188
    providing access, 48
    regulation in, 180, 234–235
    studies on, 335–337
    and suicides, 169–181
    trust in, 19
    types of, 338, 339
Microfinance Act, 235, 251
microfinance institutions (MFIs)
    becoming banks, 313
    capital for, 123–124
    as commercial ventures, 10, 42–43
    government regulation of, 203–204
    and group training, 176–180
    regulation in, 319

ABOUT THE AUTHOR

 **Vikram Akula** has been at the forefront of creating market-based solutions for financial inclusion. He founded Bharat Financial Inclusion (formerly SKS Microfinance) in India, one of the world's largest microfinance companies. In 2006, *TIME* magazine named him one of the world's 100 most influential people. His awards include the Schwab Social Entrepreneur of the Year in India (2006), the Ernst & Young Start-Up Entrepreneur of the Year in India (2006), and the Ernst & Young Business Transformation Entrepreneur of the Year in India (2009). He has also been named a Young Global Leader of the World Economic Forum and an Echoing Green Fellow. He has been profiled in media ranging from CNN to the front page of the *Wall Street Journal.*

Vikram is also an investor in and serves as chairperson of Vaya, which uses tablet banking technology to deliver financial services to low-income people in India. He is an angel investor in fintech start-up ArthImpact, which uses an app to provide credit to small entrepreneurs, the "missing middle," in India. He is also an angel investor in AgSri, a sustainable agriculture company working in India and Africa focused on helping small sugarcane farmers reduce water use. He is the founder and chairperson of the Bodhi School, which provides education for underprivileged children in rural Telangana, India.

He has worked with McKinsey & Company and the Worldwatch Institute and authored *A Fistful of Rice: My Unexpected Quest to End Poverty Through Profitability* (Harvard Business Review Press, 2010). He studied at Tufts University (BA in philosophy), Yale University (MA in international relations), and the University of Chicago (PhD in political science) and was a Fulbright Scholar.